It's Not Personal, but it is PERSONAL

A deep dive of self-reflection during loss, love, trauma, and a spiritual awakening to heal, all while attempting to live without feeling shame or guilt. Was transcribed from the timeline of 2019-2024 from private love letters to a spouse incarcerated and authentic journal entries.
Shana Christine Dillon

Spoken4Eternity

Description: First edition. | Oregon : Spoken4Eternity [2024]

Identifiers: ISBN 979-8-9913389-2-9 (Hardcover)

ISBN 979-8-9913389-0-5 (Paperback)

ISBN 979-8-9913389-3-6 (Paperback)

ISBN 979-8-9913389-4-3 (Paperback)

ISBN 979-8-9913389-1-2 (eBook) ISBN 979-8-9913389-5-0 (eBook)

Subjects: Memoir. | Emotional maturity. | Mental health. | Self love. | Healing journey.

Book cover/picture taken by Justina Woods on 7.30.2016 @ 11:01 am in Oregon on Ramona Falls Trail

Picture of Author taken by Sheila Glo on 10.01.2023 @ 4:55 pm in Kahului, Hi

This book is dedicated to my 6 year old self.
May you recognize that you are loved
and safe at every age.

Me gazing fondly at my little brother
Michael Angel Perez
1984

Contents

It's Not Personal,

but it is

PERSONAL

Chapter One
2019 End Of Spring

When it rains, it pours

I am currently writing this from memory before I dive into my journal entries and letters I wrote. I was at my son's baseball game. The sky was full of angry clouds ready to give way at any moment. A few sprinkles, then some rain. I was excited to watch my son play. I loved watching him at any sport he played. He was a natural. I can't remember if it was the middle of the game or towards the end when I got the phone call. On the other end of the call was Rob's sister telling me the Feds got both her brothers. I immediately felt panic, my heart torn out of my body and helpless. One of her brothers is my husband. I don't remember the next pieces but I am sure the old me tried my hardest to stay face and act like nothing was wrong for my son's sake. Once the game was over I would figure out what to do next. I remember the rain showed up in full throttle after the phone call because I tried to find cover yet be in a bird's-eye view of the game. Or at least for when the game did start again since all players were off the field during the downpour.

On May 15, 2019, my world came crashing in on me and I was in a fight or flight response for many years to follow. Again. Apparently, I have been getting really good at this, since the age of two.

Journal entry

May 21, 2019

Tuesday

Friday night I was asked to journal every day for 30 days! 3 pages!

My thoughts have been all over the place, I wasn't sure when and how to begin.

Well, today I'm off work and overwhelmed. I have a horrible pain in my chest, a lump in my throat, and my entire body aches – of death!

6 days ago today my husband was taken. He is in Nevada in the FUCKING Federal Jail. ICE on top of that and I have no idea if they will let him come home before serving time! I pray he can, I hope he can, I miss him.

I miss feeling safe. Talking to him whenever I can.

I am so pissed off, and sick, I hurt ALL OVER! It feels like I have holes throughout my entire body. It's so exhausting. I know I should take it one day at a time yet I look ahead and see years flash in front of me of what we will miss out on (together). I feel guilty for even trying to live. Go to a concert or laugh.... I am supposed to go to my cousin's wedding in Sac in 2 weeks and I want to cancel. How the hell am I supposed to smile, feel loved, and be happy when my heart is locked up?!

I have no air to breathe...

...it feels like I am suffocating.

I have only spoken to my kids about what has happened, my bestie Marquita... and my counselor.

I was gonna go talk to my mom today. But somehow her friend knew and got to her first. I know she's heartbroken too, but I don't feel like it's the same. I don't trust her now, because she said horrible things to my husband at the end of March that caused him to deny her and not speak to her. He didn't even try to see her on her holiday. I don't blame him. I heard what she said, it was awful! This is probably why he is in this position too!

Journal entry

May 23, 2019

Yesterday I was so angry! From the time I woke up... till I went to sleep.

And today I am just exhausted.

I hope and pray the worst part is over.

Journal entry

June 4th, 2019

It's the end of the day, 9:33 pm.

I'm exhausted.

I feel sad.

I feel like, I should break down and cry. . . but I haven't ...not all the way. Or maybe I feel like I shouldn't do it again.

I just flew back from Sacramento yesterday. I worked yesterday and I worked today.

I feel like I'm not sure what or how to proceed. What do I need to look forward to? My chest hurts, my heart feels like it's in pieces.

Journal entry

June 14, 2019

Friday

I noticed I try to fill a void, by keeping busy with anyone or myself.

I say this because it doesn't feel good to sit still in my thoughts.

Because I have so many holes in my heart.

Mail

June 15, 2019

My Dearest Husband

I would like to ask, how are you - but we both know the answer.

I can't believe we are at that place again.

When you asked me to not write to you, the first week, I was actually relieved. Because it gave me hope that you would be home any day. ...and now we are a month later.

1st letter I am writing. Is killing me. I feel sick, sad, angry, heartbroken, and in grief.

I feel like I should have spoken sooner and delayed your flight one more day, been selfish, and kept you with me at home, safe.

If only ...

I'm just lost. I know we weren't in the best place, yet the few days before you left we were working on communicating, our friendship, and our relationship! My heart and soul were looking forward to the steps we were taking together.

I miss you!

I miss you SO BAD!

This feeling. Is exactly like how you feel in there, except I HAVE to go through life still. The everyday tasks, and somehow do this as if my heart and spirit are not shattered.

I miss you!

I love you PaPi!

New day

6/16/19

Happy Father's Day my love! Wish I could hug you, love you, all day here with me in the present! I love you so much mi amore! xoxoxoxo

Last night's writing was tough.

Today is a new day.

I hope you feel a little lighter. I hope we both do.

Jr and I will be cleaning up the backyard for you love.

...a gift. Happy Father's Day PaPi!

I love you!

Love always & forever

Your wife

Shana C

Ps.

I have a few other gifts for you, one is beneath the sheets!

Xoxo

Journal entry

June 15, 2019

Saturday

Night 10:18 pm

I feel like my whole life, I am constantly swimming. Just to keep my head above water ...at work, at home, finances. I am tired of swimming.

I'm tired of feeling sad when I sit still and heartbroken when I move.

Never thought I would feel this empty and broken again.

SHANA CHRISTINE DILLON

Journal entry

June 16, 2019

Today is Father's Day.

No real dad to say this to, well not my blood. But I have stepdad's. Both I reached out to. Both appreciative.

I stayed busy today. On very little sleep. I was active, pulled weeds for three and half hours, walked everywhere, did laundry, cleaned, and cooked.

Simply stayed busy.

10:49 pm I'm going to put my feet up now and try to sleep. In an empty bed. I wake up all hours of the night... again. Just like years ago. Why?! Because I think someone is in the house, or I am woken up by a nightmare of needing to check to see if someone did break into the house!

Journal entry

June 17, 2019

12:20 am

Monday night

Reflecting.

Today I did a Tova test.

Tomorrow I will go over the results with the doctor.

I found some music I can relate my feelings with, the artist is Russ. The songs are 'Alright', 'Fix This,' and 'Nobody Knows."

Tonight was a full moon. Might be why all the feelings are all over the place with extreme lows.

IT'S NOT PERSONAL, BUT IT IS PERSONAL

Journal entry

June 18, 2019

Tuesday

Today felt very overwhelming. From beginning to end.

I know this morning I was super amped because I drank coffee with my asthma medicine which I haven't been prescribed for over 6 years. (a steroid prescription, to help me breathe) I remember being up... just not this up! My heart was super racing at work. ..all the way till lunch. I felt like I couldn't sit still. Then I crashed directly after my dr appointment at 5:45 pm.

My heart felt heavy. My chest felt heavy. My neck hurt. I was overwhelmed with disappointment in myself. I guess I didn't expect nor did I believe that I have ADHD. The provider gave me the results from the TOVA test which leaned heavily towards combination type. Which is both hyperactive impulsive and inattentive.

This hit hard

But then she said she has a few more diagnoses, one being anxiety disorder and the second major depression disorder.

This felt like knives to my throat and chest.

Because YA, I'm depressed! I have a lot of shit going on right now, but that has not been my whole life. I mentioned this part to her including 4 recent deaths, one Big one, my little brother, and now I am really trying to cope with the grief and figure out tools to heal including seeing a counselor that has helped.

It truly was a hard pill to swallow. After I told her she said she would evaluate that and sounds like this is more associated with grief and she will not put this diagnosis into the chart.

It still hurts... either way. It felt like any and all the pain came crashing down at once on my chest and I was to blame. It was extremely hard to hear so many clinical diagnoses now from a different counselor, about what is wrong with me.

Journal entry

June 19, 2019

I woke up wanting and planning to run! Yet, I began reading and looking further into how /what I was diagnosed with, to only run out of time.

I exercised at home for 15 min. That was the only time that was left. Before I went to work. I felt overwhelmed like I wanted to break down and cry.

But I didn't. Instead, I pushed forward.

I didn't make it far... around 8 am I noticed my bank account was overdrafted by $400. I was under the impression the fraud dispute was handled in May. The circle of phone calls and my emotions on high caused more stress. Then to have Rob's lawyer call, not once but twice. The call was almost 30 minutes of NOTHING. Only that maybe I can be a 3rd party custodian and go to court on his behalf. Basically, vouch for him. That he will go to court and not cause trouble. Which would get me in trouble. He asked for a letter from my job and a letter from his mom's provider. Stating that Rob is her caregiver.

All this while I am at work taking several emergent calls or calls that are a high priority of patients who have depression or anxiety.

A fucking merry-go-round!

I truly felt overwhelmed. Like I was stuck anyway I turned and the urge to break down and cry and to make it all stop. Was pounding at my head.

But I didn't...

I just kept my head up and kept pushing as if it was just a normal day.

I have a horrible headache.

Chapter Two
Summer Of 2019

June 22, 2019

8:09 am

I had a goal to write in here yesterday. I had the worst headache. My whole left side (neck and shoulder) was so tight and painful, it hurt to move. I recognize this. It's happened to me before with my ex. I carry my stress there, till it locks up. With the absolute worst migraine ever ALL day, yesterday.

Today as I wake I feel pressure again throughout my entire head. I pray it subsides. My left side is super tender and sore as if I lifted weights for a solid hour. I pray this lessens too.

Sounds and feels like I need to put yoga back into my diet.

My husband called me. Woke me up around 2:30 am. Our conversation was short. He basically snapped at me after I described my day and how horrible I felt. For him to say you need to listen to your Dr and take care of yourself first, not the kids. Or watch a movie.

It made me feel less of a person. Frustrated because I actually am trying to take care of myself.

His tone and approach really got to me. That I ended our call

IT'S NOT PERSONAL, BUT IT IS PERSONAL

because I could feel his energy tightening on my left side. The energy came through the electric current of a cell phone. Go figure.

Today - I will tackle today only.

Journal entry

June 25, 2019

6:38 am

I ran this morning, trying to beat the sunrise, instead, I joined Mother Nature crying a light dust of tears, as the sun joined the sky and at the end of my run a double rainbow appeared.

I am grateful

To be healthy and strong enough to fight through the pain.

I am grateful to witness such beauty.

Journal entry

June 26, 2019

11:16 pm

I saw my counselor today.

She told me to keep journaling. Don't stop. This will help.

Maybe I will take a second journal with me. To keep on me, so...when I am ready to spill... I can.

Mail

Card mailed out

June 26, 2019

To my husband

You are the stars to my night

You make my loneliness disappear whenever I see you

Thank you for putting up with my many moods. I'm so grateful that you are my husband!

I fucking LOVE you!

My Dearest Husband,

How I miss all the little things... like your beautiful smile, and your caring ways. Texting you when I get somewhere safely, asking a question when I please, or kissing you at my leisure. I miss the Big things too! Feeling safe, (Especially at home at night) Being in your arms, in your embrace, you sleeping in our bed (or not sleeping (wink)) Playing is always fun! Having date night. Having my best friend here to conversate at any time. Your unconditional love!

I miss it all!! I feel gypped! I bet you are feeling the same too!

I pray it all turns around and we never have to look back, only forward. Lost time we can never get back and it sucks knowing you are there and I am here, and that I am expected to keep living, even though my heart is gone and shattered.

How can I keep living, and happily at that? I don't know love. I miss you! I love you!

love your wife

Shana C

Journal entry

June 28, 2019

late...

I started my day doing for others, which made me feel good and happy. I gave 8 employees flowers and cards (thank you cards) to acknowledge appreciation. Most of the day I felt some joy.

...but there were several downpoints.

IT'S NOT PERSONAL, BUT IT IS PERSONAL

Including when I finally spoke with Rob. 2 days late. He bought us concert tickets and insurance on those tickets. Well –you cannot just get your money back without there being a legitimate reason -per Insurance Alliance Policy! Rob, believes it's easy and if I am not trying to get the money I BETTER GO! Or send someone in our place! $1200.00, for 2 tickets! LOL!

ME - For our anniversary, when he was home. I bought NFL football tickets and during that time we had a fight. One we could not resolve in time to drive together to Seattle to make it work for a gift I bought with NO insurance.

I never said you better go. I don't want the tickets to go to waste. I do not care for a double-edged sword, but come on.

The NFL tickets just went to waste.

We never went.

But his gift.

(sigh)... I am supposed to go. Smile. Dance. And all with a broken heart or give my gift away because the money with insurance is a FUCKING JOKE!

Maybe I will see about going to the fucking concert!

If it's meant to be it's meant to be.

Journal entry

July 1st, 2019

late..

actually 7/2

12:12 am

June came and went... just like that. The days kept moving.

My husband surprised me with concert tickets. He got them in

April.

I ended up going tonight with Marquita. It was the first concert I felt sad and alone at. It was beautiful music. Beautiful voice and all were great entertainers.

I was just sad. I felt alone even though I was surrounded by thousands of people and I was lost in all the memories I had of my husband.

I miss us and the love.

Journal entry

4th of July, 2019
9:20 am

First day off in 10 days!

And I feel yucky!

Pretty sure I will go on a hike because I don't want to stay inside on my day off, plus the sun came out!

I have been out of bed since 7 am and already cleaned the house, so I should go do what I love most and push all the aches and pains aside.

Explore a new trail!

Journal entry

July 7th, 2019

July will be wonderful! Full of wonderful memories. Full of hope, wonder, love, and riches!

I know this because I have a few events to look forward to! Today was one! I watched the Oakland A's kick Seattle's butt in Seattle! My son and daughter Destiny were with me and one of my nephews!

Both Gemini's first time going to an MLB game! The score was 7-4 and we almost caught a ball! And there was a RUNNER on the field! First time I saw that LIVE! Just some random person who ran out on the field. Not naked, but running around being chased. I have been to many MLB games. So to see this in person too, was quite the entertainment!

Great day with a new fun memory!

Mail

7.7.2019

My Dearest Husband,

Thank you for calling so I could hear your voice. I wish I could see you. I miss you. I love you! I do crave you, to be in your lap and by my side. I'm looking forward to that day!

In the meantime, I am trying to fill a void. I have planned a few things this month to keep me busy. Your Khalid concert kicked it off. ...and well baseball yesterday. It was nice to create the 1st baseball game memory for Q and Destiny! It brought back great memories! From my grandpa to us, and the kids. Joy can be found even during hardships. So I've heard.

The other morning I listened to a Podcast Eckhart Tolle mentioned at the end - If you tell another person (for example your partner). "Make me happy" usually ends in divorce.

I do not want this, so ...we both need to find and create our own happiness and then the rest will align. I don't want to depend on you to 'make me happy' and I don't want you to depend on me 'to make you happy.' Yet, I know we will create opportunities for happiness to experience together. I guess I can't wait till it all aligns again.

One day.

FUCK!

This Wednesday is 8 weeks! 2 months you are away from me! :(

I miss you PaPi!

That podcast I listened to also spoke of the essence dimension, which is self dimension and a higher spirit, one that can connect with earth and humans. When Eckhart spoke it resonated with me. I feel like I have this self dimension, the consciousness. I say this because he gave me a few examples. He spoke of people, he said humans either have empathy or not for humans and nature. Mentioning that humanity is a work in progress for most, yet there are some who constantly demonstrate goodwill, and bellavance, manifest, compassion towards others, and are very aware.

The other example was the forest. Most will walk through the forest and point out what everything is, that's a bluejay, a spruce, etc... explaining in depth which is great but then you have one that can walk in the forest and connect with their mind. Where the mind will become very still, able to be in a conscious present being aware of the sacredness, connecting on a deep level.

I feel this way when I hike, maybe this is why I am drawn to it. He also mentioned an old Ancient saying. I wrote it down so I could remember.

"Consciousness sleeps in the stone

Consciousness dreams in the plant

Consciousness awakens in the animals

Consciousness awakens to itself in the human."

Also called spiritual awakening. When you are still, you never move, essentially yourself than when you are still.

I feel still when I am in nature.

I thought I would share. Love you PaPi!

IT'S NOT PERSONAL, BUT IT IS PERSONAL

Love Always your wife

Shana C

Ps

If you ever go outside

Stare at the sky

You will find me,

I will be in awe, with you

Journal entry

July 13, 2019

almost midnight

I feel sad, angry, unsure, uneasy, lost, frustrated, alone, defeated

...for the last several hours... and probably most days.

I hope tomorrow some of this pain can subside

Mail

(Moose & bear card mailed out)

July 15, 2019

Sorry, ~~you're~~ WE are feeling mooserable!

Bear hugs and feel better wishes

I love you very much and miss you like crazy mi amor!

Love wifey

Shana C

xoxo

Journal entry

July 20, 2019

...late

I have not written...because I have kept myself busy

with doubt

pain

sadness

and questioning my space... as I go out to concerts or late-night chats or drink, or watch TV shows... one after another after another...

...if I come back to silence and being still in my home... It's too loud for me.

Mail

7.21.2019

Sometime after noon-

Literally

My Dearest Husband,

I am currently at Salmon Falls to gather my thoughts. Not sure a Sunday afternoon in the middle of summer is the best time ... Ten different families out here, all loud with noisy kids, screaming, crying, or throwing rocks. I am trying to focus only on the sound of white rushing waterfalls.

I am grateful you got to experience this place with me. When everything is still and nature performs at its best.

I miss you.

I miss us.

I am extremely sad, torn, and heartbroken that most of our married life ...

IT'S NOT PERSONAL, BUT IT IS PERSONAL

We will live apart... and have been, and will again.

I am questioning how I can do it all over again.

I keep searching for strength.

I found a few songs... a month or so ago... that I can identify with, and that my pain can relate to. Russ is the artist on 3 of the songs.

The first one is called 'Alright'

"If you reminisce, I hope you find some shit that helps you benefit

& alright

These are crucial times

I wish the pain in me committed suicide, & alright...

(the hook on repeat) (above)

You know my stress stretches zip codes

...if death comes in threes, then pain comes in twos.

... they see me strong, so I can't come off as very weak.

Alright.

The 2nd one is called 'Nobody knows'

Mask up my pain, hold back my tears

I'm going insane, nobody knows

All by myself, let the rain hit me

I'm going insane, nobody knows

(the hook)

...I'm talking to myself, I hope I'm listening...

heavens where you get when you fight through hell."

3rd one is called 'Fix This'

"I have nightmares daily, I feel crazy ...rock a fake smile

Momma, I had enough

Fix this

Sometimes it's just too much
Fix this ...
I'm dealin with a lot of pain
I don't know which way to go, tell it all to go away
but it be coming back for more
Momma, I had enough
Fix this ...
(the hook)
Sleep is my only escape from all of the pain, but I hardly sleep"

The other artist is Smino - actually had the song for a while, but just started playing it again. Called 'Long Run'

"Give me a sign
Show me the way
I've been alone
I've been afraid
You was suppose to be there for me, for the long run.
Why. why. Why. What I do"

I have been playing the songs less ...but they still ring loud. Especially during this time.

I don't want to go back in time, but when I sit here in the middle of the beautiful picture. My feet wading in the crystal clear water (ice cold, may I add!) I'm reminded of that beautiful peaceful day. When we read our books, people watched and found that snake. Maybe we should have spoken more, of a new path to take.

It's a little after 5 pm now. I took a break from the music and 'poor me' feelings. I people watched. I read. I got my feet wet. Read some more. People watched some more... a lot of people. Families came and gone. I would say at least a little over 400 (over the last 5 hours). Crazy how popular this spot is now. I've already packed up my belongings except for my backpack & this notepad. I figured I would go to the top of the waterfall to finish writing. Super quiet up here... no screaming kids. Just the river flowing to meet the fall and the wind whistling in between the dark green lush trees and branches.

Feels tranquil.

Like I found peace. (finally)

The sun is still high in the sky beaming down across the rocks and water. The sky is crystal clear blue, not a cloud in sight. I bet the stars would be beautiful out here.

I love you.

I miss you.

When I get home I will enclose a copy of a page I took from the new book I got. I highlighted the one I was asked to read out loud.

Survivor Guilt   July 5

"We begin recovering. We begin taking care of ourselves. Our recovery program starts to work in our life, and we begin to feel good about ourselves.

Then it hits. Guilt.

Whenever we begin to experience the fullness and joy of life, we may feel guilty about those we've left behind- those not recovering, those still in pain. This survivor guilt is a symptom of codependency.

We may think about the husband we've divorced who is still drinking. We may dwell on a child, grown or adult, still in pain. We may get a phone call from a non-recovering parent who relates his or her misery to us. And we feel pulled into their pain.

21

How can we feel so happy, so good, when those we love are still in misery? Can we really break away and lead satisfying lives, despite their circumstances? Yes, we can.

And yes, it hurts to leave behind those we love. But keep moving forward anyway. Be patient. Other people's recovery is not our job. We cannot make them recover. We cannot make them happy.

We may ask why we were chosen for a fuller life. We may never know the answer. Some may catch up in their own time, but their recovery is not our business. The only recovery we can truly claim is our own.

We can let go of others with love, and love ourselves without guilt.

Today, I am willing to work through my sadness and guilt. I will let myself be healthy and happy, even though someone I love has not chosen the same path."

(The Language of Letting Go by Melody Beattie, June 1990, page 183)

I do hope this letter finds you well and your heart slowly mending. You're in my heart and thoughts. I love you.

I will put $$ on the phone again soon. Just this month I have already paid over $500. It adds up. I will try to figure out the other # soon.

Until then, keep me close, as I do you.

Love Always

Your wife

Shana C

IT'S NOT PERSONAL, BUT IT IS PERSONAL

Journal entry

July 23, 2019

Today was a big day.

I interviewed for another position, well the same position at a different clinic. The reason - I wanted my 10s back. I was hired to work 10-hour shifts. 4 days on 3 days off. And I have always been flexible.

I wasn't going to say anything but I let the manager know on Friday. In hopes she would change her mind, nothing.

Then today we had an all-staff meeting and ironically one of the MA's gave kudos in front of everyone. Then one of the doctors did the same on her own time. What felt good was how she fought for me, she asked me if she could say something on my behalf to management. I told her sure.

The letter was immediate, within 5 minutes after our conversation, and powerful. She spoke in the letter/email very highly of me. She even said I was invaluable to her during her time at the department.

If things don't stay and I do move on, I am ok with this. Because I know I am of great value in any position or place of employment. I have always taken pride in my work and it feels good to know I am appreciated, recognized, and worth a great deal.

Journal entry

July 31, 2019

Disneyland comes to an end - 7.31.19 Today I am a little sad as I reflect on our trip...

E- 24

D-20

Jr-15

Only because I hoped every day we would be together & instead, the flu came and interrupted the flow.

Took Nonni down 1st for almost 2 1/2 days, then Jr for the last 2 days

It sucked

Even tho they were under the weather they tried to push through and join in - but they could not do past a few hours

I should be happy. I am thankful for being able to provide this, we did get great photos & experience some rides all together. I did get some one on one w/both my girls. I just hope they will have a great memory to look back on & one day want to do the same for their family.

Being together was wonderful. It just was in pieces... I guess life is that type of ride right now.

Mail
(Postcard from Disneyland in California)

Aug, 02, 2019

My Dearest Husband
Sending you love and magic from the happiest place on earth!

We miss you! Lots of love!

Love your wife!

xoxo

Shana C

IT'S NOT PERSONAL, BUT IT IS PERSONAL

Late night Sunday

8/18/19 10:02 pm

My Dearest Husband ~

I hope the pics and this letter find you in good spirits.

I'm sorry our time is short this week, fucking phone costs are becoming a car payment! And I need to start budgeting it in as a bill, or I'm going to get behind again. My mom just caught me up for the 2nd time and I don't want to keep asking. I shouldn't, at my age.

Back to our photos! I love these ones! I'm going to frame mines and put it by the bedside soon. We look like we have it all figured out! And we look happy! I miss US! I miss you!

Some moments are easier to accept than others. This was one of those great moments.

I love you!

I crave you!

I miss you!

Love your wife

Shana C

xoxo

Journal entry

Aug 25, 2019

I am overwhelmed with sadness. The last few days.

Yesterday I hoped for a call from my husband. I felt so alone and broken.

Today I woke up to the same ...too familiar feeling and the pain is sickening.

I am tired of this feeling.

I am not a fan of gluing my shattered heart together over and over again! It is exhausting!

I started packing my husband's clothes. Away... until who knows when.

How do I even deal with this heavy, sad, angry, broken feeling?!

Mail

11:06 pm
Late Saturday night
Sep 7, 2019

My Dearest Husband -

I hope this letter finds you with hope and love still in your heart.

I miss you. I love you.

I know we are both in extreme places, that neither of us ... (alone) ... wants to be in.

It's hard to find the words to put on paper. I'll try again tomorrow. I wanted you to know that I was thinking of you, that I love you and I am trying my hardest to go through life without breaking. It is so fucking hard.

It is 2:11 am and I can't sleep.

Alone in this bed. Alone in the house. I don't like being alone, and yet I am married. I just realized maybe this is 1000 times harder because this is the first time having absolutely NO contact, no physical touching. I can't see you! We can only do so much for 30 minutes on the phone once a day if we are lucky in a 24-hour period! It's fucking insane, driving me crazy, angry and sad! I can't believe I haven't seen you since May. Or touched you since May. hugged you, and made love to you...since forever ago! I FUCKING MISS YOU! This empty broken lost feeling is horrible! Last time I survived on our love, connection, your hug of security every Sunday, and passionate sweet kiss that I longed to go back to because we would actually sit still and talk, communicate anything and everything. We had a plan then, we did, we spoke of what we would do after you had not been home for over 3 years. More than 1,100 days apart. In an empty bed, but married...

Hey love, it's Monday night now.

The article/pages I included surprised me that 'Pain' was the topic. Ironically I am doing my best to feel the pain... and let it go. Yet, I do have tendencies to try and cope (by not coping) and keeping busy...to avoid the pain. So this part is yesterday... yet a lot of my life.

Stopping Our Pain September 8

"Some of my feelings have been stored so long they have freezer burn. -beyond Codependency

"There are many sources of pain in our life. Those of us recovering from adult children and codependency issues frequently have a cesspool of unresolved pain from the past. We have feelings, sometimes from early childhood to the present, that either hurt too much to feel or that we had no support and permission to deal with.

There are other inevitable sources of pain in our life too. There is the sadness and grief that comes when we experience change, even good change, as we let go of one part of our life, and begin our journey into the new.

There is pain in recovery, as we begin allowing ourselves to feel while dropping our protective shield of denial. There is the pain that leads and guides us into better choices for our future.

We have many choices about how to stop this pain. We may have experimented with different options. Compulsive and addictive behaviors stop pain - temporarily. We may have used alcohol, other drugs, relationships, or sex to stop our pain.

We may talk compulsively or compulsively focus on other people and their needs as a way to avoid or stop our pain.

We may use religion to avoid our feelings.

We may resort to denial of how we are feeling to stop our pain.

We may stay so busy that we don't have time to feel. We may use money, exercise, or food to stop our pain.

We have many choices. To survive, we may have used some of these options, only to find that these were Band-Aids –temporary pain relievers that did not solve the problem. They did not really stop our pain: they postponed it.

In recovery, there is a better choice about how we may stop pain. We can face it and feel it. When we are ready, with our Higher Power's help, we can summon the courage to feel the pain, let it go, and let the pain move us forward–into a new decision, a better life.

We can stop the behaviors we are doing that cause pain, if that's appropriate. We can make a decision to remove ourselves from situations that cause repeated, similar pain. We can learn the lesson our pain is trying to teach us.

If we are being pelleted by pain, there is a lesson. Trust that idea. Something is being worked out in us. The answer will not come from addictive or other compulsive behaviors; we will receive the answer when we feel our feelings.

It takes courage to be willing to stand still and feel what we must feel. Sometimes, we have what seems like endless layers of pain inside us. Pain hurts. Grief hurts. Sadness hurts. It does not feel good. But neither does denying what is already there; neither does living a lifetime with old and new pockets of pain packed, stored, and stacked within.

It will only hurt for a while, no longer than necessary, to heal us. We can trust that if we must feel pain, it is part of healing, and it is good. We can become willing to surrender to and accept the inevitable painful feelings that are a good part of recovery.

Go with the flow, even when the flow takes us through uncomfortable feelings. Release, freedom, healing, and good feelings are on the other side.

Today, I am open and willing to feel what I need to feel. I am willing to stop my compulsive behaviors. I am willing to let go of my denial. I am willing to feel what I need to feel to be healed, healthy, and whole."

(Melody Beattie, June 1990, pgs 256, 257, 258)

I drove Nonni back home yesterday. That took all day, plus the drive was a mess ...it was dumping pools of water, similar to that time we were driving back down from the Mirror Lake Mt Hood area. Freakn nuts! Today too, crazy wet out there looked like a few flash floods!

Well, I'm excited to hear your voice tomorrow.

I miss you! I love you!

I wrote/saved a few quotes that I try to read... maybe once or twice a week. Thought I would share. I love you.

Love your wife

Shana

"When you do things from your soul,
you feel a river moving in you, a joy."
-Rumi

"You can be rich in spirit, kindness, love and all those things that you can't put a dollar sign on."
-Dolly Parton
"If you can find a path with no obstacles,
it probably doesn't lead anywhere."
-Frank A. Clark

Journal entry

Sep 8, 2019

Sunday

I saw my counselor on Friday. The last 2 Fridays actually. She gave me homework. Make 2 lists. What I am angry about and what hurts and feels sad... I guess.

ANGRY

Being married, but I'm alone

Money

Rob is in jail (in a different state and I can't see him)

Myself

My choices

Always working

Not working out! WHY? Because I am depressed and can't find the damn mental space to do it! This pisses me off!

FUCKING STUFF -boxes everywhere in my house! Again! (I am going to work on this today!)

HURT/ SAD

I feel like I'm in the middle of a breakup. My heart is crushed to pieces.

IT'S NOT PERSONAL, BUT IT IS PERSONAL

My brother didn't get to live his life. I mean, he did live a great life, but he didn't live past 32 and get to see his 2 little girls keep living and growing. So basically my brother's death at too young of an age hurts me deeply.

Chapter Three
Falling Of 2019

M^{ail}

September 26, 2019
8:58 am Thursday
At work, on break
with heavy thoughts
of you my love

My Dearest Husband,

How I long for your touch, your warmth, your love, your kiss, your hugs ... (fuck you give the best ones!)

I miss you

I miss you

I MISSSSSSSS YOU!

I hope these photos keep you strong in health, love, and faith.

This could honestly be one of the most testing times yet, for both of us. Emotions are high, I know, from both of us.

I love you dearly. I always will. I know I may not always sound this way over the phone ...it is extremely challenging to show you this ...by voice only.

I am doing my best ...with pieces of my heart missing.

I look forward to living again. One day soon, I hope.

...late afternoon. Had to go back to work and it got really busy. So happy tomorrow is Friday even though I work Saturday too! Anyhow

I love you! I look forward to hearing my favorite song! (your voice! <3)

Love your wife

Shana C

xoxo

"Peace with the Past September 25

Even God cannot change the past.

-Agathon

"Holding on to the past, either through guilt, longing, denial, or resentment, is a waste of valuable energy – energy that can be used to transform today and tomorrow.

"I used to live in my past," said one recovering woman. "I was either trying to change it, or I was letting it control me. Usually both.

"I constantly felt guilty about things that had happened. Things I had done; things others had done to me –even though I had made amends for most everything, the guilt ran deep. Everything was somehow my fault. I could never just let it go.

"I held on to anger for years, telling myself it was justified. I was in denial about a lot of things. Sometimes, I'd try to absolutely forget about my past, but I never really stopped and sorted through it; my past was like a dark cloud that followed me around, and I couldn't shake clear of it. I guess I was scared to let it go, afraid of today, afraid of tomorrow.

"I've been recovering now for years, and it has taken me almost as many years to gain the proper perspective on my past. I'm learning I can't forget it; I need to heal from it. I need to feel and let go of any feelings I still have, especially anger.

"I need to stop blaming myself for painful events that took place, and trust that everything has happened on schedule, and truly all is okay. I've learned to stop regretting and to start being grateful.

"When I think about the past, I thank God for the healing and the memory. If something occurs that needs an amend, I make it and am done with it. I've learned to look at my past with compassion for myself, trusting that my Higher Power was in control, even then.

"I've healed from some of the worst things that happened to me. I've made peace with myself about these issues, and I've learned that healing from some of these issues has enabled me to help others to heal too. I'm able to see how the worst things helped form my character and developed some of my finer points.

"I've even developed gratitude for my failed relationships because they have brought me to who and where I am today.

"What I've learned has been acceptance– without guilt, anger, blame, or shame. I've even had to learn to accept the years I spent feeling guilty, angry, shameful, and blaming."

We cannot control the past. But we can transform it by allowing ourselves to heal from it and by accepting it with love for ourselves and others. I know, because that woman is me.

Today, I will begin being grateful for my past. I cannot change what happened, but I can transform the past by owning my power now, to accept, heal, and learn from it."

(Melody Beattie, June 1990, pg 274, 275)

IT'S NOT PERSONAL, BUT IT IS PERSONAL

Mail

Oct 6, 2019

8:34 pm

Sunday night

My Dearest Husband,

Thank you for this morning. Sharing one of your greatest accomplishments. That memory was beautiful. November of 2013 was grand! You played a huge part in making it magical. Thank you for not allowing the ocean to stop you from exploring and agreeing (or giving in) should I say!? For me to explore. The paddle boards! I remember you were pretty persistent on not having me go out by myself in the ocean. It was so beautiful out there. On the waves, the free turtles we saw swimming, the salty sand, and all the golden sunsets! What about parasailing!? At sunset! That was fucking amazing!! I loved that! One of my favorite memories! Hawaii had a way of keeping us high! And it all started with us celebrating you! For your birthday of 34! We came back and did it BIGGER! By celebrating US!

The photos I printed a while ago, and wanted you to remember your 43rd birthday! Being with you on any beach is the BEST! And I'm pretty sure I kicked your ass in Casino! (wink) Exploring, making love all day, our own hot tub time, and napping!

Fuck, I MISS YOU!

I love you

I miss you mi amor!

Keep me close to your heart, as I do you, with all my love.

Your wife

Shana C

Xoxo

35

I miss you, I miss us, I am grateful we have our memories - NO ONE can take that from us, or our love!

Oct 23, 2019

5:10 pm

My Dearest Husband ~

I hope this letter finds you in good spirits. I leave tomorrow for Mexico. Am I ready, nope of course not. ALL last minute, you know me. But hopefully tonight I can get organized.

I just jammed so many things in, including selling my enchiladas. Apparently, they were so good one person said, "Oh, I don't normally eat the red ones," yet once consumed she said, "They were sooo good!!!" quoting (because she sent it to me by text.) LOL, another one (well someone) LOVED them soooo much they stole someone else's plate, to have as their own. WTF! Right?!

I love you so much. I will keep you close to me while I travel and yes I will be safe. I will be back late Monday night. Says to arrive at 9: 30 pm.

I love you.

Love your wife

Shana C

xoxo

Ps

I included the story posted in

The New York Times, back in August

about Raphael Saadiq

  Reflection & photos from my trip building houses in Mexico

IT'S NOT PERSONAL, BUT IT IS PERSONAL

10.25.2019

Gloria, Mexico

The morning started at 5:55 am with a burnt smell and trees wrestling outside amongst themselves, you could feel their liveliness enter the open windows as we slept in our bunk beds.

I decided to climb out of bed before the alarm, to grab hot coffee, and catch the sunrise.

As I sat outside I realized the burnt smell was from the wildfires in California and somehow the ashes began to sprinkle on the greenery and ground of Mexico.

I read my daily meditation from author Melody Beattle as I adopted this new daily habit a few months back.

Which I will share, because it was so fitting for what was ahead.

It read: October 25th

"Some people believe that each of our days were planned, Divinely Ordered, before we were born. God knew, they say, and planned exactly what was to transpire.

Others suggest we chose, we participated in planning our life- the events, the people, the circumstances that were to take place, in order to work through our issues and learn the lessons we needed to master.

Whatever our philosophy, our interpretation can be similar: Our past is neither an accident nor a mistake. We have been where we needed to be, with the necessary people. We can embrace our history, with its pain, its imperfections, its mistakes, even its tragedies. It is uniquely ours; it was intended just for us.

Today, we are right where we need to be. Our present circumstances are exactly as they need to be- for now.."

SHANA CHRISTINE DILLON

(Melody Beattie, June 1990, pg 306)

As I finished reading the page, I looked up to see the sun rising as the crescent moon glistened above La Posada, and a new day would be beautiful with all its imperfections.

Shortly after St Joseph & Providence group that will soon be family was greeted with breakfast that was prepared by Santiago y Olivia. Two beautiful souls who woke up before dawn to prepare a warm breakfast that would fuel our day of 20. Breakfast was fresh fruit, hot cakes, & avena/oatmeal. After our meal, we gathered in a circle with Eduardo from Esperanza to speak of what the day ahead would consist of.

We would drive to a Community, Gabriel Rodriguez. We would meet Leticia Cruz Alejandra & help mix concrete to build the floor out in the hot 90-degree weather.

Eduardo & Victor drove us to the site. Eduardo has been with Esperanza for 21 years & once we were at the site his heart came alive. He began designating tasks, he grabbed equipment that needed all the men's assistance to move out of the area where the foundation was. Which I learned was what would help mix the concrete. Thankfully I thought to myself we are not mixing it by hand as we had to in 2017 when I was in Guatemala. It was very rewarding work on the soul, yet exhausting on the body, as I reflected.

Inside where the home would be we had lines of people 7 on one side and 5 on the other. These lines would help pass the buckets of all ready mixed concrete to be laid on the foundation to create a floor. Then another 4 stationed on the other side, cutting concrete bags in half, to cut the weight down once poured. Thirty, 100-pound bags of concrete to lift in fast motion, under the hot blazing sun is not a lot to ask from one person. Don't you agree? The task was shared of course, yet a huge physical task at that. Then there were anywhere from 3 to 7 people across the Street shoveling rocks into buckets -we needed five to be exact and sand into buckets, four to be exact, and not halfway.

"Make sure it is all the way full," said Eduardo, telling me in Spanish to tell them in English. He was definitely at home. Oh let's not forget 2 and 1/2 buckets of water and all of this for almost 3 hours in constant motion.

What a beautiful, sweaty, pain in our muscles yet with grateful hearts, manual labor kind of a day! With Spanish music blasting in the background and Eduardo yelling, "Agua!" which was our cue, after a minute of 'catch your breath,' which felt like 5 seconds. To begin our tasks again!

What an honor to be part of Leticia's family. Esperanza familia. And now our family Providence St Joseph's extended familia, from Oregon, Washington, Texas, California y Tijuana Mexico. What an honor to be here.

To be present.

To be part of something greater than us.

We were part of an enriching community, a family. Where we all were embraced as equal. Today was a beautiful imperfect day in Tijuana, Mexico.

Days after giving
This morning's reflection,
8:11 am Sunday

Sharing my last day, reflection, and pictures from volunteering at Esperanza

Life is supposed to go back in order.

You are supposed to wake up at the sound of an alarm clock, instead of roosters cawing, and staff chatting with love preparing breakfast for their guests.

You are supposed to prepare for the constant motion of what your work day instills no matter the struggle of a mending heart or physical barrier upon your spirit.

How do you process what you were part of, what you accomplished, and need the world to recognize to be present and move forward with giving hearts not one made of stone?

To simply be grateful for what we have, life's simple treasures are truly the greatest ones.

A home with a roof

A roof not leaking

Running water

Running hot water

Water you can drink from a facet

Electricity

Heat

Shoes

...life's simple things that many take for granted.

Be grateful

Move forward in your day with awareness and an open loving heart.

Small steps forward of giving will multiply in a ripple effect of why 'We' are truly here.

Spread love.

Create a wave of giving unconditionally.

One of my favorite sayings.

"Water is more precious than gold." (children of Flint, MI) ...and any other parts of the world struggling for clean water.

Mail

Anniversary card mailed out on 11/8/2019

11/13/2019

(front of card) image of the lady and the tramp eating spaghetti

Love you

My Dearest Husband,

6 years feels like a lifetime ago we got married. I wish I could tell you these words in person and you can make our favorite pasta dish! Maybe we can reenact this card one day. Maybe.

Well, I would like to wish you beautiful memories and I hope your heart and soul can feel the love we've shared.

Love you. Cheers to another year connected by spirit!

Sending Hugs, Kisses, and Love your way!

Love your Wife

Shana C

XOXO

Journal entry

Nov 21, 2019

Been awhile

The assignment I got last week, I am doing today.

What do I need and want from my husband? (that is still locked up)

-I couldn't think of what to write so I went through our old text messages.

And then you happened to call me.

20 minutes later

41

Still not sure what to write

...I want you to be the man you said you would be.

I need you to never put yourself in this position again, (because I feel like it was somehow knowingly) yet wrong place, wrong time.

I want you to want better for yourself.

We had dreams together and vacations we were supposed to experience together ...now they are on fucking hold.

I need you to want to stay the fuck out of jail!

I want you to stop breaking my heart

I need you to want to be FREE and stay FREE!

I want you to fight harder next time

I need my husband ...if I am staying married

I want to be at peace with myself.

I want to be happy, but you in there has me broken ...but not like last time ...this time I feel shattered!

Journal entry

Dec 4, 2019

I will now use this journal for my new therapy group class.

In class, we completed a guided meditation with the visions of the answers we wrote to questions given by email.

I enjoyed having the feeling of no burdens. Being able to wake up without having to run and clock in somewhere. I was able to catch a sunrise, live by the ocean, do yoga, help my kids if they needed it, travel, and go on mission trips to serve others in other countries. Help serve here in our country, and make a difference in others' lives because I made a change to mine. Smiling from within, having found a balance, spiritually, mentally, and physically! Feeling at peace. Letting go of any hardships.

                    ... later, still 12/4 I am at home now 9:38 pm

In my room

By myself

Surrounded by clutter ...with a very heavy heart.

I don't know if my heart is breaking for the woman I met and the stories they shared or if it's my own grief that sat inside stored up tightly for no one to see.

All I know is it feels so heavy it hurts like hell. The kind where it hurts to swallow.

Journal entry

                                                        Dec 18, 2019

In group, we drew ourselves in 3 different environments. I shared more this time. I don't feel heavy or light...just in the middle, this time.

Chapter Four
Winter Of 2019

M^{ail}
Holiday Card

(In front of the card is a Red Cardinal in bushes of cranberries covered in snow)

Peace is Always Beautiful. -Walt Whitman

12-25-2019

'Wishing you all the peace and joy the season has to offer'

My Dearest Husband

Hurts to write, so I typed. Love you!

Should have 5 things with this card

(typed)

Hi love

Wasn't sure how to write you, knowing we are a part again

I really hoped you would have been home, even if only for a few months.

I wish this wasn't so hard & we could have a Christmas miracle

I found this photo of us when you came home and things were simple. My heart yearns for you, your love, and peace of mind.

I hope the light is shed next year and our paths no longer have to be separated

    I miss you

    I love you

            Love your wifey

            Shana C

"Worry does not empty tomorrow of its sorrow, it empties today of its strength."

-Corrie Ten Boom

"Breathing in, I calm my body. Breathing out, I smile. Dwelling in the present moment I know this is a wonderful moment."

-Thich Nhat Hanh

"I finally figured out the only reason to be alive is to enjoy it."

-Rita Mae Brown

Chapter Five
Still Winter, New Year 2020

*J*ournal entry

Reflecting on 2019

What challenges brought the greatest learning last year?

I was diagnosed with ADHD (2 types) by a licensed NP and then my counselor said that I am Codependent. Hearing this news honestly felt defeating, which had me dig deeper to truly learn who I was. It was as if I was meeting a stranger yet, I had lived with her my whole life.

All of this was within weeks of my husband being torn from our home. I am still struggling with this and trying to find what is best for me while learning.

The important thing from this is I am able to get to the root of how I have been and why I would act a certain way. Now I know there are resources and tools to help me navigate.

2019 was the year of hard, tough, shattered pain and crucial facts.

IT'S NOT PERSONAL, BUT IT IS PERSONAL

2020 will be the year of self-care, healing, and learning myself in a new positive light.

My Intentions for 2020

I want to feel stress-free and not guilty for living.

I want to experience more nature in other states and countries.

I want to release any pain physically or emotionally.

I want to receive love, happiness, riches, and peace of mind.

Journal entry

Jan 7, 2020

The big rocks or storm clouds ...

I may experience this on my journey

Would simulate me... falling back into old habits, staying comfortable in a place I don't want to be in only because it is familiar, and not prioritizing by putting myself first.

I can see past these challenges on my journey. I will stop and remind myself to not fall back into old habits.

Journal entry

Jan 22, 2020

...half way through. ..In group

after meditation and imagery

By Martin Rossman & Andrew Weil

Exercise

The safe place was filled with a beautiful warmth, the sun was shining, and the water was crystal blue-green. The sound was tranquil of small waves opening doors on the sand. The light of the sun felt light and safe. I felt happy and at peace.

Relaxation is a tool for healing

Journal entry

Feb 5, 2020

Mediation Imagery

The advisor I met -came to me as a white silhouette that came to me by floating, engaging in the scenery ...in a flower garden near a warm beach.

I asked the advisor her name ...softly spoke saying spirit

The question I asked was will I live alone long ...again with a broken heart?

Response - didn't get any, instead, the image changed... everything turned gray around me

I tried asking again in a different way

Is this right? To not give up during this time of heartbreak and leave...

Again no answer

Write 4 affirmations for this year

I am healing

I am prioritizing

I am a new positive light

(I came up with 3)

-be mindful of self-care daily

-continue to create serenity in the middle of chaos

Now with affirmations... feels closer to 8/9

IT'S NOT PERSONAL, BUT IT IS PERSONAL

Journal entry

Feb 19, 2020

Sample dialog

'A problem or issue, or concern...'

Reference: Dr Gordon

Conversation for pain in the neck

Left Side Pain (LSP) - Guess I will call you by name

I noticed you are back and it's been a while, maybe 9 months.

Pretty sure I already know the answer - you are stress-related.

How do I get rid of you?

(LSP) - well you have to stop taking on so much.

Ask a question. I have a statement instead. This is easier said than done. If I don't stay busy I will be more stressed and sad about the reality I am living. So do you have a new idea or suggestion?

(LSP) - continue to be gentle as you tread. Go back into good self-care habits.

Mail

late night Feb, 2020

11 pm

My Dearest Husband

It feels like forever, how I long for your touch, your love, your embrace, affection, your strength, your lips, your everything ...I miss it all. Every bit of you I fucking misssssssss!

...even the stubbornness.

I wish I could hug you, kiss you, dance on you, straddle you, love on you, lick you, suck on you, fuck you, be with you, ALL OF YOU!

I FUCKING MISS YOU!

Missing you is an understatement.

Some days I am dying slowly inside as if I was cursed with aging 20 years per our one year.

I need you. I want you. I am yearning for you. I am craving you. I desire you.

It's a new year, 2020, how the fuck are you not home with me, with your wife?! Why are these years on repeat again!?

I went to Mom's for a little bit ...for the Super Bowl. Shit ...I thought I was fucking going crazy! Folks are on a whole other level, I couldn't even tell you.

I am telling you this because there was an old family friend there. She has been our family friend for almost 25 years. Her husband died 11 years ago. Well, she was there and she brought her boyfriend. She said, "I never thought that I would love again... & then this man showed up in my life, outta nowhere." ...then she started showing pictures of her new home in Oregon, living in a senior community, on a golf course ... then about 15 minutes or so, she asked my brother about his wife and kids, and then she asked me how I was doing and if I have someone special or a man in my life.

The whole house got quiet.

I responded. Yes, I'm married, I've been married.

...I came home ...wondered why she would ask. She knows I got married. Is it because my mom speaks of me, working all the time, being by myself, or because you weren't there...

I don't fucking know. But it felt surreal and lonely to say it out loud, and me knowing that YOU are NOT here.

Where I could just smile, conversation with you at any given time, without a fucking limit.

IT'S NOT PERSONAL, BUT IT IS PERSONAL

I fucking miss you! I miss you like crazy, like I'm addicted, sooooo in love, and everything is crushed inside. To have you there and me here. Some days it's hard to breathe ...I try really hard to not think about it. But then when I do, I can't swallow, and I just cry. It feels like grief, the feeling won't fucking go away. And I am trying. Man, I am fucking trying, for real I am.

I don't want you coming home when I'm old. We were supposed to do this shit together, not fucking apart. Grow old together. Instead, we are growing old rapidly from heartache, broken hearts, and shattered souls ...separately.

FUCK

I pray this is the last time god breaks me while I'm on this damn earth, my strength is dissipating. It is taking all of me to stay sane, and to move forward with how life should be.

Ya, I've planned a few things and every single one of 'em I want to cancel! I literally have a debate with myself on canceling ...every last one of 'em, since you've been gone.

Because I have to muster up the energy to go, be some type of way, happy, preferred since I will be out in public and suck up the pain, and suck up the guilt I feel for living.

I'm just so sad babe

I miss you

I miss us

I miss your smile, your laugh, I miss your hands, I miss our showers, I miss you making love to me. I miss you even telling me, "I've already told you ...you know I don't like to repeat things."

I miss coming home to you.

This missing. ..Sounds like a fucking broken record!

Fuck

PaPi I love you! Please meet me in our dreams, let's go to Hawaii ...make love on the beach. Kiss every part of me and I will kiss every inch of you. They can't take our dreams or our love.

xxxooooxoxo

Ps

Still hurts to write or hold a pen.

The only reason I decided to type it...& I needed you to know I love you. I miss you. I can't live without you. And this shit fucking hurts and it's driving me crazy!

Love always & forever

Your wife

Shana C

(valentines card)

2-14-2020

Front says

WE CAN STILL DO IT ALL NIGHT LONG

(inside says) ONE MORE EPISODE? Happy Valentine's Day

With a cartoon image of a couple sitting on the couch watching TV

My Dearest Husband ~

Craving you even more during this time of year. Love you & miss you! I got this card thinking it was funny ...we good for one more episode! HaHa!!

I hope this card finds you remembering all the good runs we did have! And all the special candle-lit dinners! I bet you would love to have me covered in chocolate-covered strawberries and champagne! Fuck I wish! And can't wait! Loving you & missing you!

IT'S NOT PERSONAL, BUT IT IS PERSONAL

Love your wife

Shana C

Journal entry

February 21, 2020

another year wiser...

During 2019 I decided to truly dig in, with a lot of soul searching, and healing ... I am still doing the work.

Healing is never-ending. (I am jumping with joy!)

NOT!

2020 and forward I decided I will be grateful for the gift of life.

How precious it is. Each living soul that will cross your path.

Although I am still extremely heartbroken that my little brother Miguel is no longer here dancing beside me in human form, he is a million times in spirit! And Ohhhhhhh How He Has Proven That!!

He came to me in several forms during the last 2 months.

To remind me that he is actually still here, dancing with me or skating ...each step of the way.

Thank you, little brother.

For the past 6 years, I have struggled with the thought of celebrating my life. Especially on My Birthday ...with the loss of you so close to this date. When your life was taken so abruptly it killed me.

Part of healing...

Is to live without guilt.

Today I will celebrate living.

Continue to count my blessings.

Live 1,000% with no regrets.

I will dance on this earth with a grateful heart.

I am proud that my little brother is still beside me.

Because tomorrow is never promised, and when life gives you Lemons ...well We ALL Know

...You paint That Shit GOLD!

Journal entry

March 4, 2020

In group

Take stalk of energy

40% Who I have unresolved guilt with

0% unresolved jealousy

35% Where do I have doubt? (future)

55% What do I actively worry about? (bills)

40% Where is my anger at now? (work)

25% Hurt that still lingers ... my brother

30% is shame

20% Where or who do I blame? (myself)

20% Regret -(not speaking up more and setting boundaries) ...causing resentment

55% actively fear - that I may make the wrong decision with work or my relationship if I change and choose a new path.

I am willing to let go of 40%

Next, write an intention letter

My intention in writing this letter is to release any regrets and to be free of the past. I feel angry at myself for not placing more boundaries in my path with relationships. I feel afraid that I may have caused damage to my kids. I feel hurt that I am married yet separated with circumstances out of my control. I accept the fact I have no control, it just sucks and feels like a whirlwind. I am slowly accepting living without my husband. The deep desire of my heart now is to feel whole. (not shattered glass)

What am I doing to support myself now?

I am practicing meditation and listening to wellness talks.

What I am asking myself for now...is forgiveness and patience. What I am asking for help from god or the universe is strength and signs ...so that I can travel the lighter path.

I am grateful that I can work on self-healing. My loving and powerful intention going forward is to continue with self-love, forgiveness, and healing.

Mail

Saturday

March 14, 2020

20 pics

My Dearest Husband,

Here are the photos you requested.

The ones you printed.

I'm not really sure I understand why "things" matter to you, but if it will bring you peace ...then so be it.

I would rather have a life full of laughter, love, and memories than to have something bought.

A planned or even a surprise picnic. One rose, not a dozen. A card with your feelings for me written, not a necklace. A long hug with a passionate kiss. A small getaway, to a state we have never been to. You. Just you, being present, being here with me for the rest of our days. You alone would be enough, as long as we continue to build on a foundation of trust, of what we truly want in this life.

What do you want in this short life we are given? What are you happiest doing?

Sending all my love your way with the longest hug & passionate kiss to follow. I love you! I miss you!

Love your wife,

Shana C

(Card mailed)

Front of card - couple holding hands in the field of dandelions

This is really hard, but we can do this.

Inside

Sometimes I'm overwhelmed with all we're going through. I can only imagine what it's like for you -bouncing from hope to fear and back again. When it feels like too much, we'll hold each other's hands. Some days will be easier than others, but I'm walking this road with you the whole way.

Sunday, March 15, 2020

12:50 pm

My Dearest Husband

Some days are harder than others, trying to catch my breath and stop the tears from falling from not knowing the unknown. My heart will never be whole again until I know you are safe, healthy, and free. Sending you all my love, long hugs, and kisses! I love you. I know we are both doing our best to hang in there with so many shattered pieces. I miss you!

Love Always & Forever, Xoxoxo

Shana C

IT'S NOT PERSONAL, BUT IT IS PERSONAL

Journal entry

March 18, 2020

No "in-person" group meeting
Instead, we logged in, online
Be at home
By yourself
Yet ...with each other
Two and half weeks ...deep into the chaos of the coronavirus
And ALL the closures around us including schools.
Now.
Draw how you feel.

Mail

(Good mail card)
Front of the card (many red and pink lips, no words)
Inside card (3 lips, saying "All the kisses. All for you.)

1:20 am
late Tuesday night
Wed morning 3.18.2020

~My Dearest Husband

I woke up trying to put my arm around you or climb on you ...to make love to you till the sun decided to peek through. It's late... a little past 1 am and the bed is empty. Again. Still empty. I want you home. I miss you. I need you home. I miss my husband! Missing your hands grabbing & gripping my ass, while you are deep inside me. I need you to kiss my neck, caress my breasts, suck and kiss below my hips, cum back to me. Cum suck on my neck, bite me, love me, fuck me, want me, need me, be with me, cum with me...

Fuck I Miss You! If only you knew how much....

I love you PaPi!

Love always & forever

your wife

Shana C

Chapter Six

Sick Spring Of 2020

*J*ournal entry

My life

My fucking life

...is faced with obstacles and you will have many detours thrown at you Shana

and you will adjust those sails

and remind yourself to breathe

and go with the flow

not against the current

& those who truly know me

Know...

I seem to love that damn current

Because I'm not that person who goes with the flow or plays follow the leader

I am a leader!

So I will adjust the sail and take it in one wave at a time ~ ~ ~

Happy Damn Friday!

I was summoned for Grand Jury Duty in the middle of an epidemic for Covid-19!

World Wide!

Businesses were closing in different states and placing bans for people to stay home, across countries.

Stating we have to stay 6-10 feet apart (calling this social distancing)

The courthouse did not open its doors till about 5-10 minutes after the fact of a few hundred people waiting outside spread as far as you could see, there was no single line, or any line for that matter to get inside.

A lady came outside and said, "You have a choice to leave or stay, this will be the only time we do this due to the circumstances. Please understand this does not dismiss you from jury duty you will be called back at the next one, but you are free to go if you are not comfortable coming inside. We will not all go in one room. We will all be in several separate rooms, so we can social distance."

A person asked if they could get their form signed for work to show they did attend.

The response was you have to attend the entire process if you want that signed.

(I thought to myself, they answered my question, I guess I am staying) About 4 hours later, sitting in a room 3 seats apart from any other person. 15 people in my room, 70 chairs. They announce that instead of 35 people they will pick 14. The reason being we could not be in a group of 10 or more. (this would be 2 groups of 7)

My # was 114 out of 257 people called to show.

I was the 5th person picked

IT'S NOT PERSONAL, BUT IT IS PERSONAL

I start on Monday, for 2 days every week.

For the next 5 weeks!

Honestly, I wanted to laugh. What the fuck!?

A lady asked a question (the exact thoughts that I was thinking) while we were waiting. She said, " California just shut down, we are in the middle of a pandemic, do we really need to come if we are picked?"

The response was, "Yes you still need to come. The pandemic does not mean the government is closed down."

I am pretty sure I did laugh.

Out loud.

Journal entry

March 20, 2020

Sunday is when I water my plants

...Somehow the last 2 Sundays I did not get to this task, w/ the overwhelming outside world ...piled on my inside world. It is a lot to manage...

This last week I looked up at this one plant and from what I could see a yellow leaf is now forming... dying under the green one

Shoot!!!

I told myself on my way out the door heading to work. To water my plants! (My work is in healthcare, at a medical office) ...this whole week, I just kept forgetting. Maybe it is because I am working all the time trying to just stay afloat during the chaos and bills. I start an hour earlier and stay an hour later, for many days now.

This Sunday I will remember to care for you and get rid of the dying leaf...

Journal entry

March 23, 2020

Monday

First day of Grand Jury Duty

We started at 11 am and ended at 4:44 pm

There were 4 different possible federal cases

Strangulation, burglary, intent to distribute drugs with possession of drugs, and sodomy.

Journal entry

March 24, 2020

You know how sometimes you are right in the middle of it... and you second guess the signs or don't understand the lesson till later?

Two things

First, when I was chosen I thought one reason for this was to give me a break from my current job and I still get paid. The 2nd thought... I get to understand behind the scenes. Gain knowledge and insight into the system and the irony of my current situation.

Journal entry

March 25, 2020

Wednesday

We, "America, the state of Oregon" are officially supposed to stay in the home unless there is an urgent need or you work for a place approved to stay open.

Well, I work in healthcare and my lovely new gig (smirk face) 'Grand Jury Duty' is approved to stay OPEN!

IT'S NOT PERSONAL, BUT IT IS PERSONAL

Yesterday's caseload was:

2 different robberies and an assault.

After the cases were viewed, discussed and dismissed, or agreed upon, I went to work, back at the clinic.

How can one job cause anxiety ALL damn day?!

Journal entry

New week, same month

Monday, 9:20 pm

March 30, 2020

Today's Grand Jury Duty schedule was supposed to be from 9:30 am - 4:30 pm with a one-hour lunch break. Instead, it was 9:30 am -6 pm with only a 25 minute lunch.

We had 6 cases

Aggravated Harassment

Arson 1

Unlawful use of a weapon

Burglary 1

Attempted Arson 1

Assault 2nd & Attempted Murder

Exhausting long day.

The last case was traumatizing. The victim was clearly shaken up and after she spoke of this person who she met the same day had tried to stab her with a knife and was out to kill her, he said. When she was done sharing her story, she was told she was free to go.

My heart went out to her.

What in the world?!

Free to go?! With no one to console her, to help her, and no resources provided. Very heartbreaking to see. Especially with our government.

After a very long traumatic day, I got a voicemail from my supervisor saying some things changed with work and to give her a call.

No one answered. (double sad face)

I got in touch with a coworker, and they said we got split up into 2 groups within the clinic. To help with social distancing. Half would come to work one week while the other half would be on-call.

I am on call this week.

Then after all this... my husband calls with expectations of me communicating with his lawyer. Now. Not later. Right now!

Asking me to send the text messages out. Again.

Oh ya... (sad face) and my acupuncture got canceled for tomorrow, due to COVID-19 and the new ban is in place until April 30th.

Is this a sign? 4/30 is someone's birthday!

Lol

My stress level is HIGH!!!

Journal entry

still 2020
Date unknown

Notes for myself to destress...

Energy field tapping ~ eft

Thought field tapping

Use the oils

Remember 'subconscious'.

Pay attention to what we are feeding our mind

Feed healthy cells, not the coronavirus

IT'S NOT PERSONAL, BUT IT IS PERSONAL

Journal entry

April 7, 2020

The driving to get to Grand Jury and to work... complete opposite directions is wild to be part of during the Pandemic. It feels like the twilight zone. Or that old movie called Night of the Comet, from the 80's! The feeling of driving anywhere right now ...is eerie.

Yesterday Grand Jury was a blur. ...four or 5 cases. I remember 2 were burglaries.

Today, there was only one.

Strangulation

5 pm today, exactly. I received a response from Rob's lawyer, Todd. He is no longer Rob's lawyer. Rob asked me to text him saying he wanted him to remove himself from his case.

I sent that message 3 days ago.

Not really sure how I feel about this. More so because I don't know who will take his case in the middle of a pandemic. Whoever this new lawyer will be, will they fight hard for my husband, or will it all be half-ass assessed?!

Rob has been gone for 11 months. His trial was supposed to be next month and now I have no answers again.

Not sure how I feel, maybe lost again, worried, and a little upset with myself for being the middle person, again.

Rob sent a letter, a motion to release the lawyer, as well.

Did I really need to send the message too?

Mail

(Sympathy Card)

Front of card - Forest

It's so hard to lose someone you love, especially when it happens so unexpectedly.

Inside card

Always remember that you have the love and concern of family and friends. So many people care about you and are keeping you in their thoughts & hearts.

4.11.2020

My Dearest Husband

My heart breaks as I write this.

I am crying.

At the pain, I know you feel, for the loss of such a beautiful friend, a true gem. For having to give you a card instead of a hug. I am so sorry for this horrible pain and loss.

I wish I could say something that will make these days easier. I can only say to treasure the memories and cherish the conversations. Keep Earl's spirit alive by speaking or remembering all the gifts you 2 shared. He was an Angel ...long before he left us. My deepest condolences, my love. Your heart and spirit are in my prayers daily for healing. I pray one day peace will find you. I love you PaPi, with all I am.

Love your wife

Shana C

xoxoxo

Journal entry

April 15, 2020

Back at work.

The vibe and energy is still off. Super overwhelming.

I learned something new about myself during the last few weeks.

I am absolutely an empath.

IT'S NOT PERSONAL, BUT IT IS PERSONAL

Now I know why I can read the rooms I enter, it is simply the energy.

I will work on learning more... about myself.

...also. I was supposed to write another letter, to forgive someone... Not sure who that someone is yet.

Journal entry

late entry for
Grand Jury Duty
April 13 & 14

Assault 2

Attempt Elude

DCS Methamphetamine

Attempt Assault 2

Assault 2

On the 14th, we continued the case for DCS Meth

Well a repeat

Because the officer was not sworn in and continued finishing the Assault 2 case

Then we had another Assault 2 case and a Strangulation & Possible Rape

EXTREMELY HEAVY

Journal entry

still 2020
Date unknown

10 Things that are good from our Pandemic of COVID-19

When I was on call -I got to stay home, this reminded me of what I am grateful for

- connection with my kids, during their time of staying home, to help prevent any sickness or illness

-I am able to help others while working in the healthcare field

-I feel like my neighbor and I will be more than just neighbors, I know it is weird but we just met (and we have been living next store to one another for a couple of years now) all because of Grand Jury Duty ...I was called to finally introduce myself

-Currently, I still get one on-call day, so kinda like an extra day off

-I learned a new coping skill (tapping)

-less driving (which normally would be school events, sporting events, orthodontist, etc....)

I guess I can only come up with 7 good things

Gratitude and Forgiveness

The 2 most important letters

Work on separating my energy and or not allowing the negative energy to absorb me

Work on writing a letter to continue the healing

Work on being kinder and gentler to myself. Do not be so hard on myself

-4 steps of A/A

Journal entry

April 19, 2020

Sunday

8:34 pm

My son is in his room watching YouTube of people playing video games. I am solo in my room with boxes everywhere still ...you would think there were 10 of us living in this house. So many boxes...

As I write ... my entire arm and hand still hurt to grip and hold a pen. I guess I really did injure myself when I was in Mexico, volunteering to build houses.

Tomorrow is the LAST week of Grand Jury Duty. THANK GOODNESS!!!

...the only thing I will miss are the half days, going away.

I posted 21 empty sticky notes on the mirror. The plan is to motivate myself back into a workout routine or start running again. Something to get myself out of depression. After I complete the task, then I will remove a sticky note. ...eventually to see a partially healed person in the mirror.

We are still in the beginning stages of a pandemic with a fucking idiot in the president's seat!

My husband has NO lawyer, who knows when he will go to court for trial now with Las Vegas shutting down!

Truth ...the whole world, has shut down!

Crazy to think this is the last page of this book. This journal was gifted to me 4 years ago, from a kindred spirit. My beautiful friend Justina. I guess she knew back then... I would need it.

...wish me LUCK on my new 21-day habit 4-life!

Until the next journal!

Deuces!!

The first page of this journal (was/is) 2.21.2016
"Positive Mind
Positive Vibes
Positive Life
Happy Birthday Beautiful

We don't meet people by accident. They are meant to cross our paths for a reason. Thankful you've crossed mine." <3
Justina

Mail

8:22 pm
Monday night
4.20.2020

My Dearest Husband,

After Grand Jury Duty I came home, ate, cleaned up a little, and then walked over to the park to be warmed by the sun. It felt good, almost like a hug with several birds around singing that spring was near.

I sat out there for almost an hour reading. I finished a book full of poems. Several jumped out at me, and I decided I would write some down to share with you.

Most are really short, yet have a powerful feeling or message behind the delivery.

Thinking of you

Miss you

Love you

& I hope this letter finds you in better spirits ...or at least on the mend.

Love your wife
Shana C
Xoxo

Poems by Atticus
LOVE HER WILD

LOVE (pg. 30)

"If I had all the treasure in the world, I would follow my dreams, play with my children, and spend time with my wife."

"No," said the old man.

"If you followed your dreams, played with your children, and spent time with your wife. You would have all the treasure in the world."

LOVE (pg 49)

"It's A LONELY THING, PROTECTING A BREAKABLE HEART."

LOVE (pg 70)

"I aspire to be an old man with an old wife laughing at old jokes from wild youth."

LOVE (pg 55)

"I let her go because I knew she could do better and now she's gone, I wonder if I should've just been better."

HER (pg. 100)

"I promised to kiss her a million times before I died.

Fifty a day for the rest of my life – so when I was gone she could smile knowing there wasn't a place on her I missed."

HER (pg110)

"Brushing a girl's hair behind her ear once a day will solve more problems than all those therapists and drugs."

HER (pg 126)

"Angels must be warm to fly -that's why she always slept in socks."

HER (pg 134)

"She had been through hell and though no one could see her demons they could see the face that conquered them."

HER (pg 137)

"That was her magic – she could still see the sunset even on those darkest days."

WILD (pg 154)

"AN ASHTRAY WITH A GOOD STORY

MAKES THE SMOKE TASTE BETTER."

WILD (pg 173)

"The hardest step we all must take is to blindly trust in who we are."

WILD (pg 175)

"What a strange world we trade our days for things."

WILD (pg 191)

"I worry there is something broken in our generation, there are too many sad eyes on happy faces."

WILD (pg 192)

"There is always a glimmer in those who have been through the dark."

WILD (pg 223)

"I hope to arrive at my death late, In love and a little drunk."

New journal

Purchased in 2019 at Common's concert

"Let Love Have the Last Word."-Common

Journal entry

April 21, 2020

Today is my cuzzy's bday

Signs and numbers. I keep seeing them. This last month and a whole lot this week... the last few days.

555

4444

IT'S NOT PERSONAL, BUT IT IS PERSONAL

1144

111

114

and hummingbirds

Today was the last day of Grand Jury Duty

We had one case today and 3 yesterday

Today ended with possession of meth and intent to distribute methamphetamine

Crazy!

The person was pulled over because the car had no LP in front of the vehicle. He had 9 grams on him. Apparently, the rule book is if you carry more than a point something or more than 2 grams you are a dealer. Even though there was no act of the person selling ...they can charge you.

Yesterday's case might have been the worst yet... or should I say caused the most trauma.

We had to listen to a 911 call of a woman asking for help. Asking her roommate to leave and she feared for her life. He grabbed a knife...

Supposedly had left the apartment only to come back punching the lady over and over and over... again in the face and head.

It was excruciating to hear ...to listen to the painful event unfold.

It was sickening, I felt sick.

Then it got worse, we saw the victim on live video chat. Her whole face was black and blue. Two black eyes swollen shut, on the 1st day.

This reminded me of how scared I was to stay at my aunt's house when I was younger. Age 11 or 12... reason, her boyfriend at that time would beat my aunt. One of my cousins later shared that he abused each of my cousins too.

So sickening how people can treat others this way. I hope I never have to hear such horrible life stories again.

This makes me feel helpless and awful for the victims involved.

4/20 was

Assault 2

Assault 2

DUII x2

...going through a Pandemic and facing these unsafe acts are extremely uneasy and overwhelming.

All in person

...for this.

I am glad it is over.

I don't have the stomach for it.

Journal entry

April 24, 2020

I woke up today to a not-so-good text message.

From my step-dad

"Good morning. Happy Friday! Not so much for me, I'm home today trying to find a Dr to get a mental assessment for her. It's gotten verrryyy bad. Had to leave work yesterday. She had another mental breakdown! I'm so so worried. (sad cry face) and there's more I can't tell you about or I will be in trouble! I have someone I will call and hope they can get things started! Sorry for all this. Love you!"

At 5:58 am

I called

IT'S NOT PERSONAL, BUT IT IS PERSONAL

We spoke

Eventually, he said what he could not say

Because I guessed it

I asked.

"Did my mom steal again?!"

He said, "Yes, but it's worse!"

My mom not only stole... she stole a whole grocery cart full of food. She was stopped outside as she was putting items in her car. They asked her for a receipt and instead of cooperating she hurried into her car, drove off in a panic, and sideswiped 2 cars.

So she did a hit and run, on top of theft!

The police were looking for her, and she told her husband, and he advised her to call the police to talk.

Due to many witnesses and video footage, she has 2 charges she is facing. Court is on May 20, 2020!

Since we are currently in a pandemic they did not put her in jail! The only reason why, they assured her.

So... maybe I can now put # 8, 9, and 10 on my list of what I am grateful for during the Pandemic! Her not being placed in Jail **absolutely** takes number 8, 9, and 10! My mom staying free! *That* I am grateful for.

To top all this off! Grand Jury Duty is NOT over, The judge extended the term until May 29th!

Why?!

Again, due to COVID-19!

They also mentioned that we did such a good job that it only makes sense to keep who they have instead of requesting new people.

I laughed. Out loud. Again.

Journal entry

April 24, 2020

Letter

My assignment from 'Group Class'

Write a 2nd letter

Took me a while to figure out who I needed to forgive.

Well, what better way to heal than to forgive the past?!

My intention in writing this letter is to forgive the past. To release any resentment or regret and to be free of the past. My intention is to release any anger or hurt so that I may move forward in peace and freedom

To my X, I feel angry that you lied several times and made me feel like shit as if I was the bad guy. I feel afraid that if I do not forgive you, you still have some kind of power over me. I feel hurt that you abused me mentally, and physically, and you did this with no remorse. I feel sad that you are my children's father and you played victim several times to them making the kids feel bad about their choices. When anyone in their right mind would know that adults should lead by example. To be accountable and to never blame a child for being busy with sports or bettering themselves in their education.

I accept the life I once had with you because it taught me many lessons, I will not repeat. I accept that you may never apologize or be accountable for your actions and the pain you have caused.

The deep desire of my heart now is to not cause trauma or heartache to my kids.

What I am asking for is help from the universe or a higher power for strength and guidance in raising honest, compassionate humans.

I am grateful for surviving many dark days, months, years... with you.

My loving and powerful intention going forward is to love myself, and my kids unconditionally regardless of any pain and to not place blame.

signed, the healing me

Journal entry

April 27, 2020

Man life is funny

Right back at it

Grand Jury Duty Agenda was 9:30 am -3:30 pm with a one hour lunch

But at 11:30 am the schedule got rearranged & lunch will now be 30 minutes

The first one took a little over 2 hours - Unlawful use of a weapon with 6 charges and 3 different victims

The 2nd case was Attempt Rape in 1st degree with 3 charges including 2 counts of sexual abuse, robbery with one victim

3rd was taken off the docket - ~~Strangulation~~

Last case - Arson, manufacture of cannabinoid extract, and unlawful use of marijuana

Mail

(Birthday Card)

Front of card -Sunflowers w/gold trim

A day full of sunshine, good wishes, and happiness.

Inside Card - Have that kind of birthday. Enjoy Your Day.

4.30.2020

My Dearest Husband ~

Thinking of you, a lot more these days. With your birthday here
...and you there. Sure wish I could give you a birthday hug, kiss, loving,
and make breakfast with my bootie out for you to grab kinda day!
Happy 44th Birthday my sweet husband. Wish I could be your present
and you could just unwrap me!

I miss you. I love you. Found this old photo ...thought you might
want it. Also, I sent you 2 books, for your birthday and put a little
money ...towards what you may need. I wish I could celebrate you in
person. I wish our wishes came true.

Love you. Wishing you feel love & some joy on your birthday PaPi.
Words by M.L.K.

"There can be no deep disappointment where there is not deep
love."

Words by William Shakespeare

"The course of true love never did run smooth."

Words by Mother Teresa

"The hunger for love is much more difficult to remove than the
hunger for bread."

Words by Leo Buscaglia

"Love is life. And if you miss love. You miss life."

Words by Shana Dillon

"I miss the taste of your sweet MaCallan lips, against mine."

Feliz Cumpleanos mi amor!

Love Su Esposa

Xo

IT'S NOT PERSONAL, BUT IT IS PERSONAL

Journal entry

May 6, 2020

Today is my little brother's birthday!

Big 36!

Heading out to celebrate him! We started early ...last night!

Late entry

For May 4th & May 5th

Grand Jury Duty -

Monday

-Tampering with witness

-Sex abuse 1 and Attempt Rape 2x (2 victims)

This did not sit well with me. I was able to envision all of it, the exact place, where, and what the home looked like. Why? I lived in the exact address for a few years, almost 20 years ago. Listening to this was extremely traumatizing.

-Aggravated Harassment

-Assault one and unlawful use of a weapon (this was a horrible stabbing)

-DCS /PCS Meth

Tuesday

-Coercion with a firearm

-Kidnapping in 2nd

-Unlawful use of weapon, 4 counts

-Menacing, 2 counts

-Pointing firearm, 4 counts

-Harassment, 4 counts

-Stalking

-Computer Crime, Identity theft, Encouraging child sexual abuse in 1st degree, Unlawful dissemination on an intimate image, 8 victims, 1 minor

HORRIBLE!!!

So done listening to this sickness, corrupted part of the world!

Journal entry

May 6, 2020

Group 6-8 pm

Self-sabotage

Self Worth, worthiness

-The problem will exist until the lesson is learned.

Take note of where I numb out and what am I trying to escape

Repetition compulsion- Where do I see this (not so good) habit in my life?

Shame is different than guilt

Self medicate -

Anything we do to distract us from how 'I FEEL'

Be aware of this

List 5 things for benefits of choosing self-med

-sometimes distress

-don't have to face the work

-depending on what it is, can help me escape

-easier way out

-makes me feel

What is most appealing?

-instant gratification

IT'S NOT PERSONAL, BUT IT IS PERSONAL

Are you avoiding doing things that are more adventurous or emotionally demanding? What are you avoiding?

-Emotionally demanding

I am avoiding my current state, my husband in jail and only my family knows. Feels very painful, and shameful, this feels personal to me. I do not want to feel judged.

Journal entry

date unknown

Still 2020

Be full of grace and be compassionate with yourself during this time.

Reminder - work is not who I am or adds value

We will continue to have consequences until we learn what we need to know

Whenever we are resentful of a person it is because they crossed a boundary

Make NO apologies for SELF-CARE

Journal entry

May 31, 2020

Late entry

Today is Sunday night almost 10 pm

A Lot has happened this week... a few different milestones ...feels like.

Grand Jury Duty is finally over!

Is it ironic to have done this during a Pandemic for 10 weeks!?

Hard to say

Tuesday's load was a bit lighter since 3 of the cases got put off for another day. LOL and for the first time, we actually had a lunch break longer than 25 minutes

It was wayyy too early for lunch, but it was a long needed one.

10:45 am -12:30 pm

5/26/2020 - Schedule was 9-5 - 9 cases on the docket

-Theft 1

-~~Strangulation~~

-ID Theft

-~~Unlawful use of weapon~~

-Unlawful use of weapon

-Burglary 2 & Criminal Mischief 1

-UU MV

-Strangulation

-~~Strangulation~~

(the 3 crossed out were removed from the docket) and we still got done after 5

Lessons learned and things came to light.

Done!

SO DONE! Finally!

Then Wednesday after work I had a meeting with a loan officer and I was approved for a home!

Finally, GREAT NEWS!

(big smiley face) I am approved to buy a home! Beach here we come!

Now today, Sunday... I finally went through half of our bags and boxes... at least the ones that are here at the house. All this stuff was from back in the day when our other home was torn apart in 2014. There was A LOT. It was crazy to go through 6 years of memories on paper and to be doing it all by myself.

Again. All by myself, again.

Mail
(Card)
Front of card - 2 bears hugging
I wish I was there to give you a hug
Inside card - blank

June 1st, 2020

Or you were here with me...

My Dearest Husband,

How has it already been a whole year? (sad face)

It's 5:40 am, Monday morning now, June 1st of 2020.

Yesterday, I started going through our things around 9 am and stopped at 4. There was so much. Sorting through all the paperwork wasn't the hard part. It was revisiting our past, knowing our privacy was invaded. It was hard going through memories we built together and many memories we did not. It reminded me I needed much more than super glue and wine to piece my heart back together. For 6 years I packed all of this away and took this weight from place to place ...at least my room is no longer in the living room. I don't know why it took me so long to go through it. 2,190 days ...plus some. Bittersweet. Bitter because it reminded me again of how much time we lost NOT holding each other. Sweet, fewer bags I have to carry on the next move. I wish this card was more uplifting. Yet the reality is our life ...well, at this time ...our life is like a yo-yo. I feel like we need a professional to yo-yo our life, so we can have more ups than downs. I miss you. I miss your strong hands and your warm hugs. Your sweet kisses. I do love you, very much ...even through all this pain. I just wish I could hug you & kiss you. Make it all go away. I love you PaPi

Love Always your wife

Xoxoxo

Journal entry

June 3, 2020

Group 6-8 pm

Grief is not to be treated.

Grief is a natural process for the mind and the body.

When grief is not processed and when it gets stuck in the body it will make the body sick.

Grief is how we perceive it.

Where is the bar? (look back at the letter written to yourself for 6 months of work)

What are my gifts or talents to help me achieve my goals?

-follow my intuition

What are the blessings I need to recognize to move through this journey?

Journal entry

June 6, 2020

All day

Saturday

Woke at 6 am

Left house at 8 am

Picked up my mom at 8:10 am

Got gas

IT'S NOT PERSONAL, BUT IT IS PERSONAL

Drove 1.5 hours to the coast so I could look at homes to buy! My son was with us too!

We saw 1, 2, 3, 4, 5, 6 -homes!

6 homes in Lincoln City

I have to say pictures online and being in person are very different!

Now to decide, do I really want to spend 3 hours a day in my car driving ...or start looking for a new job?!

The homes were nice. There was not one home that had everything I liked and all had pros and cons. I am happy Jr was there to take videos.

Journal entry

June 7, 2020

Full Moon

Listening to a full moon in Sagittarius workshop

Focus on Tribe in the ever changing circle

I need to detach from old belief systems

Energy is fluid, not linear

Pisces ~ Listen and pay attention to your body

Too much effort -

Pride is driving a force that keeps saying to make it work, but I need to step back because it is toxic and it is time to not force it. Even if I am committed.

I need to release what no longer serves me

Pay attention to my soul, to my soul tribe, to my divine energy

Pay attention to who is aligned and who I am

Need my space

Need time for myself

Need a break... especially during healing for codependency
Release any oppressed relationships

Chapter Seven
Stifling Summer Of 2020

*J**ournal entry*

July 1, 2020

8:05 pm

I had my group class tonight

Today was the first time I told the class that my husband is in jail.

My trauma and what I spoke out loud was inspiring to my counselor to change our exercise to a few writing topics, from Dr James Hollis

2 people from our class were not there. So it was much smaller and intimate. (only 2 judges instead of 4) I am not sure how this feels, saying it out loud.

Yet, my trauma inspired others. I guess it sparked an interest in digging deeper into our own wounds. And now a suggestion of tools or resources that can be used for one with trauma.

Living an Examined Life by Dr James Hollis

Being Vulnerable (pg 164)

Where do you need to grow up?

I need to grow up by slowing down. Not taking on everyone else's problems before I have a chance to resolve my own.

I need to grow up by not taking things so personally mainly at work, when conversations are not had.

I need to grow up by allowing my kids to grow and learn from their own mistakes.

I need to grow up by being more gentle with myself. Be kind, be like a kid who has not been tainted by the harshness of the world.

Instead of feeling like you need to be a certain standard, be authentically you.

Set your boundaries as you please. You are your own person and you can choose growth with happiness.

You can be light and easy on your soul.

Everyone grows at their own pace.

Grow at your own pace, let go, and grow at your pace.

(drew a pic of a full tree)

Mail
(Good mail Card)
Front of card - Lemons
Life won't always be like this.
Inside card -
Sweeter days are coming

7/8/2020

6:44 am

sunrise

IT'S NOT PERSONAL, BUT IT IS PERSONAL

My Dearest Husband ~

I do hope sweeter days are coming. How I long ...and miss them so!! I know you do too.......

I know this time around has been extremely difficult and challenging for both of us, for many reasons. Now we just have to figure out the underlying message. The lesson ...and never repeat it again.

I know part of mine... It is figuring out myself and creating boundaries. This is a HUGE lesson in itself... and seems to be a rollercoaster of emotions during a pandemic and my husband locked up for who knows how long. Extremely hard to find balance. ...but I know it's in us. I know it's in me, I know it's in you... so we can't give up. Right!? ...can't give up.

I miss you. I love you. I will end the note with words from Rupi Kaur ~

"It was when I stopped searching for home within others and lifted the foundations of home within myself, I found there were no roots more intimate than those between a mind and body that have decided to be whole."

Love your wife

Shana C

Journal entry

July 15, 2020

Happiness comes from happenings
The more we attach to things, the more suffering
How do we break the cycle of suffering?
-Inspired

-In spirit
-Inspiration
Mail

7/19/2020
1:25 pm

My Dearest Husband

Currently, at work, typing seems to be easier than actually using a pen, since it is extremely difficult to hold a pen... let alone write.

Thank you for my letter last night. The underlying message ...I do not think I know all of it, I just know it has been a long road, and while on this long road, a few things have surfaced ...which makes me believe I may know part of the reason we are on this path again.

A very rough path for sure, for me, for you, for both of us ...the dips and grooves are insane.

So rough that every other day I try not to cry, I find myself simply holding back all the tears. I am exhausted and depressed, more than ever ...back to not sleeping well and just sad about the unknown...

I know there are a few things in the making (that could be positive), yet I am unable to find the strength to truly be excited for these events... my counselor said I needed to ask myself why.

She said, "Why am I not excited that I am buying a house?"

She said to journal this

I am not really sure the reason, only that I know I am sad, that it is an overwhelming feeling to do this all on my own because I have to, not that I want to. I am in a position that if it does not change... I will just continue to suffer. So I guess I am not excited because I have so much pain, heartache, and a million and one things to do during this insane Pandemic time... And how do I maneuver, not to mention my body is broken, I stress about me usually being able to move anything during moving, but how can I lift things when sometimes I can barely lift a handful of dishes without pain or causing more damage, and then there is the part that I am married yet I am doing things as a single person... from so many levels not by choice.

I know you don't want to hear my heartache, or really I do not want to hear my own heartache. It is just a constant reminder of where we are at... another reason I really don't write as much. Because I don't always know what to say... hard to say and express how much pain I feel and then try and be hopeful all in one breath.

I recently read a statement, that said, "Girl if your boyfriend agrees you can do better, then you need to do better." Under this, it said, "because if this statement is said, then that person agrees they cannot change and will not accept the challenge of growing for themselves or the relationship." When I read this I wondered about you. How do you truly feel, if you feel that when you are home you would be able to work on yourself and what is best for you?

Tuesday

6:33 am

I never got to finish typing...

I made a copy of this article because I thought we could conversate about it. Remember the good ole days when we would have all the gossip magazines? Back then we even said, "If only we knew everything we know now, back then."

LOL, I'm sure our thoughts will resort to that again! Tonight is an MRI of the shoulder ... let's see if they see anything!

I sure do miss you PaPi! A LOT!

Have to go to work, it's that time ...need to get this all out in the mail so you have something.

I love you! XOXO

Love me forever

Your wife

Shana C

Copy of Will & Jada -How They Saved Their Marriage from People Magazine July 27, 2020

Copy of house/layout property, to purchase

In Salem, Oregon - wrote next to Street Address -

—------> our home. Off Astronaut Ave, "When I was little I used to think I would be an Astronaut."

(Good mail Card)

Front of card - Pink lotus

Hello over there

Inside card -

Love FROM OVER HERE.

July 27, 2020

My Dearest Husband

I know life is so different for both of us right now. Funny thing you and I have been dealing with uncertainty since May of 2019. And the world just started to deal with the unknown this year and uncertainty. Looks like you and I have a head start against everyone! HaHa!! You and me against the world. Who knew this lesson had a silver lining ...strength, another lesson in disguise ...to never waste valuable time or mental peace of mind, on the affairs of others –that is too high a price to pay.

IT'S NOT PERSONAL, BUT IT IS PERSONAL

I looked through some of my old photos last night.

I miss you.

Remember the surprise outing I did for us when we went out to eat and went and got churros from the spot you heard about? I think they were mentioned on the Food Network channel. That was such a fun day...just being in the moment. The presence was a gift in itself. You were so surprised! I am so happy we got to experience that together before it closed. They even had cuts playing!

I love you PaPi. I hope this is good mail! (wink)

Love your wife

Shana C

Being is Enough July 21

"We are not always clear about what we are experiencing, or why.

In the midst of grief, transition, transformation, learning, healing, or discipline -it's difficult to have perspective.

That's because we have not learned the lesson yet. We are in the midst of it. The gift of clarity has not yet arrived.

Our need to control can manifest itself as a need to know exactly what's going on. We cannot always know. Sometimes, we need to let ourselves be and trust that clarity will come later, in retrospect.

If we are confused, that is what we are supposed to be. The confusion is temporary. We shall see. The lesson, the purpose, shall reveal itself — in time, in its own time.

It will all make perfect sense — later.

Today, I will stop straining to know what I don't know, to see what I can't see, to understand what I don't yet understand. I will trust that being is sufficient, and let go of my need to figure things out."

(Melody Beattie, June 1990, pg 200)

Mail

Aug 2nd, 2020
4:44 pm

(Card)

Front of card - Picture of Hay, yo-yo, halo, Aloe plant

Hay, Yoyo, Halo, Aloe

Inside card - JUST WANTED TO SAY I'M THINKING OF YOU

My Dearest Husband

I just got back from camping. I realized ...we have yet to go together. One day. Right? It was peaceful, the weather was perfect ...a little bittersweet not having my brother there. Yet I know it would be just part of life. ..to grow in different directions.

I miss you. I thought of you often. Sat with my feelings and thoughts ...most of the hours. Reflected on what was... and what will be. (Of course, I don't really know what that means) Yet I have to be grateful for all of it because there is a time and place for everything and a reason why the puzzle pieces are hardly fitting together. Even if it's not exactly how I envisioned it. If I have learned anything ... life is never how we envision it but it will unfold like a gift if each day we are fully present.

This is a challenge ...and may take me a lifetime to master it. I know it will be worth it because I will not miss the gifts each day brings by only being in the present moment. So as much as I would like to look forward and as often as I reminisce I am challenging myself to be grateful for now. To be in the moment... the best I can. One day at a time.

Feels like a lifetime since I have been in your arms. I miss you and I love you.

I hope this card finds you well. I hope your heart and mind are feeling some peace. I am wishing each day to carry us to the next ...pain free.

...in the meantime, I will hold on to the memories of laughter, lovemaking, good company, home-cooked meals, your smile, your laughter, your love, your magic hands... that make all the aches and pains disappear. Till very soon mi amor...

Love your wife

Shana C

xoxoxo

Journal entry

August 5, 2020

I did yoga and breath work today

My success today was the choices I made to support my body

Journal entry

August 6, 2020

One more week and I have a new job!

Still in the middle of a pandemic and I am still in the medical field, but after being at one clinic for almost 5 years. My time will serve me most elsewhere. I will now be with the hospital in the Diagnostic department. After 2 months of training on-site, I go remote. I will work from home. The main and the BEST reason for transferring, aside from why I applied.

Because I am buying a HOME! I found a house and it is in a new city for me, one that I am not familiar with. Salem. (smile face)

-My intention for today is to focus on my happiness, any joy, and to be grateful during the chaos.

-My goal for today is to pack one box and write a thank you card.

What I love and appreciate in myself... that I am finally being honest with myself. About EVERYTHING.

Journal entry

August 7, 2020
5:35 am

-My intention for today is to recognize my feelings, be ok with what I feel today, and embrace the feelings. Regardless of what type of feeling. (for today)

-My goal for today is to sit down, pay bills, and make a bill list for next year.

What I love and appreciate about me ...I am 42 and finally figuring out how to feel and live.

Journal entry

August 9, 2020
4:44 am

I woke up early today, in hopes of seeing the stars sparkle out in the sky before sunrise

...no. It still looks like a giant black cloud. That covered our sky.

IT'S NOT PERSONAL, BUT IT IS PERSONAL

I am so heartbroken

The fires started where I camp. 2 weeks ago at Green Peter Lake, then a week ago at the Santiam near 3 pools, Henline Falls and Salmon Falls. All the homes, all the trees, all the animals, my heart just hurts... for all of them. To my core, it hurts.

Then we had a crazy wind storm that started Monday. 40+ miles an hour winds ...more or less in some places of Oregon. Trees were torn down, ripped out of the ground, and more fires, jumped or got out of control.

I don't know if I should stay home or go to work today. There are fires all up and down the West Coast, causing people to evacuate and having me feel worried, anxious, scared, and uneasy. The air is toxic to breathe, if anyone is out and about.

I want to help those who need help, but how?! Go to a Red Cross, and start volunteering ... it's different now. You have to go through steps because of COVID and the Pandemic.

Our new home I put a bid in is in Salem. I know it's not fully ready yet, but I hope the fires can be contained before entering those neighborhoods.

This is another part that scares me.

I looked up the news, and some cities around this area went into evacuation last night... this town is next to where I live right now.

I pray we'll all be safe. No one else will lose a home or get hurt.

Please protect us.

Journal entry

August 13, 2020

5:36 am

Today will officially be my last day at the clinic, shy 2 months of 5 years.

I poured my heart into this job... sweat and tears. Time for a new chapter.

On Monday I will train at the Hospital for a few months with DX imaging.

New job. New people. For a new phase of my life. It's time.

-My intentions for today... be present, if my mind wanders bring it back to the present moment.

-My goal for today ...pack for camping, and put everything by the front door.

What I love and appreciate about myself...that I am accepting my feelings even if sad or angry. I no longer hide them or push them away. I just accept them and then release them.

Mail

(Card)

Front of card - All green with images of different stick planted trees in pots

Inside card - blank to write

8/14/2020

My Dearest Husband,

Thought I would share this email. LOL sent out one day before I left.

My last day was actually really good.

Kinda crazy good.

Got all kinds of gifts and cards and a big poster signed! Kinda surreal really and I am now heading off to camp! I enclosed the email that was written about me from work.

I love you
Love your wife
Shana C

Wednesday

August 12, 2020

12:15 pm

(Email) from work to the whole clinic

Subject: Shana Dillon!

"Hard to believe, but it is true!

Shana's last day is tomorrow, Thursday. I was in total denial and thought it was next week. Time flies.

I know that we will all miss Shana as she does so much for each of us! I can't tell you the number of times she has reminded me of something and/or has done something extremely thoughtful. We all get caught up in the day-to-day grind, but Shana has always found a time to make a small gesture to lift our spirits. Shana is always willing to help out when and where needed and I know works endless hours at other healthcare locations.

I am grateful that with her life changes that our company has a spot for her! Shana has been at Mercantile for what ...about 5 years! Let's just pretend that Shana is on an extended vacation.

In honor of Shana, let's do something we know she will enjoy:

1. Thursday, 08/13th will be recognized as Shana's day

2. It will be sports day; meaning jeans and wear your favorite sports shirt!

3. We'll roll over phones at lunch, so you can enjoy sitting

outside. I know Shana enjoys the sunshine and outdoors.

- Bring your lunch

- We'll supply ice cream, individually wrapped and available in the freezer

Shana, from all of us here, thank you so much for your dedication to the Team!"

You rock!

Mary and Team!

Journal entry

August 19, 2020

Wednesday

Our last group class will be outside at a park

We are to bring a 'Heart gift' something that I treasure that I already own, it is called 'Tribal Gifting'

Exercise today

Draw 3 photos

As you are now

How do you want to see yourself or where

How will you get there

Journal entry

August 20, 2020

6 pm

I just finished a virtual visit with my counselor.

It was deep, heavy, and needed.

I had no idea that I had been enabling my mom since I was little. I am now 42. I was scared she might try to take her life.

I will now help me.

I will start some inner child work.

I will talk to the younger me, that little girl, and let her know it is ok. She no longer needs to be or feel responsible for our mom's life.

I am giving my mom's life back to her.

I am no longer responsible for her life. We are no longer responsible. (sad, relieved face)

Journal entry

Aug, 21, 2020

5:24 am

"Schools are caught in a coronavirus catch-22. They need to navigate the uncharted territory of virtual learning or risk a coronavirus outbreak by going back." Waking up to this type of news.

Mail

8/24/2020

Monday

My Dearest Husband,

I hope this card finds you in better spirits and on the mend towards healing. I also hope that the next one is the LAST one. HOPE!

That book I read daily... well I try to at least... The Codependency book, called "The Language of Letting Go."

The last few dates/topics are a lot of work... and I know I read this last year, but it did not sink in like it does now. The topics are

'Letting go of shame,' and 'Honesty in Relationships,' 'Detaching in Relationships,' 'Responsibility for Family Members,' 'Self-Care,' 'Step Eight' and 'Willing to Make Amends.'

When I read each one and the specifics, it's hard to not be hard on myself for the years I have lived thinking I was responsible for so many people, before myself. To be honest, this whole week feels like a lifetime of work. I have realized also that not only is it extremely hard work, but it's heart-breaking and also freeing. If this makes any sense..?

My arm and hand are on fire... (sad face) super hard to write. I will leave us with a quote. It's a tough one, but it's from the book.

"Today, I will work on a change of heart if hard-heartedness, defensiveness, guilt, or bitterness are present. I will become willing to let go of those feelings and have them replaced by the healing energy of love." Melody Beattie

-sending love and healing thoughts to both of us. I love you.

Love Shana C

Mail

September...

.. 2020

My Dearest Husband,

Hey... it's Thursday night, we just hung up.

I decided to write to you as much as I could today. First I would like to say I cut everyone off for a few weeks.

It wasn't just you.

My mom, the kids, Marquita ...my counselor ... anyone who wants my time. I just can't right now.

IT'S NOT PERSONAL, BUT IT IS PERSONAL

My list is forever long and it just keeps fucking growing.

And no one can do anything about it.

Except me

So I apologize if I hurt your feelings. Clearly, I do not know how to communicate under stress. So my words did not come out compassionately.

I should have said, I am under so much stress that I am at a breaking point, and I am so sorry but I really need a few weeks before I can talk or probably communicate genuinely without breaking down or losing my cool.

Here is my list of shit!

Claim with medical insurance for my arm.

Buying a house

Give my notice to move (I did this already because I WAS so excited)

Don't know if I have a place to live yet (is the feeling now)

Jr's school (did not give him books yet, so have to figure out time off work to get them)

Jr's sports (wants more papers, and get a clearance from his Dr)

Nonni is moving

Selling 2 cars online during a pandemic

Who will actually come through to buy the Monte?

21 questions about the Monte

No questions or inquiries about the Mitsubishi

Packing

Not enough money to cover bills

Oh but I am trying to buy a house

New day .... 30 plus hours have passed now
Late Friday night, 12:02 am ... Saturday morning

I decided to open my emails. Guess what, the other lender could not pull it off either. NO house. I'm not buying. What a fucking joke my life is... and it's not even fucking Tuesday!

Now I have to wait till fucking Monday to pray and hope that the landlord is ok with me saying, "Sorry never mind. Can I sign the lease again and pay your house off because I am not buying my own?! At least not this year!"

What a fucking mess. I hoped and prayed I could figure this out in the next few weeks before I was supposed to do the walk-through...

Literally in a few weeks

What the fuck

My heart is broken

What am I supposed to tell my kids

What am I supposed to tell Jr

What the fuck, what the fuck

WHAT THE FUCK

Now I really don't want to talk to anybody, because all I am going to do is start crying ... by the way I am not capable of buying a fucking house.

Maybe if I did it last year... it could have worked... What the fuck is this damn lesson!?

Oh, I know. You did not do it. Fuck you, Shana!

...feels like death. ...I'm tired of grieving

(sticky note posted on Congratulations letter, of purchase)

Why did they even give me this fucking bullshit paperwork!!? Beyond me!

Shana C

IT'S NOT PERSONAL, BUT IT IS PERSONAL

Journal entry

September 19, 2020

This fire... It's maddening

Heartbreaking, traumatic .... sickening

I am sooo broken from this...

I am counting my blessings

I have a bed

I have a house

Yet

I am just so heartbroken

The fires did more than take our trees, our homes, our air.

The fire broke my heart & crushed my spirit

I am at tug-of-war with my emotions

The fire has taken so much from so many, including me.

The forest

The hikes

The healing trails

The peaceful beautiful luscious greenery burnt till no end

I am grateful to have been given the opportunity over the last 7 years to grow and heal amongst the wisest souls.

Yet I am at a loss for words, the heaviness that surrounds me is surreal...

Journal entry

September 21, 2020

Monday

5:50 am

I made a conscious decision on Saturday to stop wearing my wedding ring.

WHY?

Because I am doing

EVERYTHING

By Myself!

Journal entry

evening now

5:53 pm

I am overwhelmed with anxiety and paperwork going in circles with the home needing documents. Three weeks ago I reached what I thought was the correct department to retrieve the court order of child support that was needed to complete the process for underwriting, only to find out they cannot help me.

LOL

So I called literally 6 different phone #s including a person from Grand Jury Duty to try to help me get the correct documents.

I paid for them

They sent them

But now I cannot retrieve them, because they decided to encrypt them.

LOL

So did the folks I started the claim with on my arm.

Everything I am trying to complete, be done... is instead in never-ending circles.

I feel sooo beyond not my relaxed, go-with-the-flow self!

I am VERY STRESSED and ready for the calm!

NO MORE STORMS Please.

no more.

Oh, I forgot to mention... I did get that steroid injection in my arm on Thursday. As you can tell my handwriting is a little nicer.

The pain is still there and me writing right now is increasing the pain. (sad face)

Chapter Eight
Bleak Fall Of 2020

Journal entry

September 22, 2020

I don't know if I got horrible news… but everything dropped in me when it was spoken out loud to me at 4:10 pm, no options to buy my home. At least with the folks I have been working with.

I almost let it defeat me…

So I made some phone calls …what is the worst that could happen, when it already happened?!

LOL

The first person I spoke to I told them the scenario, they then said I don't know if I can help but let me put you on hold and speak to my supervisor.

I waited for what felt like forever with elevator music playing through my car speakers, as I sat parked in front of the townhouse …waiting.

She returned saying we could not help, but maybe another office could and provided another phone number.

The phone number was the same number I called yesterday.

At this point I truly have done all that I can that is in my power without asking for others to co-sign. LOL

Ya, they asked me who could help do that!

So.... at this point I am ok to let the higher powers put it into place if this is truly meant to be.

Journal entry

Oct 16, 2020

New Moon workshop

Trust my guides, trust my path, trust what is in front of me.

Start taking time to actually heal. Heal my arm. Heal my heart. Heal my spirit.

I need to have 'the conversation' with Rob that I will be traveling in a new direction in a new light. I will no longer hold on to hardships that are not mine to begin with. It is not healthy.

I will find a way to work less, have more money, travel more, explore more, and be at peace as I move.

Mail

Oct 20, 2020

4:40 am

My Dearest Husband,

How did we get to this place?

How are we so far apart yet can feel each other's heartbreak...daily?

Why is it this time around, I am not allowed to see or visit you...

The crushing feeling I have within my entire being... questions my mind.

Can I live this way for another year?

Can we keep living this way?

Since I have not heard your voice... I have cried every night again. It hurts me deeply knowing that you are now sick, and again fighting with every ounce to stay well in such a cold inhumane space. (sad crying face)

I wish I could hug you, comfort you in your time of need, love on you, binge-watch whatever you please. ...but like I said before... this time around won't let us. So we have to dig real deep to figure out ourselves on why we are on repeat with this fucking lesson.

A card

I picked this out a month or 2 ago ...it reminded me of Hawaii, the feeling just by looking at it, then the words... well ...they are fitting for this time stamp. So I decided to ask the kids to write some encouraging words or think of any good memories to help you through this time.

It's our cup of tea, hot soup, hugs, love, and any cold medicine you may need ... to heal quickly love.

My best friend, my heart, my love. I am wishing you a speedy recovery and this memory is in hopes ...that it can be the medicine you need to recover.

2018, 12th of November... We walked, we talked, we laughed at our jokes, as we trailed through the trees of the Tualatin National Wildlife Refuge. We had our hot drinks in hand, saw the red-tailed hawks perched on the trees, we felt the spirits of the wisest souls (the trees) next to us, watched a beautiful sunset, sat on the bench, and toked some mota. (smiley face) Smiled and laughed at what was, how far we have come, and what would be... We made plans to continue that special vibe ...forever.

Hahahahahah, I even got you to moonwalk across the yellow crisp leaves that were scattered everywhere on one of the bridges ...as we walked back towards ...the end of the trail. I have a video of it too! LOL. I asked you to do the "Michael Jackson," and you knew what I meant (smiley face) You said, "Away from you or towards you!?"

Dang Papi

Always towards me

Please

I'm tired of you being away from me. Fuck. I didn't mean to break down again.

That memory. That day. Was 5 years married. It was so special, it felt so good. Just to laugh, be ourselves, act like teenagers, be in your presence, wrapped in your love, safe, and what felt like the beginning of forever ever after. PaPi your love and company always made me feel secure and safe ...and truly this was all I ever needed.

Get better PaPi. Michael Jackson your way out of this horrible sickness and B.S.!!

I love you

I miss you

For every lifetime.

Love Always & Forever

Your wife

Shana C

Xoxoxo

Journal entry

Oct 31, 2020

Blue Full Moon

Workshop

Letting go of what I cannot control

Letting go of the pain

Letting go of...

My broken heart

Relationships that no longer serve me

Not buying my house

Rob having COVID

Me with possible breast cancer

Rob not coming home

...him not being my husband

Letting go of long-distance relationships

Letting go of scrubbing other people's toilets

...letting go of all the heartache

Mail

11/04/2020

Wednesday

My Dearest Husband,

Good Morning. It's 7:23 am, last I spoke to you was Sunday. I got the letter on Monday. It's a horrible heartbreaking truth, our reality. (broken heart) Hurts like no other. It's also not fair to put it all on me.

Your words say, "I just ask only. To believe in us! In our love! And if this is not enough I leave it up to you."

"To find what it is that your heart needs."

IT'S NOT PERSONAL, BUT IT IS PERSONAL

Rob, I have always believed in us and OUR LOVE, I STILL DO! You know what I want. I want you to be home, to be free. To be where you feel the most love and peace. And I want that feeling too!

I want my heart to stop breaking

I want the pain to go away

I want to stop feeling grief, anger, and sadness every day.

I want to stop hearing and seeing people who are married live life together, while mine is apart. I want all 'ten of swords' to stop stabbing me in MY HEART! I feel like I am dying a slow death of heartache!

I want to heal

I want peace

I only want to cry, shedding happy tears. I want ALL the pain to leave and the only way for this feeling of less pain... to happen... is to start accepting the truth. And to take one step at a time instead of focusing on the whole staircase.

Every ounce of me LOVES YOU SOOO FUCKING much!

The way I am moving through life is not healthy. The way we are both living is not healthy. We need to have a conversation and have a plan to heal to somehow live healthier.

I want to stop grieving and I want to start healing.

We just need to talk without being interrupted.

I miss you. I love you.

I love you always & forever

Love

Shana C

Ps

I made these copies last month or 2...

I just didn't have the strength to send it and

The letter you wrote ... yes Dillon's do not give up, yet my bloodline is Padilla. I am not giving up. I am making a choice.

We are our own individuals, yet the same bonded by spirit, your my twin flame.

'Recovery,' 'Being Gentle with Ourselves During Times of Grief,' 'Transformation Through Grief,' 'The Grief Process.'

(Melody Beattie, June 1990, pgs 292, 293, 314, 315)

Journal entry

Nov 10, 2020

More has happened and plenty has stayed the same.

I am still in the same townhouse. Renting. Paying someone else's mortgage.

I will start working from where I live, starting tomorrow. 4 days a week, with Tuesdays, Saturdays, and Sundays off.

Rob may or may not come home early. He believes he has a chance for an early release. He has had 2 court dates and still no actual hearing ...they just keep pushing the case back, due to COVID.

I think I can move forward with healing if I now say I am separated instead of saying I am married.

I just started having the conversation with Rob. Hopefully we ...I can figure this out, this month.

I don't want to feel broken, sad, angry, unbalanced, shattered... any longer.

Then we have the pandemic if you are following the directions... should be home most of the days with a lot of self reflection.

IT'S NOT PERSONAL, BUT IT IS PERSONAL

Mail

11-12-2020

Written Nov, 7 Saturday

(7-year Anniversary Card)

Front of card- images of hearts and pencils

Just for fun, I made a list of the top hundred things I like to do with you.

Inside card -

1. Kiss and hug & stuff.

2. Repeat 99 times.

My Dearest Husband,

I just got off the phone with you, not too long ago.

My heart aches too, to just have a normal life with you. Especially in 5 days Nov 12! How is it that we will be married for 7 years and physically together only 2 years?!

We sure know how to create the BEST memories. All our beautiful trips or romantic picnics. Bed and floors covered in roses. Popping champagne for days... in any state, we went to visit! Our breathtaking hikes, even the ones you were mad at me on because the trail seemed never ending. (smiley face) What beautiful memories we got to share together. ALL so priceless. Well, my love... I know it doesn't seem or even feel right this year. Because you're there and I'm here, and we are separated. We don't have our Sundays this time where we could simply kiss and hold hands. We both have cold empty beds. (sad crying face) Our hearts are filled with shattered glass. 2020 being married does not feel like marriage ...it feels like I'm all alone. And ALL I want to do on our 7-year anniversary is Kiss, Hug, and Fuck and REPEAT 99 times!!

I miss you. I love you.

xoxo

Journal entry

Nov 12, 2020

7 years ago today I got married. I cried when I made my entrance, while I was walking down the aisle. I look back ...and I know why now. I had no one to actually have a conversation with about all my emotions leading up to that point. I brought anything and everything that I felt to that day. I was so happy that I found a forever after.

The spirits were with us and most of our loved ones were there. It truly was a beautiful time for that moment.

Who knew we had so much work ahead of us

So much past trauma

So much past pain

So much current pain

So much healing ...put directly in our lap while we are forced to be completely apart.

This type of commitment is not for the weak

And if you have been shattered to pieces over and over and over again... I would not fault you for choosing differently! For choosing you and only you.

I choose me

Myself

I want to survive

I am tired of picking up the shattered pieces.

I am tired of feeling like a battered woman.

It is exhausting

IT'S NOT PERSONAL, BUT IT IS PERSONAL

Journal entry

Nov 15, 2020

Under this new moon in Scorpio

I invite in

Power

Good health, wealth, richness with light

I will soon travel without any worries. I will feel powerful again. I will be free to live, practice yoga in other countries, and feel joy and peace on this next journey. It will feel liberating. I will no longer have pain or any concern of hardship. I will have tons to share, give, and live off of!

Journal entry

Nov 30, 2020

Full Moon

The Penumbral lunar eclipse

I am letting go of the hurt, the pain, the sorrow, the life I once had. The sad broken version of me.

I am letting go of a relationship that is not an equal marriage.

I am letting go of my shattered soul.

It is time to heal, all the way

Journal entry

Dec 5, 2020

Today - outside, the view is a blue sky with empty tree branches.

I know the air is crisp, clean, cold, and clearing ...later I will walk amongst nature.

I read today's daily meditation from the Language of Letting Go, titled, "Difficult People."

I know I have grown when I recognize most of the words as the past for myself.

"I will continue to learn to love and care differently in a way that takes reality into account."

I will enter my relationships - on new terms.

I am still growing, in many directions.

(I drew a solid tree under these words with heart leaves)

I am a beautiful blossoming tree with strong healthy roots grounded in a healthy nurturing vibrant, aging, longevity foundation!

Looking at this tree feels like I am looking in a mirror.

I feel peace coming

I feel happy on its way

I feel tranquil

I feel love

I love myself

I love seeing I am growing

I love seeing I am healing

I love seeing I am healthy

<3 <3

Journal entry

Dec 6, 2020

Many may not know

Last year I injured myself during my trip to Mexico

I have been dealing with it ever since the end of October 2019.

IT'S NOT PERSONAL, BUT IT IS PERSONAL

In July I finally found the source of my pain by getting an MRI

I am dominantly right-handed.

I have taught myself to be left-handed so my right arm can heal. Excruciating pain and swelling played a huge factor.

MRI Findings say- I have a "Severe rotator cuff supraspinatus tendinopathy with partial-thickness tearing".

This comes from age, being an athlete, or some repetitive trauma to the shoulder...

Mine is repetitive trauma /repetitive motion. I have numbness in my right arm, tingling all the way through my fingertips. Pain that wakes me up at night if I happen to roll over and sleep on my other shoulder. It used to hurt like hell to simply write with a pen or brush my teeth. Hints why I taught myself to be left-handed. Now the pain is less, yet still very noticeable. (Many days banging down the door to say, "Hey I am still here!") Mind over matter can seem to only work for me half days now.

So not only have I been healing mentally and spiritually, from past traumas.

I have been trying to heal physically too!

LITERALLY

It has truly been a struggle to not be able to do exercise routines daily. Ones that I am accustomed to, with weights, or doing planks. Putting dishes away, baking cakes, cooking, and even working (typing). I took my body for granted. I thought I would never be put at a standstill.

I have found new ways.

Through technics, my PT taught me, plus hiking, and more...

I was so used to doing many different types of exercises on my own for years. This was a routine, a daily habit I had chosen in life since I was young.

I was always counting on my body to push through ...as I tried to do this last year too.

On the last day in Mexico, working construction the physically demanding day of labor building homes, caught up to me. I did not listen to my body, when it said, "Stop!"

Instead, I pushed through ...which I am sure caused more damage. Lesson learned.

I will never do that again. Keep working when clearly injured.

My routines are now modified

with this said

My goal is to continue to heal, whether it's taking time and listening to my body even if surgery may have to be the route.

One day again

I will be back

...to beast mode!

Journal entry

Dec 8, 2020

Tuesday

2:40 pm

Currently reading 'The Power of Now' by Eckhart Tolle

Page 26, Speaks of a truthful reflection from our body/ emotions when our mind is acting.

If there is an apparent conflict we feel in our body. The thought (mind) will be the lie and the emotion (body) will be the truth.

I don't know if this is ironic or not, but this happened today.

IT'S NOT PERSONAL, BUT IT IS PERSONAL

I recognized it immediately. I got a letter from Rob requesting me to do a handful of things.

I had an overwhelming feeling in my body. I could feel anxiety at its highest, I felt angry. I was actually mad when I opened the letter. I thought this letter would be something else.

Knowing I wanted nothing to do with the request. My emotions were very real, very valid, and very true.

Journal entry

Dec 12, 2020

Finished listening to a podcast from Super Soul Oprah's OWN.

A few healing notes I took

Listen to your heart, What's my best intention?

Have a conversation with yourself. Listen to yourself.

Learn the inner art

Have compassion and forgiveness without forgiveness the world is lost.

It is like those 2 prisoners of war that met years later

One said to the other, "Have you forgiven your captors yet?"

And the other said, "No, I never will."

Then he responds, "Well, then they still have you in prison, don't they?"

You can free yourself from the past through forgiveness.

Mail

12-14-2020

My Dearest Husband

Look at what gem of a letter I came across. I only sent you a copy of the last 2 pages, it was written when you were in Carson City on 11-08-2007. The poem was the original reason I decided to copy the letter and send it. Then you spoke of the Erotic Exotic Ball, looks like we never made it. You got to go to those Santa Crawls tho, remind me again who all you went with? Because I know it was not with me.

This letter. Wow, it flooded me with memories. So much love we had for each other back then, (I know we still do, have love, it just feels different like a puzzle missing 2 parts) we had so much hope, faith, and dreams... we were somehow *the brightest star* in each, of each other's lives. How can we get to that again? I miss us. I miss us soooooooooooo fucking bad... it hurts like crazy! Some days it drives me crazy & angry.

You said, "Whatever I do means more when you are there!"

"Whatever happens to me, means more if I can share it with you!"

I believed this. *DEEP Deep, deep within my soul.*

You have always been deep within my soul, my heart, my bones, and my spirit. We have always been one. I will always love you like no other.

I just wish I knew how to do it, without you. Life is so much harder, without you. We had some crazy shit happen... from so many different levels of pain, hurt, loss, grief... and so many beautiful things ... memories... from love making, fucking, traveling, road trips, celebrating, moving, reading to eachother, cooking together, going to wine tastings, hiking, you sharing your peaceful trail in Nevada, to me sharing the healing trail and blue waters in Oregon on New Years Day, kissing, hugging, taking showers together, running bubble baths, cumming in my mouth and you filling my soul when you do this, (I MISS IT ALL) holding me at night, cooking me my favorite breakfast, jewelry shopping together, date nights (in or out of the house), back rubs, foot rubs, you buying a foot spa to soak my feet when I worked all those crazy graveyard shifts, hand rubs every weekend for three and a half years, laughing, crying, loving, joking, April fool's day with my not so funny cake pops, your brothers surprise party in Cali, 2018, me dancing for you when you would visit before you moved to Oregon, you deep inside me, all the time, everytime, you felt soooo fucking good, your eyes deep gazing into my heart, our handstands out on luke warm beaches of Oregon, our Hawaii anniversary, popping champagne wherever we go, feeding eachothers souls, feeding eachother chocolate cover strawberries, lighting candles before we make love, tell you to fuck me with only my "brand new heels on" you bought me, red roses everywhere... because WE LOVE eachother sooooo fucking much, more roses for any occasion or simply because, made love on roses & rose petals, single roses, white or red roses, walked the rose garden, picnic in the rose gardens, pop some more champagne in the middle of fields of roses, laugh and smile more MORE, tell eachother we will never be apart again. NEVER.

The traveling... Seattle, Washington, Boston, Massachusetts, Reno, Lake Tahoe, Nevada, Florida, Cali, Oregon, Hawaii not once but twice Oahu and Hawaii, Las Vegas many times, Sacramento, oh and the Concerts, soooo many concerts, ***WE FUCKING LOVED HARD, YOU*** and ***ME***, we **LOVED Soooo Fucking Hard!** Sade, Lil Wayne, 2 Chainz, TI, 6lack, Lauren Hill, Miguel, Masego, Erykah Badu, Jay-Z, Kanye West, Big Boi, G-Easy (haha, remember we both called it, G-Easy would blow up), we were soooo good, so fucking GOOD Together! Shit, we got married to John Legend Rich Forever! Well, Rick Ross's song featuring John, but his hook, the Legends hook is what resonates deep within my soul. Because I was always rich forever with you! I never needed anything else, just you. Your heart, your love, your touch... just you. Just the simple things. I was rich from your love, from our love, from our bond.

We got married to this. (I defined rich forever because our love is like no other, this is why I felt so rich)

"On the way we shed some tears, every day we sacrifice, so we can be standing here, oh what a hell of a life, been waiting so many years, and the future is bright, now it's very clear, that we goin be rich forever, **FOREVER**, and ever, and ever, ***AND EVER, we goin be rich forever.***"

Why couldn't we just stay together forever as we planned (literally together, not in separate states, separate beds, or separated)... all the love we poured out, all the walks and the talks and the love we truly genuinely felt, all the lovemaking, grinding, spanking ...feel soooo good moments and memories. I miss us. I miss you. I miss my husband. I wish I could make love to you, kiss and suck on every part of you, right now!

I found another memory. A note I wrote to myself on 11-12-2018. It said, "First year of marriage we were Bonnie & Clyde."

"A true champion will fight through anything."

"The third year of marriage we learned how to communicate, especially on Sundays."

This is all I wrote... felt like I should share.

What should we do now? How should we start living? One day at a time... 13 years later... What's our next move, Rob?

I love you soooo fucking much, it's killing me slowly to be without my heart.

But fuck!!! Thank you soooo much for all the beautiful lovemaking, back-breaking, sunrise to sunset loving. Thank you for saying yes to so many adventures in our home, wherever that home was, and outside of the home. We had some priceless memories we shared together. I am soooo fucking rich because of these beautiful treasured memories and because of how we loved.

With all my love

Love your wife

Shana C

(I am including some Zen stories I came across)

Printed /typed out on ... 12-12-2020

From Niklas Goke (published in Personal Growth Jan 10, 2019)

"My theme for 2019 'should be EVERY Year' is 'focus.' Focus on the work and projects that matter, the people I really care about, and most of all, focus of the mind. If You're anything like me –overthinking introvert with a mind that's always on –that last one is especially difficult.

Part of it's just human nature. Our brains are wired to look for problems. To obsess over an issue we can fix. Until we create a solution, which gives us a short burst of relief. Then, it's on to the next thing.

But for introverts, it's particularly easy to get stuck on the obsession part. Our default response to almost anything is to think up a maze in our mind, then zip through it until we've explored every corner. Like a mouse looking for cheese, even if there's none to be found.

One of the few things that's helped me stop spinning in circles in my own head is Zen stories. I'm not sure why. Maybe, I can relate to the imagery associated with Buddhist monks. Maybe, I'm a sucker for allegories. In any case, while some people might think they're cheesy, they work for me.

When my mind is cloudy, a Zen story can clear it up. When I'm frantic, it calms me down. And when I'm too close to the trees to see the forest, it helps me see.

You may not be an introvert or compulsive thinker, but I hope you'll still benefit from the following seven stories. I know they've done wonders for me."

".1 The Man Who Said Yes

A man went to a Buddhist monastery for a silent retreat. After he finished, he felt better, calmer, stronger, but something was missing. The teacher said he could talk to one of the monks before he left.

The man thought for a while, then asked: "How do you find peace?"

The monk said: "I say yes. To everything that happens, I say yes."

When the man returned home, he was enlightened.

This one is actually real. The man is Kamal Ravikant. In an interview, he shares his interpretation of the monk's advice:

"Most of our pain, most of our suffering comes from resistance to what is. Life is. And when we resist what life is, we suffer. When you can say yes to life, surrender to life, and say: "Okay, what should I be now?" That's where power comes from."

When the weather is bad, when your crush won't answer, when the obstacle won't budge, don't say no. Don't dig in your heels and push and shove until your veins pop out in frustration. Say yes. Accept. Breathe. Life is flowing. Always. It's us trying to swim upstream. Let the current carry you instead."

".2 The Girl At The River

A senior monk and a junior monk were traveling together. At one point, they came to a river with a strong current. As the monks were preparing to cross the river, they saw a very young and beautiful woman also attempting to cross. The young woman asked if they could help her cross to the other side.

The two monks glanced at one another because they had taken vows not to touch a woman.

Then, without a word, the older monk picked up the woman, carried her across the river, placed her gently on the other side, and carried on his journey.

The younger monk couldn't believe what had just happened. After rejoining his companion, he was speechless, and an hour passed without a word between them.

Two more hours passed, then three. Finally, the younger monk could not contain himself any longer and blurted out: "As monks, we are not permitted a woman, how could you then carry that woman on your shoulders?"

The older monk looked at him and replied: "Brother, I set her down on the other side of the river, why are you still carrying her?"

Resisting what life is trying to tell you is exhausting, but resisting to what life has already told you is guaranteed to be in vain. What's done is done.

If you feel guilty, it was a mistake you can fix. If you feel ashamed, it was a mistake you shouldn't repeat. But regret? That's just dragging a past event into the present. It's a toxic attempt to twist reality. And it always backfires."

".3 The Crystal Cup

A Zen master was given a beautifully crafted crystal cup. It was a gift from a former student.

He was very grateful. Every day, he enjoyed drinking out of his glass.

He would show it to visitors and tell them about the kindness of his student.

But every morning, he held the cup in his hand for a few seconds and reminded himself: "This glass is already broken."

One day, a clumsy visitor toppled the glass on its shelf. The cup fell down. When it hit the floor, it was smashed into thousands of tiny pieces.

The other visitors gasped in shock, but the Zen master remained calm. Looking at the mess in front of his feet, he said: "Ah. Yes. Let's begin."

He picked up a broom and started sweeping.

I found the idea for this in The Daily Stoic, by Ryan Holiday. About a year ago, I wrote that "half of happiness is being okay with what you don't get." Now, I think I know what the other half is: being okay with losing what you have.

The man who remembers to be grateful for his possessions is ahead of most. But the man who knows they won't last is ahead of him still. Be the second."

".4 The Bowl

A monk told Joshu: "I have just entered the monastery. Please teach me."

Joshu asked: "Have you eaten your rice porridge?"

The monk replied: "I have eaten."

Joshu said: "Then you had better wash your bowl."

At that moment the monk was enlightened.

I can only echo what Leo Babauta said about this story:

"There is something profound and yet minimalist about this advice. It's: don't get your head caught up in all this thinking about the meaning of life... instead, just do. Just wash your bowl. And in the washing, you'll find all you need."

We think we do, but most of the time, there's no need to think or plan or strategize, because ultimately it won't make a big difference which option we choose. There's always one or multiple next steps to take. So we might as well take any one of them. Often, there's more satisfaction to be drawn from doing."

".5 The Move

Two men visit a Zen master.

The first man says: "I'm thinking of moving to this town. What's it like?"

The Zen master asks: "What was your old town like?"

The first man responds: It was dreadful. Everyone was hateful. I hated it."

The Zen master says: "This town is very much the same. I don't think you should move here."

The first man leaves and the second man comes in.

The second man says: "I'm thinking of moving to this town. What's it like?"

The Zen master asks: "What was your old town like?"

The second man responds: "It was wonderful. Everyone was friendly and I was happy. Just interested in a change now."

The Zen master says: "This town is very much the same. I think you will like it here."

What we seek is what we find. The reasons why you do what you do matter as much, if not more, as what you end up doing. Because they shape how you seek. So, ultimately, they'll also determine what you find."

".6 The Teacup

A learned man once went to visit a Zen teacher to inquire about Zen. As the Zen teacher talked, the learned man frequently interrupted to express his own opinion about this or that. Finally, the Zen teacher stopped talking and began to serve tea to the learned man. He poured the cup full, then kept pouring until the cup overflowed.

"Stop," said the learned man. "The cup is full, no more can be poured in."

"Like this cup, you are full of your own opinions," replied the Zen teacher. "If you do not first empty your cup, how can you taste my cup of tea?"

".7 The Four Candles

Four monks decided to meditate silently without speaking for two weeks. They lit a candle as a symbol of their practice and began. By nightfall on the first day, the candle flickered and then went out.

The first monk said: "Oh, no! The candle is out."

The second monk said: "We're not supposed to talk!"

The third monk said: "Why must you two break the silence?"

The fourth monk laughed and said: "Ha! I'm the only one who didn't speak."

They all had different reasons, but each of the four monks shared his thoughts without filtering them – none of which improved the situation. Had there been a fifth, wiser monk, he would've remained silent and kept meditating.

This way, he would've pointed out their mistakes without a single word. Without breaking his own quest for better. Done long enough, talking inevitably leads to embarrassing yourself. Listening leads to learning.

IT'S NOT PERSONAL, BUT IT IS PERSONAL

The less you speak, the smarter you get. And, maybe not quite coincidentally, the smarter you get, the less you speak.

Maybe, we're not meant to roam the world in a perpetual state of carefree, ignorant bliss. But we're also not mere rats in a maze. Thinking is good. Solving problems is useful. Overthinking problems is not.

Like Zen, focus is a lifelong practice. We'll fail many times along the way but remember: the best distraction is a good story. Who knows? It just might get you back on track."

(website Medium, written by Niklas Goke published in Personal Growth 1/10/2019)

Journal entry

Dec 14, 2020
Monday
New Moon

Eclipse workshop
What I saw for my future self
Healthy
Happy
Financially secure
Traveling
In sunny new countries

I feel joy, I will feel bliss and no longer have concern for $$$, I will be on the right path for wealth, health, and pure joy with my familia and any extended familia.

3 things I am proud of this year

Setting boundaries

Recognizing what does not serve me

Learning to let go of what does not serve me, while finding my healing path towards a healthier version of self.

Self-love & gratitude

Keep trusting my intuition

Chapter Nine
Dark Winter Of 2020

Journal entry

Dec 21, 2020

Jupiter and Saturn will align creating what looks like the brightest star from Earth tonight. These 2 planets only align about once every 20 years.

A lot can happen in 2 decades.

Journal entry

Dec 24, 2020

Reflecting

WOW!

What a fucking YEAR!

So many different puzzle pieces. So many heartbreaks and yet so much growth.

I have finally learned it is ok to sit with my feelings. That I do not have to push them aside.

It is good to be present. To be 'all the way' in the now. Regardless of what is released from emotions or feelings.

To love as hard as you can and for as long as you can.

It is ok to have friends

It is ok to be alone

Setting boundaries is a must

This is what healthy looks and feels like

This is healing

This is loving myself and showing up for myself

...giving my inner child all the love and nurturing that was missed

I have learned I will never know the future ...and I am now ok with this.

I will only live one day at a time ...pain or love, one day at a time.

I've learned not to set expectations on others. This is unrealistic, and it will cause a domino effect. A boomerang to breaking my own heart.

I have learned the recipe for "happiness" is through "ourself" ...we are the core to our own bliss.

I learned meditation is key to a "higher self"

I learned to "release and rest" because some things no longer serve me.

I am grateful for the experience. All the downs, and the ups ...is why I am currently on a more peaceful path. And because I did not push away the feelings... I did the work and I will continue to do the work.

I deserve serenity

I deserve love

I deserve peace

IT'S NOT PERSONAL, BUT IT IS PERSONAL

Journal entry

Dec 28, 2020

Monday morning

6:44 am

What challenges brought the greatest learning, during the year of 2020?

A huge challenge was to not follow others with their energies. (especially any negative ones, to pay attention to how I feel). To learn that it is ok to disconnect from them in order to connect with myself.

Another challenge that brought learning was sitting with my hard feelings. When I am sad or angry, it is ok to sit with these feelings. Do not cover them up by keeping busy all the time or pushing them down deep and aside from recognition. Instead, acknowledge the difficult feelings and sit with them, because they are valid and it is part of you. Then when I am ready I can release them, especially when they do not serve you!

2020

Was the year of growth, was the year of creating a more solid foundation for myself. The year had many broken bridges and I had to learn to leap across them, trusting myself that the pathway I chose was towards peace. My heart was broken several times this year, and yet I was able to pick up the pieces and slowly glue them back while moving forward into a deeper state of healing.

2021

Intentions - I will stay empowered. I will connect with my higher self and the higher power. I will continue to heal my ancestry wounds within me. I will continue to ground my roots into a loving, healing, healthy foundation.

I will remember to check in with myself first before giving my energy away. I will feel loved and safe throughout my whole entire being, with no doubts of self, while connecting to my higher purpose.

I will experience the serenity and stillness of self consciousness and the beautiful light that flows within from the universe.

I will honor my path.

I will honor me.

Journal entry

Dec 29/30, 2020
late
close to midnight
Full moon

8 -means listen to yourself, the intuition. As above, so below. Focus on your internal compass, 8 also means completion of new cycles.

What I feel in my soul is what I will follow

On this evening under the full moon in cancer, I choose to let go of the past controlling negative energies. While out on my boat I let go of other people's traumas and their energies, beliefs, and egos. I choose to let go of what no longer serves me. Moving forward.

I am following MY internal compass!

ALL SELF LOVE

Mail

(Holiday Card)

Front card - Christmas bulbs

Just a little note to remind you how much YOU mean

Inside Card -

...and that's A LOT and That's For ALWAYS! Merry Christmas

12-25-2020

My Dearest Husband ~

I wish we had a Christmas miracle and this was not another holiday spent apart. I wish.

Everything is so heavy again, especially during this time. Jr and I put up the tree and while we did this I realized the next year or 2, I will be ALL by myself. All will be grown and on their own and I will be married but all by myself.

This is reality and is a hard pill to swallow. Hmmmm.... Maybe our Christmas miracle can be that neither of us will be diagnosed with cancer. Then we can be thankful because this would be a Christmas Miracle! I will wish, hope, and pray for this miracle.

I MISS my husband.

Love you

Love

Shana C

Chapter Ten
Dire Cold Abyss, Yet A New year, 2021

*J*ournal entry

Jan 3, 2021

The other day I pulled a card from the Lantern Oracle Deck

#29 = 11

Radical Self acceptance

-name all the things about self I had ever wished to change

I used to wish that I didn't grow up so quickly. I felt like I never really was able to be a child, that my childhood was robbed from me.

I had kids at a young age and had a miscarriage.

I also had abortions at a younger age.

I wished I had a mom, instead of a friend. I wish I was taught to follow my intuition and not have to fend for myself and act like an adult at such a young age.

IT'S NOT PERSONAL, BUT IT IS PERSONAL

I was rejecting my mom for not allowing me to be a kid and for always pushing me to be in a relationship, this was as young as preschool. The realization has surfaced for never really having stability or boundaries growing up.

This feeling is showing up because I have been working on myself. For over a year now specifically working on codependency habits. I have learned this is a behavior I was taught. I now know my mom never healed her own self-traumas. I am choosing to break the barriers and teach my kids and myself so our past traumas are not being resurfaced in our present life. So I can now love and live healthier.

I am grateful for all my experiences, hard or easy and I know now it was all needed to grow into the person I am today.

Journal entry

Jan 3, 2021

I signed up for another group healing course, this one will be led by Alex Elle

~Pathway to Peace ~

A few journal questions were given

-What does my inner child need today? Describe the feelings

I need love. I need to not feel abandoned.

When I say this out loud I feel sad and heartbroken. I am reminded of how many times I have been abandoned.

By both my mom and dad. My mom left him when I was a baby because he was extremely abusive. So I could now only imagine why she truly was not always there for me.

By my step dad who is both my brother's dad. (biologically) He was around from age 2 till 8 or 9, and then occasionally during my

139

teenage years. The abandonment was that I did not know he wasn't "my biological dad" so when he and my mom separated, he would pick us kids up on the weekend and then slowly would not take me. I remember we would all be so happy waiting to hear his musical horn honk to pick us up, and one weekend he pulled me aside and said sorry you can't go this time. And then the next time, and the next, and the next. That is when I learned he was not my dad by blood. I also learned I had a different last name.

Today I will show up for my inner child. I will love her and not abandon her.

-Where can you make room for more play and creativity in your life?

I can learn to say yes more without having the burden of guilt. I can do things that I enjoyed as a kid, like jumping rope or doing things I never got to do ...

I will make room by adding new child play dates with myself on my calendar.

-How are you leaning in and getting curious about what your inner child has to say?

I am envisioning myself as a child and asking her what she needs. Talking to her and listening to her.

Journal entry

Jan 10, 2021

~Pathway to peace ~

zoom class (Alex Elle)

Look at our past and release

Unclench our hands, and our hearts, and let go.

IT'S NOT PERSONAL, BUT IT IS PERSONAL

Peace requires acknowledgement

A drawing of an 'Emotional Suitcase'

Inside the suitcase is

Shame

ALL family traumas

Loss

Mistakes

Grief

No dad

Not good enough

Blocked memories

Being an adult at a very young age

Word of the week - Decompress

What am I carrying:

I am carrying heartache, for all the mistakes I have made. I have had 2 dads, (both that are my stepdads) but never really parented me ...and neither did my mom.

I was always the parent.

The roles were reversed. I feel the constant weight and pressure of responsibility of everyone in my family... (and just this last year) I am finally learning I do not need to carry everyone else's suitcase.

What am I releasing:

I am releasing all my family's emotional suitcases, one by one. They are not mine to hold on to. I am slowly recognizing the pain it brings, and that this is not my pain to carry. So I am gently giving these back to all the rightful owners. I am releasing any guilt. I do not need to feel guilty about these massive burdens. It is okay to give this weight back. I did nothing wrong. I do not need to feel guilty. It is ok to give all the suitcases back. I am releasing the chronic sadness and weight of steel that does not belong to me.

My peace offering

It is ok to feel uncertain at this crossroad. This is a new healthy way to travel. Travel light and in peace. Be gentle with yourself, and be compassionate as you travel towards love and joy. You deserve to feel peace, with no conditions attached. ~~You~~ I deserve to feel light as air and free as the flowing streams I have passed on this path. I am making peace with my whole self. Beginning with my 3-year-old self, I will hold you close as we travel lightly on our healing path together towards our higher self and the enlightenment of peace of mind.

I will keep giving grace to all of ME.

Journal entry

Jan 12/13, 2021
After midnight
New moon

New moon in Capricorn

I will be full of abundance

Wealthy

Happy

Healthy

Plan to have/buy a house at the beach

Successful with Powered by MJ

Successful with my 1st book

I will be strategic on how I move and who I move with

I will live my best life

IT'S NOT PERSONAL, BUT IT IS PERSONAL

Journal entry

Jan 17, 2021

& Jan 23, 2021

all in sticky notes

~ Pathway to Peace ~

zoom class (Alex Elle)

Inner Child Work - using the small i for little me

Past Fear -

Abandoned

Alone

Not enough

Death

Being a bad mom

Will i be loved

Fear

Will i ever heal the trauma

Present Fear -

Overcoming past trauma

Broken heart

Will my marriage survive

Abandonment

Let's meet both fears -

... never detour ever again from being my true authentic self

Tending to both fears with an understanding

I can show up for myself

Loving myself first

Give myself grace
You are human
We are not perfect
Mail
(CARD)
Front of card -
EVERYTHING ABOUT THIS IS so hard
Inside card-
BUT YOU ARE so Strong

Jan 26, 2021

My Dearest Husband,

I am currently reading a book ...actually, it's poetry by Rupi Kaur. And when I read this, I thought of you.

"You are a soul. A world. A portal. A spirit. You are never alone. You are organs and blood and flesh and muscle. A colony of miracles weaving into each other."

This also reminded me of both of our pains internally and physically.

Reason: Stress. We are both under such extraordinary stress and this will break the body down... if we allow it. Both internally and physically ... food for thought... because I know each of us is more powerful than this dark hole each of us is in. I am choosing to claw my way out of my dark hole. What about you?

Sending happy healing vibes.

Sending belly laughs, till you cry and ALL the love you can bear! XOXO Love you!

Love
Shana C

IT'S NOT PERSONAL, BUT IT IS PERSONAL

Journal entry

Jan 28, 2021
Full moon

Full moon workshop, Leo/ wolf moon

Let go and release it in the form of 4 balloons. Fill them up with what you want to release and then let each one go floating, releasing far away from you.

Balloon 1 - let go of the mind frame of being poor

Balloon 2 - let go of Rob's current situation

Balloon 3 - let go of anger

Balloon 4 - let go of procrastination

What are you grateful for-

I am grateful for knowing the meaning of power and how to survive.

I am grateful for Rob and the time spent together and all the mirrors, lessons ...reflected for me to learn.

I am grateful for learning me and learning how to break out of old habits.

I am grateful I have feelings. That I now know they no longer need to be shoved aside, that it is ok to sit with them, and just let them be.

I am grateful for my growth, my spirits, my intuition, my inner child, and my whole self.

Letter

Sacred Letter to Self comes from Pathway to Peace

Jan 31, 2021

My Dearest Shana,

You have come so far on your healing journey... that I have faith you will rise on so many levels; as you continue this path. Never forget all the lessons and people that have crossed your path. Everyone & everything will arrive in divine timing, all to teach you ...your truest most authentic self.

Yes, even the painful ones.

Always remember to be true to yourself, and listen to your intuition. Your mind is one of your most powerful tools. Do not let it get lost in self-doubt, or even tainted by other people's opinions. You are in charge of your own thoughts and power. Believe the saying, "mind over matter." This is one of your gifts.

Speaking of one of your gifts, your body is one that holds an abundance of energy. I am here to tell you that this is yours, and yours alone. You do not owe anyone or belong to anyone but yourself. It is ok to be a kid for as long as you can. It is ok to be a teenager for as long as you can. You do not need to give your body away, in order to be loved or feel love. *(please soak this in and reread what I just said) (repeat as often as needed.)*

Once you open the door to being sexually active it opens a flood of doors that comes with adulting and responsibility. There is no reason to grow up... too fast. You will have plenty of time to be an adult. When you are older you will figure out how ... and you will figure out that it is ok to speak your mind and communicate how you feel when it comes to any type of relationship.

Just remember to be true and honest with yourself first. Be selfish with your energy, as a child, as an adolescent, and as an adult. You tend to consume energy, and you can protect your energy by choosing who to give it to, at all times.

Your strongest gift is your gift to love from your soul. Your spirit. All deep within your heart. This is a reminder to be kind, gentle, and loving to yourself. Your soul is where your energy is coming from. You are full of light, love and truly are a unique genuine soul.

(repeat ~ to self)

Be mindful as you continue to tread on the earth side. Give yourself grace when it is called for. Follow your intuition, your higher self is your guide.

You are a child of God.
You are the light.
You are a spiritual being.
You are loved and you are love.

With love & light

Your older & wiser self,

Shana C

Journal entry

Feb 5, 2021

LOL

I need to find a new GREAT paying job that does not break my spirit down!

I just had a meeting and they said maybe this job is not the right fit for you...

Are you fucking kidding me?!

Let me just say working in diagnostic is no joke and scheduling for ALL modalities is crazy. The resources needed and always having to double check if the provider actually placed the order correctly on top of any new changes the system makes to do our job NOT efficiently is A LOT, to say the least.

I made 3 or 4 different mistakes, out of several 100s I have scheduled and I know in this field, there is NO room for error. The reason there is a system in place for ALL 5 people who touch this after me, can FIX it if one person missed it or if it was overlooked, or yatti yatti....

I cried this whole time. WHY?!

I think because it hurts to think or know someone is quick to judge and or point out mistakes versus acknowledging where they contribute to, or even sympathize with how much work, effort, and mind structure goes behind the scenes. This is not a no-brainer job.

I just need freedom with millions of dollars in my bank account!

Journal entry

Feb 14, 2021

<3 My Intentions for Healing <3

Be honest with myself

Honor my feelings

Never put myself last again

Love myself more than yesterday

Set myself free (be my truest authentic self, no more hiding)

Be kind and gracious during this healing journey, to SELF

Be honest with myself also means being honest with anyone I have a relationship with husband, kids, friends ...etc

Do not give excuses to yourself or say sorry for how I feel

IT'S NOT PERSONAL, BUT IT IS PERSONAL

My #1 intention for healing is to be at peace and find balance

Mail

Tuesday

Feb 15, 2021

9:05 pm

My Dearest Robert ~

I hope this letter finds you in better spirits. ...and on the mend. Finally got those photos you asked for. We had a bit of a delay.

We finally got snow! Along with a whole bunch of ICE! 4-5 days of it! (smile) It was beautiful! And we were one of the lucky ones! Our power stayed on and no falling trees on the cars. Can't say this about too many other folks though.

Today, the sun is shining and everything is melting like crazy! As if it never happened.

Funny how that works, when an extreme storm shows up and your life can be turned upside down because of it! Then if you're lucky all is close to normal again and you feel safe and happy as if it never happened.

Life.

miss you. love you

xoxo

Love

Shana C

Journal entry

Feb 15, 2021

Dream

...a monarch butterfly came and landed on my left hand before I woke.

On February 17 & 20 I also journaled about the dreams I had. This was an assignment my counselor gave me when I first met her. She helps me decode them during our sessions, especially the long detailed ones.

Journal entry

Feb 20, 2021

NOT a dream

I spoke with Rob last night. The last time I talked to him was on February 8th for about 6 or 7 minutes. Before this maybe 15 minutes on Feb 2nd or 3rd.

I am doing the math now -that is about 63 minutes or 1 hour and 3 minutes out of 20 days

20 days = 480 hours

So we spoke for 1 hour and 3 minutes out of 480 hours

We are married

And I AM PISSED OFF

That is not an equal relationship of give and receive

And still no communication by letters, another vital way to communicate since clearly the phones are not in our favor!

Journal entry

Feb 23, 2021

Another dream

I only remember bits & pieces

...& today is the anniversary of my little brother's passing. 7 years ago.

Journal entry

Feb 26, 2021

Friday evening

... after 6:30

I had physical therapy today for my right shoulder. I don't remember if I mentioned this before or not, but I have a partial tear in my rotator cuff. The reason for the constant pain still and swelling of my right hand by the end of the day. I actually learned or should I say forced myself to use my left hand. It was challenging, but I am a lefty now during most tasks.

I also had a session with my counselor today... at the end, she asked me. Where do you see yourself in 3 years?

I responded, hopefully traveling or volunteering. Living a different type of life, doing humanity work, maybe living near water or by the ocean.

...and 10 years from now?

Wow! I will be 53 in 10 years. So... still traveling. ...maybe come back to Oregon, and visit. I am not sure.

Is Rob still with you?

My response was, I don't know, maybe if he grew and did some self-work too.

She said, "Shana, you see yourself expanding and being big. You should never shrink yourself to be little while you are with someone. Think about this. No one should ever shrink for someone else or want them to."

Journal entry

Feb 27, 2021

Full moon in Virgo

-Releasing

Any shame, what has happened is not my fault

Guilt. I no longer need to feel guilty

Relationships that are not a give-and-take

Mediation is a gold box

In the gold box, the letter said it is ok to move forward with no shame or guilt and it is time to release any toxic relationships. This is the heart truth. Be kind and give yourself grace as you move through the 12th house during the full moon of Virgo.

It is ok to release all of this.

Journal entry

March 2, 2021

6 weeks of Shadow work ... starts today

IT'S NOT PERSONAL, BUT IT IS PERSONAL

With Divines Purpose

(during this course I am jotting down notes in my journal while being on the Zoom call online at 6 am, I am in Oregon and she is in Mexico)

I will work on healing Masculine & Feminine energy

The energy of yin and yang

Wounded healing

My History - Power and Control

I need to start forgiving, get rid of any guilt and shame

Work on my deep trauma

Abandonment and rejection

Forgive them (my dads)

Write 3 letters, one to each of them

Why do I say I have 3 dads?

This will help my lineage energy and emperor energy

Unconditional love

Any regret

See & feel my childhood

Kalima - - First day claiming My Power

I am the Goddess

Anytime I feel unsafe use an affirmation

-When you (I) feel lonely allow ...watch my patterns when I am lonely, what do I do?

FIRST LETTER

To The Sperm Donor
My biological blood,

Although I only met you at birth ...and spoke to you a handful of times when I was 29 years of age...

I would like to tell you now, 43 years later from the time we met.

I forgive you for abandoning me, for never truly being there or being my dad.

I have survived this long without you. I can continue for another 43 plus years. If we speak again it will truly be for my own selfish purpose. To know my heritage, to see the rest of my bloodline... until then... maybe we can meet in another lifetime and have a healthy father-daughter relationship.

For now

....good bye

your firstborn

Journal entry

March 8, 2021

When I am lonely... I tend to want to be busy or try to make plans to avoid my feelings. ...these feelings are sad and sometimes I feel afraid.

Journal entry

March 9, 2021

zoom call

Mexico/Oregon

Shadow work with Divines Purpose

Goddess Sekhmet will come through

Practice tough roles, repressed emotions

*HIGH Risk energy

Take some time off work. Give myself time to heal with neutral

154

energy.

Anxiety! It's a Red Flag!

I am at high risk. Sit still. Feel it.

Be selfish

-the lesson - Put yourself first

Galactic Council

- read 2x a day daily

A contract that needs to close out (a karmic cycle)

Exhaustion ...I see this daily

I need to surrender

-look up the dark night of the soul

-there is a tunnel I need to go through

-I need to have time off

To transmute energy

Continue to follow the moon cycles

Goddess Aphrodite

Prayers to reclaim my power

Healthy balance for myself

Hold up mirrors to my relationships

Acknowledge the masculine and awaken the energy to heal. So I can be in a union

Start dancing again, maybe even belly dancing

-allow the energy to come out

~~check in with myself. ...how do I feel when I dance and just breathe?

~pay attention to any synchronicities

Later... still

March 9th

I signed up for another group class
Heal Your Heart - (HYH) led by Alex Elle through zoom
Today is the first week -
"Let us always remember
Self-love is sacred soul work
Outgrowing outdated versions of ourselves is necessary
We deserve to be in our joy." (A. Elle)
Not everyone I love will understand or agree with my journey
Hold space for myself for healing and being in my joy
It is ok to start naming my NEEDS
Make an SSS Chart
SEEN SAFE SUPPORTED
I feel SEEN when
    1. I am recognized or a loved one reaches out

    2. ....

    3. ....

What do I want
    1. Financial Freedom

    2. Unconditional love

    3. To travel and explore

I feel SAFE when
    1. I am supported

    2. When I am not alone

3. I am trusted

I NEED

1. Joy & happiness

2. Peace

3. To honor my truth

I feel SUPPORTED when

1. I am loved unconditionally

2. I am heard and not dismissed

3. I am truly cared about and thought of as a human being

I DESERVE

1. Joy, happiness, and peace

2. A long healthy peaceful life

3. A Whole heart... not a broken one

Choose an affirmation

'I can uplift my younger self'

Why did I choose this?

I chose this affirmation because I want myself to be at eye level with my younger self, during this next chapter ... and I see this healing journey will take awhile.

I would like to continue seeing through the eyes of little me while embracing the 'healing me.'

What matters the most today? This year?

A sustained sense of well-being and internal peace.

What matters to me the most in 2021 are my kids, my spirit, my health, my happiness, mi familia, honoring the truth, and myself.

Why?

...I have neglected myself, my needs, and my wants for 42 years. It has become a tangled mess of ropes in an old basket that I am having to undue to become healthy ... happy... because it is the right thing to do.

Draw the Inner child with balloons that have fear-based words

On the next page a drawing of me, releasing the balloons

Balloons have the words

-Heartbroken

-Anxiety

-Fear

-Anger

-Depressed

Journal entry

March 13, 2021

9:36 am

My heart is broken again

I have been playing this horrible broken heart game since I was young.

I just broke up with my husband ... officially. I said the words out loud to him. I found the courage to say what the reality is ...that is that we're separated so we need to separate.

...about 44 minutes ago

my heart is heavy
I am extremely sad
I am now questioning what I did
...I need to take a drive
to the ocean
see if I can gain clarity

Journal entry   ~~2013~~

March 13, 2021

New moon in Pisces

I am not sure why I dated this originally in 2013.

But after how today went. Actually, I do know... 2013 was the year I got married. My actual journal entry says 3/13/13.

New moon in Pisces workshop

I am grateful for my husband and what he provided. He always gave when he could and the love that he did give was his best at unconditional love.

I did tell him today that I wanted to separate because it was too hard. I now have this huge lump in my throat and chest ...and now I am questioning what I did.

I am trying to release him to be happy and healthy on his own and me on my own, since we are not truly together.

I even wrote his name in the sand, before the wave washed it away...when I found myself on the Oregon coast. Trying to fully release him.

I know the next 12 months I will continue to gain clarity. I just have to do one day at a time.

Mail

3/14/2021

Early Sunday morning

My Dearest Love of My Life,

I am truly sorry to cause any heartache or pain. I know neither of us would intentionally do this to each other.

After our conversation, I realized what I said may have not been clear. So I wanted to write to you because I seem to be better at writing it out ...than verbally speaking it.

What is the reason I want to separate from you?

The reason is I can not live the way I am living any longer.

Yes, you are right, The truth is we are already separated,

Yet from the time you left in May of 2019, I have been locked up. I feel like you do not truly understand the burden I have been carrying. I am also not here to make you understand.

What we are feeling is exactly right, neither one of us is wrong, like I said before. What I am feeling is valid, and what you are feeling is valid.

I know I do not like feeling this way, I don't like feeling sad, angry, helpless, scared, not loved, abandoned. It's not healthy. This is one reason I am separating from you.

I am not free to speak with you privately, call you when I feel like it, make love to you, speak about exactly what's on my mind at whatever time of day or night it is, or simply live freely when I am free.

I do love you, I always will. I LOVE YOU SOOOUULL FUCK-ING MUCH it hurts like HELL!

I took a really hard look at my current state of living and the reasons

I do the things I do or used to do. I am doing my absolute best to break old patterns.

I struggle with abandonment.

I know this because it was triggered like crazy when you got locked up. I struggle with it from my mom, ALL my dads, and now you. I am afraid that when you return home, this will happen again. I will be left alone. Again.

This is why I am choosing me.

I don't want to be in prison any longer.

This is the reason I am asking for us to separate because I can no longer live in fear, obligation, or guilt. This FOG feeling is not healthy. Fear, because I am scared this will happen again. Obligation, because this is not how a relationship works this is part of Codependency, and these are patterns I recognize I no longer want to be a part of. Guilt, because I should not feel guilty for choosing my own happiness or a life of no more heartbreak & struggle.

Another thing I recognize, and I am pretty sure I have told you, but I get angry and have extreme anxiety when it comes to anything that has to do with the law. Court, jail, a police officer... any of it is extremely triggering. It takes me to a dark hopeless place. I dread this feeling and I am trying to get rid of this feeling. I no longer want to be tied up with the law if I do not have to. It is a horrible helpless feeling.

I thought about what you said yesterday.

Is there someone else? Again the answer is NO.

Do I long for companionship?

Yes, I do. I miss this. I miss having conversations, private conversations without being recorded or having to pay for a conversation. I miss the simple ways of living, without heartache. This is nothing new.

I have told you this all before. I miss everything about living free.

What I see and recognize daily within myself is... I am fighting for my life.

I am here on the other side of you, FREE, yet I am LOCKED UP. I AM being punished. To not be loved, feel loved, feel happiness, be in joy, or walk in love.

I did some math

There are 10,080 minutes in one week. 1 WEEK. I was lucky if I got 60 minutes with you in a week. On a phone call, not private, not between only you and me. That's 60 minutes out of 10,080 minutes, in one week.

There are about 53 weeks in a year, 52. Something to be exact. If I add all the weeks up it equals 3,180 minutes we might have had a conversation.... (this average is in a whole year) a whole year of talking by interrupted, recorded phone calls doesn't even add up to a whole week.

How is this healthy? How is this a healthy loving marriage?

Let's say you come home tomorrow. Will this happen again? Will you be taken from me again for years? If the answer is I don't know or yes. :-(

Then I will die all over again. I will just keep dying in this lifetime.

Over

And

Over

Again

I will just keep dying a slow death.

Please understand I am only telling you all of this because this is how I feel. I do not blame you or want you to feel guilty. This is not my intent. I only want to share what I am feeling and why I chose what I did. I am in charge of myself and my own feelings. I am releasing any expectations you may have had for me or thought of me. I am not carrying this any longer.

I deserve to have a companion who can be there for me if this is what I choose. I deserve to heal and not feel guilty for choosing myself first. I deserve love. Unconditional love. Always. Not just parts of my life. I am choosing me, first.

I know. The FUCKING TRUTH Sucks. Our truth sucks. Every ounce in me wishes it was different. That our love story is forever, happily ever after.

My chest hurts

My heart hurts

My soul hurts

My heart breaks a million times and I continue to die a slow death, with you not by my side. (literally not by my side)

So instead of me dying every day. I am going to try really hard to live my life. On my own. I have no idea if this is the right way, but I do know the way I am doing it now, is killing me slowly. (literally)

(the rest of this letter was sent in my handwriting)

Stating

This does not mean I don't love you or I am not in love with you. I love you deeply. This is why it hurts so fucking much! I am learning to love myself first. So I am choosing myself 1st this time. I am doing my best to break the bad habits and choices I placed on my path. It feels wrong to choose me first, but I know now it's right. It's the healthy way. So when I look in the mirror and see myself I can be proud instead of lost. I can hopefully see my 43 year old self instead of a broken 73 year old woman. So I can love and give in a healthy way to my loved ones, including myself first.

It's taking everything from me to write and fight through this shoulder pain.

I said let's be friends because I do miss my best friend, but if you cannot do this I understand. You have to do what's best for you.

I don't know if I got the chance to tell you, but I got a gift from Justina's friends for my birthday during the Bend trip. 2 books. Astrology and The Secret Language of Birthdays.

The first time I opened the book was a few days ago. WOW! Mine is very much aligned. I thought I would share both mine and yours. :-(

Again, I am deeply sorry for any and all pain I might have been part of or caused. I never wanted this or to hurt you. I truly do love you. I always will. You will always have a special place in my heart. Always and forever.

I pray one day we will heal from this pain.

I am forever grateful for our time together, for the love we shared, for the priceless memories we created, and for loving me the best you could.

Forever grateful

Shana C

Journal entry

March 15, 2021

zoom class (Alex Elle)

IT'S NOT PERSONAL, BUT IT IS PERSONAL

Week 3 HYH

...week 2 still has unanswered questions

Yesterday I completed the 'Returning to Self' collage and decided to go with the art therapy that was suggested.

...yesterday was HORRIBLE. My chest hurt so bad from the heartbreak. The exercise I did helped tremendously. It truly was divine timing. I played 3 different songs on repeat for over 4 hours, in the background. This helped me to work through the pain and sit in it. While being in art therapy.

Songs were ~ by (Omah Lay), Bad Influence, Damn (ft 6lack), and Confession

My art - Returning to Self, had clippings of nature, wine, food, and sunsets. I made myself (as the sun) and had a few words.

Lets laugh, dance, embrace yourself, from the heart, safe, The compassionate healer, inhale, exhale, Feel all the Feels, use your 5 senses, move move move, Wild things, return to paradise, be brave, look inside, prioritizing you, live in the now, find your squad.

Most of these are cut out into the shapes of a whole heart and words bursting to and from the sun (me). I cut a moon out from a clipping of a compass.

-What do people want me to be?

People want me to be perfect and show up for them at any time without questions asked...like how I used to be and show up.

People want me to show happiness, regardless of my true feelings. So really they want me to lie and be fake.

People want me to be exactly what their minds and hearts expect. They are portraying expectations of me that are not authentic or fair.

-Who are you really?

I am only human. I do not want the title of being perfect.

I am learning to stop pushing or hiding my true feelings away … regardless of other folks' expectations.

I am my own person. Who does not need to live up to anyone's expectations, but my own and even my own may change. I am not a superhuman.

Journal entry

March 15, 2021

Idea
Write a book
Title
The greatest LOVE story ever - SELF

Journal entry

March 16, 2021
zoom call
Mexico/Oregon

Shadow work with Divines Purpose
Forgiveness - - 2 sides
Spiritual journey - - death, mourning, & rebirth
I am a ritual
…take baby steps
…I can no longer abandon myself
…my deeper fear
…is being alone

IT'S NOT PERSONAL, BUT IT IS PERSONAL

Holy Rage will surface and this is how I will find myself.

This is how I will find myself!?

Trust

Trusting this process is a huge gift ...to myself

Deep inner wounds

...started at age 2- 2 1/2 years old

Processing nurturing energy

...I need to forgive my mom, my mother

...to feel safe again

Imagine your inner child

Safe

Loved

Never ever abandoned

How wonderful and joyous she is

Reflect on the inner child... what are the deeper layers, find her

...allow time to process and there is no need to sit in shame or guilt

The motion of fear will help me find my way back to my OWN power

Moon -

Eternal lessons

Follow the cycles

Break the curses

The physical, spiritual, karmic wheel, the linage

Choose your pain Shana...to be free.

Chapter Eleven
Spring Of Shadows
2021

Journal entry

March 21, 2021

I find JOY in

- Today's walk with my first born

- A clean empty sink

- My brother remembering my birthday

- The song of birds singing at sunrise

- Witnessing the sky painting a colorful sunrise

- The feeling of peace & joy while being part of a sunrise

- Spending time with my son on his 17th birthday

- Seeing him laugh smile and interact with his friends

IT'S NOT PERSONAL, BUT IT IS PERSONAL

- Hearing a hummingbird then recognizing ...it's singing just for me

- Snow falling

- Exploring new trails

- Piece of my heart showing up, authentically

- Hearing the voice of a childhood sweetheart

- The sunrise on Pisces new moon, while the birds ring confirmation out loud

- The way the sun hits my skin and warms my spirit

- Ocean views and the tranquil sound

Journal entry

March 27, 2021
5:55 am

A dream

Today I woke up from my dream, crying.

...many deep messages in that dream, then I realized what today is. It's my late brother's firstborn's birthday. She is 11 today.

SHANA CHRISTINE DILLON

Journal entry

March 28, 2021
8:08 am
Super Worm Full Moon

Currently at my moms

...by myself

...soaking in her hot tub.

Second time this week

...and it feels like medicine after hiking Angel's Rest last night ...it is much needed!

The last time I used the hot tub...my memory says maybe 10 years ago ...or even more.

...well I decided to do my homework while soaking

... 2 more Dad letters

To Dave

Thank you for doing the best you could as a stepdad.

I have several memories of where you screwed up BIG TIME ...during my adolescent years.

...but then you grew up ...and made it up by showing me and my kids that your human and people can change. You have always been a great consistent grandpa to them. Thank you for this.

I am grateful for the love you share with them and my mom. For always being constant in my mom's life.

So I would like to tell you now if I haven't before ...I forgive you for any past heartbreaks. I love you and appreciate you for trying to do your best, as life continued on.

Shana

IT'S NOT PERSONAL, BUT IT IS PERSONAL

To Dad (Miguel)

This one seems to be tougher ...

...not really sure where to start.

I have always considered you my dad.

...because you were all I knew when I was young, from before the age of 2 until now... but you stopped. You stopped actively showing up when I was 11 or 12. I remember at age 6 or 7, I was told you were not my blood dad. That I had another dad out there, just like you.

He was Mexican and had dark hair but a different last name.

I was no longer Perez, in grade school I could now use Padilla if I chose ... per my mother's words.

I remember practicing my new name in 3rd grade.

...writing it, saying it out loud, telling my friends.

Looking back ...I don't remember the trauma piece. I blocked that out.

...but the reason for my mom telling me of my new "real" last name was because I was blaming myself for your divorce. At such a young age. And again... I don't remember ...but apparently, I saw you cheating on my mom with her best friend. Later that evening after I told my mom. I was in bed. ...maybe sleeping. I don't know because again I do not remember but this is what my mom told me a few different times when I asked, and her memory is... that you came into my room yelling at me, telling me it was all my fault that the two of you were separating.

Do you remember this?

Do you still believe this? Do you believe the divorce is my fault?

...a few years passed and you would occasionally let me join my brothers for the weekend visits.

I was SOOOO EXCITED!

I was SO HAPPY!

I got MY DAD back!

In my eyes ...and in my heart, you were my dad ...and THIS I DO remember. The sound of your musical horn on the weekends and we would escape with you for the whole weekend.

Another weekend came and the sound of the musical horn was honked, so we would run to you.

Again you honked the musical horn, and again, my brothers and I RAN out to your big blue truck with our packed bags ...to sleep over. I was soooo HAPPY to be with you and you told me, "Sorry not this weekend."

...a few more weekends came and went and you did it again. I was not allowed to join.

I was 10 or 11 ...I was crushed. I was heartbroken. I questioned what I did. Why could I not be with my dad? What did I do wrong?

...me ...writing this letter is not enough. I will need to have a conversation with you.

So I can truly heal and when I say I forgive you ...mean it.

(sad face)

...in the meantime. Do you still blame me?

– - - - - I called. No answer.

He called back.

...call ended @ 10:22 am

...we talked for about 30 min

I told him I had something to speak to him about. ...and before I could say it, he knew I was crying.

He said, "Don't cry baby, what's going on? You can talk to me."

IT'S NOT PERSONAL, BUT IT IS PERSONAL

I asked...

He said he doesn't even remember and he always considers me his daughter just like Meli. That we are the same. (Meli is his biological daughter, born in 1995)

When I asked him why he did not allow me to join my brothers with the weekend visits.

He said, "I didn't have you come over because of Annie."

This was his new girlfriend, back then... he said he didn't want her to make me feel bad, so he just didn't bring me around. He also included that she always gave him a hard time saying Shana is not your kid, why is she joining all the time?

When I look back ...after they broke up, I do remember being invited again to hang out on the weekends.

Until I was a teenager, that is.

During this conversation, I found out I was 14 months old when he entered my life.

He also said I am the only kid who calls him, and whenever I am ready to visit him in Mexico he has a room ready for me.

I did not ask if he still blames me for the divorce. That will have to be a conversation for another date.

Later that evening still March 28
Full moon workshop

Sun in Aries ~ focus on I

Venus ~ focus on LOVE

Chiron ~ Self healing /love

Full moon in Libra... I will not lie to myself any longer.

...completing old cycles

This full moon is the only one that has an overlap of last year's energy!

Healing is circular

...fully finally letting go

Completed the meditation

Under this full moon in Libra, I am ready to let go of

-4 birds

One yellow canary - this is my right arm pain

One hummingbird - this is anxiety building up at work

One Bluejay - Me. Releasing past fears, past abandonment, past expectations, past sabotaging energies

One eagle - Rob

Journal entry

March 30, 2021

zoom call

Mexico/Oregon

Shadow work with Divines Purpose

- She is RISING

Heal the bruises

...reconciliation

Is my dad in a healthy balance?

-he might love ...from a wounded place

Current shadow...

...I am deep in thorns, surrounded by toxic air, not bringing love, not bringing peace to me, not bringing harmony, ...and now it's bringing me trauma.

Where am I hiding?

Why am I hiding?

The energy coming through is carried deep in my mother, it is deceitful energy

...the common denominator is my mom

Write a letter to my mom

The mother wound

...this is a lifetime of practice

It's my choice

... whatever brings me light

...what makes my heart light

...one by one I will get rid of the little fires everywhere

Journal entry

April 1, 2021

10:20 pm

I got into a heated argument with my 17 year old son. About him going with me to the beach.

I was tired of not being heard and I literally screamed bloody murder at the top of my lungs to be heard. To stop debating with me! The old me came to the surface. I shouldn't have screamed like I did. He wants to stay home, play video games, and finish his essay. (With all of the stress I am going through, my brain could not decipher his simple easy teenager request)

He said, "Mom, you didn't even ask how you can help with the class. And the reason I want to stay home is to finish my essay without distractions."

His point is valid. So I said, "OK, we will stay home."

Then he said, "No, you go to the beach you never go have fun and you don't trust me."

Trust is not the factor, but I am also not going to provide an invitation to have him be tempted for trouble.

I briefly told Destiny, and she said, "Maybe I should let him be home alone."

My thoughts are ~

One, he is a teenager

Two, I never see him or get to spend quality time with him (the main reason why I am fighting for this)

Three, I will blink and he will be gone and move away, like my other kids

Four, I will never get this time back

...later on, my son came into the room

He apologized

I apologized

We cried

...and he did his best to talk

He said it is hard to talk or share feelings ... he cried and then said please just listen, don't talk.

He said Rob is more like his dad than Doug. ...and of course, he is okay with my decision. He wants me to be happy, but he is just sad because it feels like he is losing a dad.

...and my WHOLE HEART shattered again. What did I do?

IT'S NOT PERSONAL, BUT IT IS PERSONAL

Journal entry

April 3, 2021
...would be Jade's bday
Late night in
Cape Kiwanda
Pacific Coast

Jr decided YES let's go to the beach. We drove late last night.

My best friend and her family were already there and extended the invitation to stay in the beach house they rented.

Today I spent most of my day sitting and watching the ocean and the different families ...how perfect and happy they all looked.

Jr and I rode bikes together for a good hour or so and then again for another hour UP a HILL with Johnny! It was so much fun! We ALL felt like kids! Then I went and watched the sunset, and my son joined me. It was a beautiful, flawless ending.

I am grateful for all the small moments and big memories that were created today.

Journal entry

April 6, 2021
zoom call
Mexico/Oregon

Shadow work with Divines Purpose
...last class

Energy is a confession ~ the BIG picture ~ is being a lightworker & a healer

It's time to reset

Validation = I ask and I receive

Forgiveness + Love

Check in with myself and remember to ask ...is my heart heavier than a feather?

Keep Ho'oponopono near (remember) I'm sorry. Please forgive me. Thank you. I love you. (this word is hard to forget, it was spoken at my wedding, gifted from the pastor).

Take action to no longer judge myself and not allow others to judge me.

To the Bride in the cage, it is time to live in color!

You are a goddess, master your communication ...continue to speak with conviction and power!

I am a goddess. I will transform. I will heal.

Journal entry

April 11, 2021
Sunday
New Moon

I am exhausted

I worked today. I volunteered and worked. For the COVID-19 vaccine clinic set up inside the Convention Center in Portland.

They gave over 8,000 vaccines today

The first hour was apparently a record of 1,060 people who got vaccinated.

IT'S NOT PERSONAL, BUT IT IS PERSONAL

I will be there again on Tuesday and next Sunday.

...and I am not even vaccinated yet.

LOL ... funny how I keep falling into a place of pun or irony situations.

One year later.

Still a Pandemic

I wore the face mask and face shield for almost 8 hours.

Deff DO NOT miss this part of in-person work!

The vaccine ... I will get (maybe) end of April or next month.

I was waiting to first complete my second follow-up for my mammogram since the vaccine can also cause alarming false results for patients if the vaccine is within so many weeks of the breast imaging.

Journal entry

April 11, 2021

8:33 pm

New moon in Aries

Beginning ~ first New moon of the energetic year

Abundance Love

Money Travel

I trust myself and my POWER, peace, love, and joy ... first in self.

The rest will follow

Meet other Rising Leaders ~ ~ ~

Meditate and manifest

I will have plenty of abundance, and live somewhere warm and sunny, near a body of water. I can travel anywhere and I finally love myself completely, with only a half-full suitcase.

Journal entry

April 17, 2021
Sometime after
9 am, morning

Rob called me

2x

And today we were able to do a video call, so I could see him. (my heart feels broken and happy at the same time)

We both look stressed. My face is red and broken out with acne all over. Worst in my life ever.

Rob has noticeable spots again on his head, which indicates stress. This is a stress habit he does, which is to pick at his scalp.

It was nice to see him. I finally got to show him the room. All the new big photos I put up and my plants and the small couch and he could see my new ink. (tattoo) ...yet it was also really heartbreaking. Because he calls me his wife and says he loves me and misses me and these words confuse me and make me sad. I do miss him and love him too.

It is just a heart-wrenching place we are in.

This type of life... is not for the weak.

And I am not solid... I am slowly trying to glue myself back together.

Today is also my bestie's birthday... She is in Kona, Hi.

The same place where Rob and I got married.

This also breaks my heart.

Why?

Because then... it was so special and it meant everything

IT'S NOT PERSONAL, BUT IT IS PERSONAL

...and now.... It is just a memory that in reality we cannot live like a husband and wife. And that I said the words, "Let's Separate." because it is the reality.

I am just tired of living in lies.

Journal entry

April 26, 2021
Full moon

Scorpio full moon workshop

Do not lie to yourself

It is time to complete the change

Close the door

Confirm - I will no longer give my energy away

Just keep doing YOU, keep focused

...by doing this

...Expect Powerful Change

Planet Pluto is going into retrograde, so it is important to review my foundation so I do not fall back into bad cycles.

...reminder

This summer, Jupiter will be in Pisces (sun)

There is a big shift this Friday with Uranus and the sun will come together which will create huge feelings

What came up during the meditation release

Images of 3 photos on the left to focus on are

What makes me feel safe, healthy, and loved

3 photos on the right to be released are

Old habits, any expectations, my marriage

...release, release, release

Journal entry

May 05, 2021

Yesterday I hiked. I cried. I reflected with the wise souls. I fought my demons on this trail. I will need to keep bathing in the woods for healing therapy. I need to hike my way out of depression.

I decided I will post the following words on social media.

Hiking Dog Mountain is just like life is. There are crazy hard moments especially in that last mile straight up inching your way for the beauty at the top.

Yet, there was no better reward than to say that you did it! With no one else's help except for your own courage, stamina, endurance, and your own faith to believe in yourself.

Anyone who has hiked Dog Mountain and completed the trail, especially that last mile... Not just to the first field of flowers or the 2nd field but all the way up to the top.

Then hats off to you, because that ish was extremely difficult.

Not "more difficult"... per the signs listed on the trail!

Extremely!

IT'S NOT PERSONAL, BUT IT IS PERSONAL

Journal entry

May 8, 2021

I am grateful for all the beautiful souls that have crossed my path. I know each had their own priceless gift, that they shared & the light from each one has got me to where I am today. Including my own light.

I am grateful for my friendships. The unconditional ones.

Journal entry

May 11, 2021

New moon

New moon in Taurus workshop

Focus on

Self love

Ask and receive

Rest. practice patience

Practicality = Achieving goals

A little bit every day ...adds to a lot in the end

Mars in cancer has a lot to do with ancestry, traumas, and seeing if we are emotionally ready

Believe in the impossible

After the meditation - under the new moon in Taurus I invite in

Healthy body, mind, skin

Glowing face

Abundance of peace and wealth

Strong healthy beautiful love

Mail

(Card)

Front of card- Birds flying over the ocean

In a place full of light, full of grace...

Inside card -

May it bring you some peace to know that the one you love knows only peace now.

Thinking of you with Sympathy

May 14, 2021

My Dearest Heart ~

I am thinking of you. Wishing you hope in the midst of sorrow, and comfort in the midst of pain with my deepest sympathy. I pray you find healing during this heartbreaking time. Sending you love and hugs as you remember your loved ones.

Love Shana

Journal entry

May 16, 2021

8:55 am

Another dream. This one intertwined my current job and one of my old ones.

After discussing this with my counselor, we decided that the 2 girls in the dream are stressed out and both are me (duality)

Putting money on the house, selling ourselves with no conditions (a conversation for my mom and the house)

What is harder?

I am the DJ pointing at the far end, why she felt so powerless -this is about embracing all of Shana, no longer feeling shame

It is time to accept ALL of me.

IT'S NOT PERSONAL, BUT IT IS PERSONAL

Mail

May 18, 2021
9:40 am
Tuesday

My Dearest Heart,

It has been extremely difficult to navigate life. I am trying my absolute best, but I don't know if my best is good enough anymore. I thought if I separated from you I could navigate easier ...but it's exactly the same.

I have no answers.

I'm all alone

I have to keep on climbing mountains that keep showing up on my path.

Jr is sad going through a tough time...

Nonni wants to move to Florida... So I am going to go with her in July or August to see if I can help her navigate this.

...I'm really just trying to go with the flow. Which is not always easy when I would rather crawl up in a ball, cry, and stay in bed.

Instead, I have to fight through all this pain, work, be a mom, take care of all the bills, be a cheerleader for my kids when they succeed, suck up any emotions that could be a downer to someone else ...and still try to live.

Life has a funny way of unfolding ...especially when you paint a picture in your mind of a happily ever after and the picture ends up with a whole lot of lessons to learn first. No shortcuts in life.

We have to dig deep, get dirty, and ask the hard questions. Why? How? And take responsibility for all the parts that we contribute to learning the lessons ...before we can actually live and taste the happily ever after.

I miss my best friend.

It's been a really long time since we truly communicated.

Years

Maybe one day we can start with this piece first.

I don't know if it will help ...or work for either of us. It's only a suggestion ...that you mentioned last year. You spoke of topics ...that maybe we could choose a different topic and that could help us. I remember agreeing and looking forward to this ...but it never happened.

...so I decided to write to you.

And talk... here.

Thinking of you ...

with all my love

Shana C

xoxo

I love you (drawing of rose)

"My life is part humor, part roses, part thorns." - Bret Michaels

"Forgiveness is the scent that the rose leaves on the heel that crushes it"

- anonymous

Journal entry

May 19, 2021

Watched a video on YouTube about a monk's approach to stopping jealousy and comparison

Qualities add to our self and to work on

Patience

Equanimity

IT'S NOT PERSONAL, BUT IT IS PERSONAL

Endurance

Grit

Honesty

Everyone experiences suffering

Birth

Aging

Sickness

Death

Keep cultivating my own peace, my own serenity. Allow my mind to be bright. Do my own work.

Journal entry

May 20, 2021

I opened 'The Language of Letting Go' to today's date.

Titled -'Sadness'

"Ultimately, to grieve our losses means to surrender to our feelings.

So many of us have lost so much, have said so many goodbyes, and have been through so many changes. We may want to hold back the tides of change, not because the change isn't good, but because we have had so much change, so much loss.

Sometimes, when we are in the midst of pain and grief, we become shortsighted, like members of a tribe described in the movie *Out of Africa*.

"If you put them in prison," one character said, describing this tribe, "they die."

"Why?" asked another character.

"Because they can't grasp the idea that they'll be let out one day.

They think it's permanent so, they die."

Many of us have so much grief to get through. Sometimes we begin to believe grief, or pain, is a permanent condition."

(Beattie, pg 135)

I have never watched the movie she refers to in her book, yet I know the feeling of death all too well. This tribe knows my anguished soul.

My counselor suggested that I start checking in with my body before and after phone calls from Rob

So.... I started keeping track

Feelings ~

After the phone call last night, I felt hesitant to answer

When I did answer I felt bad about his current state, constantly put in the hole to quarantine after doctor visits. Then I was frustrated that the call kept dropping... I could only hear every other word. It sucks not having clear communication.

Saturday, May 22nd

I wanted to answer the phone call, but I didn't. I was frustrated that the call was when my friend happened to show up to help cheer me up. Because I have been depressed. I felt torn.

Tuesday, May 25

An incoming call came in while I was driving home. I felt over-whelmed and really wished he would just start writing to me. Not only call. I let him know I felt like I needed to stop taking the calls for a while. Then I felt bad for feeling this way. Because I said we could be friends, yet I realized ...friends may not be realistic at this time in my life when it causes so much confusion on both ends. He said he would call me tomorrow, so we can talk.

IT'S NOT PERSONAL, BUT IT IS PERSONAL

He called

A day late, he was supposed to call yesterday.

I didn't want to answer. I felt angry when I saw it was him and anxious. I did answer the call, we talked for a little bit, and then we were silent ...the call lasted the full 20 minutes.

He asked when he could call back.

I said I don't know right now, it would be nice if you wrote to me.

Silence

...I said, I will write you.

He said, "Okay, take care of yourself." and hung up.

My chest hurts. It is not as heavy, but my heart's still broken and I don't have a lump in my throat anymore. So maybe I am healing.

As much as this hurts... maybe I can close this door.

Journal entry

May 26, 2021
Full moon

Full blood moon in Sagittarius workshop

Releasing all old belief systems

-releasing -Observe all that I have done

...now follow through

LET IT GO

...if it is not working

It is time to accept the change

...relax and chill, no need to go against the current

Spirituality + Practicality = Balance

...simply let go and trust

After the meditation what came to the surface to let go of...

I am letting GO of ...still heartache. Pain, old beliefs, relationships that are no longer there, my marriage, shame, guilt, bad health, bad skin, no house, all the bills, old traumas, what no longer serves me, and ALL the pain from the last 2 years I have held within me and ALL the pain from the last 2000 years that I no longer want to carry. I am releasing under this Blood Full Moon!

Mail

> Sunday early am
> May 30, 2021
> One more day
> & Ashanay is 26

My Dearest Heart, Rob

I've been thinking about what you asked.

"Do you know what March 13 is?"

This year. Yes, I do.

March 13, 2021, on Saturday, was when I was honest. It was when I got the courage to speak my truth of how I felt, and what the present moment truly was and is. So this was 2 and ½ months ago. And yes this is also the day I requested we separate...or as you would say, I broke up with you. I see it as - to treat our relationship how it truly is. How I have been living the last 2 years of my life, separated since May 15, 2019. It's no secret of how I have been feeling and living. I only just now said I could not continue on the same journey while you are locked up (literally) and I am locked up (yet free). The truth hurts sometimes, yet as they say ... the truth will set you free. I could no longer pretend I was happy or even ok with living the same way I already lived from August 2014 through July of 2017. Locked up yet free for over 3 years, I lived. I have been struggling with this and it was time I was honest. To myself and to you.

As days have passed ...I now realize that my request for us to be friends is extremely difficult and the circumstances haven't changed. So realistically how can I be a friend and vice versa? I don't get to call and check on you. You called it. How can we just be friends? :-(

I feel even heavier when we do have conversations, and when I am a friend to someone I care about I am all in. I realize I cannot be all in with you, because again there are constrictions in place. I also know I still love you, I know deep down I always will, and it hurts too much to give this energy with only a half-ass truth. Meaning I need to step back from this too. As much as this hurts and pains me to say...

I need to give our relationship a break. I need to be 100 and be honest about how this is affecting me. It fucking sucks, it feels like 1,000 knives continue to penetrate my spirit and heart every time we talk. Why? I cannot get past the reality we are truly living. We are living apart. And I HATE THIS! I absolutely cannot stand all the restrictions placed on us from 2 different states. I am struggling BIG time with this.

"To say goodbye is to die a little."

I don't want to say goodbye anymore. It's exhausting. I'm tired of dying while alive. At this time I can no longer talk to you on the phone. At least not right now.... This moment. This month.

If we need to communicate we can write to each other. This will provide space and the opportunity for each of us to speak, without any interruptions or a time limit. I don't know how long this will be for. *I do know* I don't want to feel guilty or be sick any longer, for choosing me first.

I looked up the meaning of Ho'oponopono. And it's more than please forgive me or I forgive you. It's part of healing.

The beautiful **Hawaiian** Prayer for **Forgiveness** is called "Ho'oponopono" (pronounced HO-oh-Po-no-Po-no), and it's lovely. This ancient **Hawaiian** practice of **forgiveness** functions as both a communication concept for reconciliation and a tool for restoring self-love and balance.

Ho'oponopono teachers refer to this practice as "cleaning," meaning that you remove or cleanse your own negative feelings to erase the negativity that is blocking you from your memory or consciousness. It's a way of expressing your wish to no longer suffer from a problem, current or past.

Ho'oponopono is an ancient Hawaiian spiritual practice that involves learning to heal all things by accepting "Total Responsibility" for everything that surrounds us – confession, repentance, and reconciliation.

I know that we have been together in a past life, several in fact. I know that we will find our way back one day. If not this lifetime, in another. I know because we are beyond soulmates, we are twin flames, Rob. The hardest yet most rewarding relationship out there. You & I. You are the love of my life. As my children are too, but I cannot continue to hold their hands and help them when they make mistakes, I can only be here when they return or if they ask for guidance. Because this is their life they are living, not mine. As this is your life you are living, not mine. At least not any longer.

IT'S NOT PERSONAL, BUT IT IS PERSONAL

Writing this I am crushed…

Ho'oponopono

…a pastor gifted this to us on our wedding day. Who knew we would truly need it or hear and feel the word again.

New day
June 3, 2021
Late night

How did we get to this point?

I can't even visit you if I wanted to

I never thought I would die 1,000 times while living.

'Face the World' by Nipsey Hussle, from his Crenshaw album in 2013

Been on repeat lately, his album, and this song

When you get the chance to listen to it… until then

Here's the lyrics (I copied them for you)

"When all dreams seem to die

The summer's gone, the breeze stops blowing

The sun just leaves the sky… So face the world now or cry

So face the world

So face the world

So face the world now or cry

Face the world now

So face the world now or cry

Face the world now" (Nipsey Hussle)

2013 was a great year …

crazy how much this song relates in 2021

Good night

Xoxo,
Shana

Journal entry

May 30, 2021
...later

Today I am grateful for the quiet. The stillness. The heartbreak. The heart mending. I am grateful for the journey back to self. This is all proof I am living in purpose and I will continue to grow with love, even when there is pain to face... I know now, the reward is gratitude. This illuminates into beautiful, spiritual, unconditional chapters that I have triumphed in my life.

Journal entry

June 1, 2021

Draw a few circles around each circle

My counselor suggested another healing exercise

I know it is due to the level of depression I am in

I drew the circles - now label them

These are circles of support

The center is your primary people who no matter what are there for you

The next circle is back up, such as a counselor

3rd circle any essential tools for my healing, such as yoga, other friends, massage therapy, support classes, or groups

IT'S NOT PERSONAL, BUT IT IS PERSONAL

The last circle is other tools - journaling, hiking, meditating, art therapy

Keep this circle in sight, near you to access

Journal entry

June 7, 2021

A dream

I only remember a few parts, but it is the second time I have dreamt of this.

Water everywhere swampy like

There are lots of houses, kinda like houseboats, surrounded by deep swamp water, trees everywhere, gloating and growing out of the deep water. While I am treading in the water, murky, dark, and thick water.

Journal entry

June 10, 2021

New Moon in Gemini

Solar eclipse and mercury are in retrograde - the last time this was aligned was 18 years ago

-Give myself what I need

-A vibe of knowing how I can improve myself

-The emotions currently, are intense

...I am just now finally releasing some of the old pent-up anger

It is overdue to release this anger ...& then the sadness shows up like a cousin

It feels like I am trying to fight for a solid foundation wrapped in a bow of safety

-it is time to create new options

...friends, connections, and write a new story

Reflect on how I have changed in 18 years

Chiron is in Aries and we are healing our healthy ego

... after the meditation, add in affirmations

I AM allowed to live

I am inviting in an abundance of joy and riches

I am inviting in a NEW strong healthy foundation with LOVE

I am inviting in a Brand New House

I am inviting in healthy new beautiful relationships with all my kids

I am inviting in travel to new places around the world

Journal entry

June 14, 2021

On June 12th, 2021 my daughter Nonni graduated from U of O with a Bachelor of Science in Psychology

To say I am proud is an understatement!

This was a monumental moment!

The Lord knows we have had obstacles over the last several years, and she has learned to triumph and pause when her spirit tells her to. I am grateful to witness such a phenomenal journey.

My heart is filled with joy!

Mail

Friday 5:33 am

June 18, 2021

I dreamt of you the last few nights

My Dearest Rob

It has been extremely difficult. The last few months I realized I am not the only one grieving.

Jr is having the hardest time, too. I spoke to both the girls... they shared their sorrow with me as well. Yet these 2 don't live with me and Jr under the same roof you lived in. Jr and I have daily reminders that you are not here.

My heart is crushed all over again, to see that my son is going through the same pain as I.

I know he wrote to you for Father's Day. He was adamant about doing this. A few weeks prior he wrote to his dad. When he told me what he had done he asked if I would like to read the letter. A two page letter full of pain, anger, & sadness. All I could think was how I did not see how much pain Jr truly had been feeling. And.... If I was the parent receiving that letter, I would feel sick. Knowing I lived in the same state and I didn't try hard enough to be consistent in my child's life, regardless of any barriers. A child should always have their parents love them unconditionally & provide a healthy loving nurturing foundation to the best of their ability. God knows I tried. Yet many times the foundation has been rocked.

Another realization I had was your youngest. I am extremely happy for the both of you to be reunited. Then there is your son, your blood. I couldn't help but think maybe he is going through the same hardships & heartbreak as Jr. I know we cannot go back in time. Yet I do wish I spoke up sooner, to let you know how I truly felt when it came to all the kids. They are never at fault. 18 and older they have more of a voice ... but as a child growing, learning, seeking love & advice. The parent is the one who should be constant, not the other way around. The child learns from what they received & what they did not receive. I would like to apologize to you now for not giving my wholehearted truth out loud when it came to all the kids. Maybe if I found my voice then, and spoke up, the relationships between all the kids and parents... wouldn't need so much work & mending now. As they are no longer children... now they are all adults, or on the verge of it.

Life is never linear. Neither is healing.

I got Jr a counselor but they are not available till next month. I will keep looking. He needs more than just me right now. I do not want him to grow up hating people and take his anger out in a way that could cause destruction to his life, later down the road. I want him to have the tools to recognize when he is hurting or in pain and to address this in a healthy manner. Amongst other things, I want for him.

New subject

I know you know Nonni graduated. Wow! What a milestone! An extremely powerful, exhilarating, proud moment!

Nonni's home screen on her phone the last few months was of me & you. Throwing up the O in front of the O building. <3

Anytime I saw this and was with her ... I paused. It felt like forever ago & just yesterday all at once, that we went to tour the school with her. Then I was reminded of how my heart hurt and was shattered because you now missed 2 monumental graduations of Nonni's. This truly tore me apart... all over again. Yet I pushed through the days, Jr and I were in Eugene... to do whatever she needed or wanted us to do. Mainly it was us supporting her and going out to eat or shop for food. LOL

We got to see her graduate virtually (on the computer) in her apartment with her, and we went to the school and watched her walk. A tearful joyous moment.

I am thankful and grateful to be part of her story.

I have to start getting ready for work now.

I do hope you are healing and hanging in there. This moment I know, feels close to hell for me. I hate to say it, but I know it is probably the same feeling for you too. :-(

I have no idea how things are going to unfold. I am no longer looking to the future. I am simply living in the present. I am taking it one day at a time. (an extremely hard discipline to practice)

If I learned anything from my brother's death. It is life is not promised tomorrow. Or today for that matter.

So I will simply just live one day at a time, and go with the flow.

Sending you a HUGE warm hug.

With lots of love. I love you. I always will.

Love Shana

Chapter Twelve
Brutal Summer Of 2021

Mail

My Dearest Rob,

Sorry I missed your phone call yesterday

Been a real busy month

Yesterday was Nonni's graduation party I threw. We had it at Alejandro & Brandy's house. Alejandro agreed to BBQ and do this on Father's Day. And well... his wife agreed to bake goods and help decorate. Overall I think it turned out pretty good. I am beyond exhausted, but can't sleep. Maybe it's the heat... or all the dreams I keep having.

Actually, I know what it is. I am drained. It took all the energy I could muster to put this together. Once it was all said and done and

IT'S NOT PERSONAL, BUT IT IS PERSONAL

I looked back to reflect, I am not good at throwing parties anymore. Or maybe it's because I only showed up as half of me. Or maybe it was the realization that I had to ask my brother & his wife to use their home to throw *my party*. This in itself was energy-consuming. Thank goodness for both of them. I guess I needed a village this time.

Either way... it's finally done.

Nonni finally got her party. (I meant to give when she was a senior but life at that time was complicated too.) When I realized she never got her grad party for senior year, and she never got to travel that year as a gift that I said I would do... Sooooo.... I told myself this year for college *she will get **both!***

We leave for Florida, at the end of next month. Instead of camping. Andddddd instead of me and her only, it will be me and all 3 kids.

So ya... just trying to be the mom I said I would be. While hanging on to this teeter-totter.

Jr said he finally got to talk with you. :-)

Nonni said she was sad she kept missing your call.

It's tough being on the receiving end... I know how it makes me feel... I always feel helpless.

I miss you. We all do.

Thinking of you and hoping for better days, one day soon.

Happy late Father's Day, love

I probably should print & mail this out now.

With all my love

Shana C

(Father's Day Card)

Front of Card - maple leaves

If thoughts bring people together, then we will be especially close this Father's Day

Inside Card - bay leaves

...because many warm thoughts will cross the miles along with wishes for your happiness.

Have a Wonderful Father's Day

6-20-2021

I miss you. Message on back

My Dearest Heart

How I long for this madness to be completely behind us. For care-free, loving, breakfast in bed days... be the only days we wake up to. I long for the simple things that made us happy. In the meantime, I hope you can reflect on how great you were when you were present in each child's life. And how one day soon you can continue with being the Great dad I know you were always meant to be.

Sending you love, joy, and simplicity.

Love you

Love Shana C

Journal entry

June 23, 2021

I flew out to Sacramento yesterday and got an Airbnb in Elk Grove, called Oasis Grove. A couple owns a good portion of the land. They made the backyard a tranquil retreat. A pool with a waterfall, several trees, plants, a huge maple tree right in the middle, and a hammock to chill on if wanted.

It's beautiful and peaceful. Even if a train heads through the other side of the fence... every few hours. The couple has 3 huge buildings, their house, and the studio I am in; which is above the apartment. Then one more apartment/studio I think a family stays in.

I think I want to come back. I have only been here a little over 24 hours …

I was supposed to connect with one of my cousins, but that didn't work out. My friend showed up though, they drove up from Reno to hang out.

We attempted to eat at Joe's Crab Shop, but instead, we ate at The Boiling Crab.

I tried fried oysters, they were actually pretty good. Then we hung out in the studio. Chilled, spoke of ALL our tattoos, and listened to slow jams.

…oh the nostalgia joined us … and then, I was left alone.

Journal entry

June 24, 2021
…early after sunrise

I woke up with a heavy heart.

I am not 100% …exactly why, yet it feels like I am sad. I am sad that I am alone again. Part of me wished my friend wanted to stay, yet I know their life is really busy and chaotic right now …and if it was me, I am not sure I would have even made the drive.

I am not sure how to process ALL these feelings. I know I need to sit still with them …try to let them just be, and then let them go …but I am just extremely sad this morning.

Today is a full moon

…and I will be mooning too, any day now.

Before I even got to Cali, I was trying to get back home a day earlier than originally scheduled ...but the cost is crazy

Maybe I am feeling like this because I am out of my comfort zone

No kids

No work

I have too much time to sit still

and I am completely alone

...I am going to drive to Alameda today. See where I spent some of the happiest parts of my childhood... but no family is left there (well not alive, they are here only in spirit)

I am going to go visit my grandparent's home

...maybe this will help my healing

Maybe I will find a piece of my broken heart in the Bay ...and glue it back.

I read a few pages of The Language of Letting Go, but I'm a few days behind... Yet, I realized I am not behind. When I decided to open the book and read, this was divine timing. The message was received and it was exactly what was needed at this time. Now. The present moment.

Later after my drive to the Bay Area

-4:54 pm same day

My grandmother's house is gone. ...GONE!

There is a home there. Just looks nothing like my grandparents' Victorian home. The house there now is ... same size, but different look. The stairs are different, the entrance is different, the backyard is different, and even the Orange tree is GONE!

I thought I was sad earlier. Driving here I knew it would be different because in one of the childhood homes I grew up in I would no longer be able to roam and walk side by side with all the memories. Due to the passing of my grandparents and then the home being sold a year or 2 after, which was in 2019. Staring at it all I felt so sad. I cried... just knowing what was once there ... is now gone.

I walked through the neighborhood. The street in front of the house Encinal Avenue and the street in back, to confirm what I was truly seeing. It was all true. The orange tree really was gone from my grandparent's backyard. It was gone. So were the stairs that led to the second story porch. Gone. It was all different. It all changed.

...I guess nothing ever stays the same.

This is my 2nd childhood home of mine ...that no longer has the same image as it did growing up. Simply ...just gone.

Journal entry

June 25, 2021

Friday

I am now going to miss this place. Especially the mornings. The birds singing, the roosters welcoming the day ...even the train. It shows life will unfold exactly how it is meant to unfold. The beautiful view this couple, mother nature, and God put in place ...to enjoy. Is truly a gift.

I am forever grateful for this healing, self-love, time ...alone. Even when it felt unbearable.

I did not know when I arrived, but I know it now, what a blessing.

My favorite is the HUGE Maple Tree sitting in the center of my balcony view! So much love, energy, and strength emerged from this spiritual living beauty.

I am grateful for the healing gifts.

Ps. My cycle aligned perfectly with the full moon ...again. (an added bonus for all the floods of emotions, the full moon was in motion) ...release.

Full Moon in Capricorn workshop

Reparent and reteach our inner child

-what we want, where do we want to continue to invest, and what we are doing?

The energy has shifted ...we can no longer forget how we felt and what we have seen.

Ask ourselves, how do we want to continue moving forward?

-Saturn is in retrograde till November (keep building a strong foundation)

-also the alignment of Pluto needs us to release our fears, I have to release the OLD fears, and doubts ...in order to shift.

Shifting through the fears is shadow work and will continue for 2 weeks after this moon cycle.

Reminder to self, SLOW DOWN

...how do I want to spend my time

I need to prioritize myself for the next 30 days

Expect POWERFUL Change

Connect with soul tribe

...continue to invite in the good energy

Under this full moon in Capricorn, I set the intention to release the following

Releasing all old patterns

Guilt and any shame for my marriage not succeeding in this life-time, the sadness (I no longer want to hold on to this pain), heartbreak

IT'S NOT PERSONAL, BUT IT IS PERSONAL

(I am now healing all my wounds), and any relationships that are not equal ...keep releasing, one day at a time.

Journal entry

June 26, 2021

Saturday in Sac

Well, Elk Grove! It is almost 7 am...I decided I am going to Lake Tahoe today, my other childhood stomping grounds!

Last minute decision, since I fly back home tonight I need to pack up and check outta here since I have a bit of a drive.

...8:24 pm I am at the Sacramento Airport

...my flight was delayed twice now

I have been here since 6:30, and the new time says my plane will not leave until 10:10 (ugg face)

I should have got a room in Tahoe!

It was so beautiful, healing, magical, and crazy busy! I've never seen it that busy. It was actually a bit chaotic... finding a parking place was like finding a needle in a haystack, glad the universe led me to where I needed to be.

I was able to hang there for about 2 hours. Since I was a little girl I have always wanted to live in Tahoe, today's trip was a reminder that I do want a home near water for sure, yet to be in the mix of 100's of people and cars, I am not 100 percent if a house in Tahoe would feel as peaceful as it did when I was young. Tahoe would be lovely to live in ... I could adjust to the busy knowing the solitude is near. Any warm majestic beach would be fine too.

I decided when I get back home I will log off social media, again. For all of July, it is time to disconnect to reconnect.

I will write 5x a week for my book. Work out every morning at least 4-5 times a week. I want to coordinate a wellness retreat. A 3 day and/or a 5 day, destination in Sacramento and include Lake Tahoe in the mix.

Mail

June 28, 2021

Early Monday morning

My Dearest Love of my life,

It was wonderful to hear your voice and see your beautiful lips with that smile!

I think it's been a month since we talked. I was busy every time you called prior or had no service... so I'm glad we connected yesterday a few times. Xoxo

Sending you soul much love, hugs, and kisses ...during this healing time.

Me getting away from the house in a different environment by myself with no agenda... to attempt a reset was needed. Feels really good.

I would love to say You and I are back exactly as we were. "We" always will be, yet the truth still stands. So ...if it's ok with you I would like to do baby steps. ...of course, I love you. This has never stopped. It is just an extremely complicated triggering time for me.

It fucks with me BIG time not being with you and it Fucks with me BIG time being with you 'on where we are at.' (sad face)

I know me. Every day is different for me. I am going to do my best to fight through the constant triggering of depression because I am a fighter. With this said, I am really trying for NOW, only one day at a time. Some days I can talk and other days I might not be able to. I will finally mail all these out. I look forward to our talk on Friday.

with all my love

Shana C

Journal entry

June 29, 2021

I'm back home in Oregon and we are having record high summer temps! 111 degrees and 115!! The car said it was 118 degrees! Stayed that number on the whole drive over to Marquita's new house with AC to cool off.

Change... a BIG shift is definitely coming!

What's been the most impactful change you've experienced in your life over the past few years? And why did you make that change?

Answered this on 6/30

The most important change I've experienced is showing up for myself first. I am now a better version of myself through self-love, creating boundaries with no expectations, and evolving in the space and place I am meant to be in. Including learning all the lessons that were on repeat for so long. (I am still navigating the repeat lessons, but I now see them)

This next year will break the cycle... This time next year I should feel lighter.

I made this change because I was tired of being exhausted and weighed down with pain. It felt like a never ending broken record. I graciously accepted what was and moved out of my own toxic habits, some were forced on me... and I am grateful for the force. This helped me create change and begin new healthy habits while slowly adapting to the new old me.

Free-spirited just like my childhood self
In July I will continue to let go of
Hindering toxic people or behaviors
Self-doubt
Pain
Any and all expectations
Hardships, any blockages, procrastination
...and of course the codependent habits.

Journal entry

July 1, 2021

...giving gratitude

Today I am grateful for having awareness and having the gift of common sense, sadly many do not.

I am also grateful for breath work, this tool feels like a lifesaver.

Journal entry

July 5, 2021

Today I went back to Naked Falls in Washington. Michael was loud and clear the last few days and very much with us today. I brought Destiny and Jr. We felt his presence. Jr climbed the side of the hill and jumped the same jump my brother did when I was with him. I captured it on my professional camera back then.

I have been telling Justina I wish I knew how to get to the swim hole my brothers took me to 10 years ago. She found it! On social media of course. Go figure. It is no longer a hidden gem, yet it is still a gem!

IT'S NOT PERSONAL, BUT IT IS PERSONAL

When I drove out with Justina on July 3rd I had this wild feeling that came over me. I recognized this road. This was my 3rd time on it now. How did I not know? The last time I traveled this road was in the summer of 2014, months after my brother Michael passed. At that time I was with my girlfriend Cynthia. As we were driving over the bridge passing Dougan Falls a flashback came to me and a message from my brother. It was surreal. The message I received was he *was* and *is* protecting me.

2014, the day Cynthia and I were out here we explored only Dougan Falls. I recall recognizing the waterfall, yet I could not remember who I was originally with. My phone had no service and the battery was low. So I decided while we were out there to just power off my phone. It was a beautiful healing day. I remember we sat on the rocks in the middle of the river. Later that day when we began to drive back to Portland, I forgot I had my phone off until we were almost to my house. 5 minutes away from the house, I powered the phone back on. I had a few messages from Rob saying don't come home. The feds are here and they are raiding the house.

I didn't know it then, but I know it now. My brother was protecting me. He was keeping me safe out in nature. Naked Falls is right around the corner down a dirt road. 1.8 miles away from Dougan Falls.

When I was with my brothers, it was 10 years ago today! After we hung out at Naked Falls for the day Michael and Alejandro decided to pull over at Dougan Falls to jump in real quick. We were there for less than 10 minutes. No wonder I could not remember who I was with yet I just knew I had been there before. I had to do some math and digging to figure out the exact date and timeline. It was July 5th, 2011. Michael, Alejandro, Meli, Destiny, and I hung out for hours at this magical water spot! Everyone jumped in except for me. That just wasn't my thing. Still isn't. Yet the other day when I was with Justina and Amy, all 3 of us jumped in for my brother.

I am so grateful to be guided back to this place! I have been speaking of it for years! The timing really is wild, yet not, because I have always believed my brother to still be here with me. With us. With everyone he loves. He truly is a guardian angel.

Journal entry

July 9, 2021

Friday

New moon

Get ready to shift

Goal for the new moon, the maternal energies

I need to reparent myself. What does security and safety truly feel like?

Feel the deep emotion and use it to navigate on this healing path

What can I do in 3's?!

It is all about taking action. Start New Cycles.

New community

New friends

New home

Under this new moon in cancer, I invite an abundance of wealth, health, love, and money to flow into my life.

IT'S NOT PERSONAL, BUT IT IS PERSONAL

Journal entry

July 15, 2021
Thursday
6:06 am

Dream

The last few dreams, there were infants in my dream, ranging from age 2-6 months

...after 8 pm

I decided later to do a deep dive, I asked my spirit self to shine through the many roles I fulfill

...What are the main roles?

-Mother

-Caretaker

-Provider

-Leader

-Daughter

-Sister

-Friend

...each one plays a huge role and each role means I need to succeed, there is NO room for failure.

Would I be more or less, if I no longer partaken in any role?

I feel like I would be both.

Journal entry

July 17, 2021

Today is my nephew Applejack's birthday, pretty sure he turns 12!

Today I woke up in a tree house. Yes, you heard that right! My son and I drove to Washington to Treepoint in Issaquah. I rented the

Trillium for the weekend!

It is so beautiful out here, kinda like luxury camping!

Last night my son and I played cribbage and I am looking forward to what the day unfolds.

Thoughts (To Rob) - in response to the letter written to me on July 22nd, 2021

First thing. I realize this letter only came to me because I mentioned you have yet to write to me. The last piece of mail I got was for Mother's Day, that card was as cold as ice.

The 2nd thing, before I read the letter you spoke to me about not reading the book we both own, that I sent to you. The one about codependency. Which made me realize you have done no work on yourself. Which means we are at a very different level, space, mentally & emotionally.

Of course, I love you. This will never change. Yes, this is true, I stopped saying it and I stopped writing it because I was trying my hardest to separate myself from you, to remove any pain I constantly felt.

Which like I said before feels like a death, like grief.

I came across a post the other day while in Florida, that said, "Grief is the last act of love we have to give to those we loved. Where there is deep grief, there was great love."

This really resonated and continues to rise in me.

I do appreciate you speaking your truth and sharing your heartfelt feelings, pain and all. It is definitely not pretty ...to hear, read, or feel. .. yet nothing about what we are going through is.

The 1st page written speaks of how you could never truly feel or understand how much pain I have been going through. You mentioned us being in a marriage. That we are not boyfriend and girlfriend and the choice I made to step back you cannot understand and that at times you find yourself hating me for making this decision and that you don't like me for this.

Rob, Hate is such a huge upsetting feeling. It breaks my heart, knowing you feel this way.

Then again, more crushing words, that you have lost trust in me and the meaning of 'for better or for worse.'

What do you want me to say to this?

...because the reality has not changed.

....

You're in jail facing who knows how much time, and I continue to be locked up as well if I say yes to the very end.

Then you said I bailed on you.

I left you...

Yet I am still here, listening and allowing some comfort or leaning upon during this chaotic, heartbreaking, neverending, storm. ...we both face. Still, writing you. Even when no letters come to me... aside from this one. I still write.

As a friend should.

I know it would be better as husband and wife, but you are not here for me. I need more than emotional support once in a while on a timed clock, at my expense or someone else's. I did absolutely EVERYTHING when you were locked up after we got married.

EVERYTHING. Rob. Did I not?

Is it truly fair to ask me to do this all over again? Knowing how hard I struggled that 1st time around.

I am pretty sure we had the conversation on one of our Sunday visits that I could not do this again. When you were locked up here in Oregon.

The bottom of page 2, you said you know the words would hurt me, and that you are not trying to hurt me, it is your truth.

Reading this

It looks and feels like both of our truths are extremely painful. There is so much trauma that has occurred in both of our hearts and souls. I cry every time this thought enters my mind.

Top of page 3 you said you do not hold my truth against me, are you sure? I am asking because you said you lost trust in me and you find yourself hating me. (this feels and sounds like resentment)

Questions you asked on page 3, that you would like answers for.

Where is it I am going in this new life I have chosen, and am I a part of that life?

Where am I going in this new life, I am trying to be happy, be at peace, love myself 1st, create healthy boundaries, heal, and move forward by gluing my broken heart together one day at a time. Will you be part of my new life? Rob, You will never not be part of my life, you have part of my heart, forever and always. Living and being together... I don't know what that looks like. Because I have changed I am no longer living for the future... I am only living in the now.

Do I still have my wife and a life with her?

I wish I had an answer, but I don't because we are both living 2 separate lives, for who knows how long.

Do I still have a home to come home to when that time comes?

I also do not know what this looks like.

I do know I would not leave you without a place to stay, my home would be open to you. Again I don't know what the future holds because we are living 2 separate lives.

Do you still want me as much as I want and need you?

YES. THIS is why it hurts so damn bad.

Do you still want this marriage and want me as your husband?

Again, yes. But the truth again and the reality is you are not here as my husband.

We both are going through pain so are we going to do it together or apart?

The answer to this is both. We are apart and yet we have formed a friendship again that only the 2 of us know how deep our pain runs, and how deep the love truly is. And well, We are both facing this apart.... Yet together. It is a horrible heartache mess. I know you are asking if we are a union. What we have and had, no one else will ever compare. I can only do one day at a time and the pain of us being separated I have to treat it as such... in order for me to survive.

Journal entry

July 18, 2021

Wow! Such a beautiful special place The Nelsons managed to build. The TreeHouse Point truly had cozy nests for humans upon the wisest souls. Trillium was floor to ceiling windows with 2 levels once inside. A wooden ladder was used to climb up onto the 2nd level where the bed resides.

I am forever grateful to experience the magic here. The stillness surrounding each tree home was breathtaking to witness. Our days consisted of river exploring, cribbage games, some reading, many walks, and 'keeping calm' while feeding the many fish was a very special experience. There were so many fish jumping, you don't see that every day!

Simply being present in the Beauty of Mother Nature felt like luxury camping. The extraordinary breakfast places a beautiful ribbon upon the get-a-way.

What a magical special place! I will absolutely be back!

Journal entry

July 23, 2021

Full moon

Full Moon workshop

It is not time to hold back, it is time I speak my truth.

Who I am today is different from the person 6 months ago, or even 1 year ago.

This is the time to create new energy

Do not believe or follow any old unstable habits

There will be 2 full moons in Aquarius, which only happens in a zodiac sign about every 19 years! The reason for the name Blue Moon is when that 2nd full moon arrives. A true full blue moon is when two full moons arrive in the same zodiac sign.

After meditation what will I release...

I will begin to release old habits that were taught to me

I will start releasing old beliefs that were passed on to me

I will release any old structures that are toxic and keep me in a wounded space

Mail

(2 Postcards from Florida)

IT'S NOT PERSONAL, BUT IT IS PERSONAL

Copied onto paper

Aug 5, 2021

Florida has been quite the adventure. E got stung by a jellyfish at Cocoa Beach. I ran almost every morning near Kissimmee lighthouse/ Lakefront Park and Jr got his first professional yet, not so professional tattoo!

Sending love

<3 Shana

"The one who observes finds all things unfolding in their proper time with grace and appropriateness. They relax inside their own silence, enjoying harmony with all of life." -Mooji

Journal entry

Aug 8, 2021

New moon

New Moon in Leo workshop

We have the choice to drop what does not serve us (any people, places, or things)

8.8 is a new portal

It is time to leave OLD emotions and structures in the past

Now is also a good time to learn a new skill

I need to focus on leveling up

Keep my eye on the prize

There is A LOT of work, but it WILL be worth it

Leo - is connected to the heart and the sun. (my moon sign) we are also very loyal!

...if you are ever with a Leo, pay attention to the lessons

Under this New Nu Moon, a new identity is born. Protection is important

    I will ask my spirit guides to help clear any negative energies

    Under this New Moon in Leo, I invite in

    Any new skills to enhance my bravery

    New skills to become joyful and have more joy

    Healing energies to help me feel at peace with my job and any relationships

    I will create a new life that will be surrounded by joy and peace

    I am joy

    I am peace

    I am happy and free with all my time walking in unconditional love

    It is My Time to SHINE!

Journal entry

Aug 15, 2021

    I spoke to Rob 2x tonight

    He called at the end of a sunset.

    How did I feel after the call?

    I felt confused. I felt like maybe my counselor is right, I am giving him hope.

    Why am I doing this?

    I love him. I don't know how to stop that, and I think I am doing this because he only has had me who was always there ... and I feel guilty if I STOP at 100%!

    I also know I should not feel guilty. He is not my responsibility.

    I feel tired.

    I am exhausted from this.

    I also did not like 2 things he said.

IT'S NOT PERSONAL, BUT IT IS PERSONAL

One was that I mentioned his sister sent a text asking me about his health and well-being. He said she should be able to do that and go to the source.

Yet the fact is, I am not the source. He is. She should be writing and asking him directly.

Second was, he said, "You haven't said you loved me yet? I love you."

The way he said it to me ...it felt like a chore.

It should not feel that way.

Journal entry

Aug 22, 2021
Sunday

Today I did not hear from Rob

Yesterday I did. We spoke 2x

Once in the morning, once at night

Afterward, I felt sad. I missed him. I felt like it had been forever since I was fully happy.

After the morning conversation, I went to Hallmark, to buy a few cards.

I wanted to buy one for our 8th anniversary ... but every card I read made me sadder knowing we had none of what they spoke of in Real Time. Only in the past. I was exhausted this weekend. I was living in the past ...and I told myself not to do this.

That living in the past was not healthy.

I need to live in the now, in the present only.

I found a song that is playing on repeat... just like my life.

'Did you/fall apart' by (Patreek Kuhad)

...later still 8/22

Blue moon

Tonight is the 2nd Full Moon in Aquarius

We are at the end of Leo season and the beginning of Virgo season (my rising sign)

I need to be intentional and reflect on how I am spending my time and energy

As I move forward I need to slow down before deciding

...I still have concrete stones I carry, very very heavy energies

...I am trying to still clear these energies.

I am still reminding myself to TRUST this process and to actually take care of myself

Have faith in my dreams

It is time to give (to myself) rather than take

REST RECOVER RELEASE

Today under this Blue Full Moon

I will release

...my old broken relationship

...my unhealthy habits

...my old stuck routines

...ALL my fears

...any resentment

...the thoughts of not being good enough

...toxic relationships

...guilt

...grief

I am grateful for ALL the lessons. I truly have learned so much. I now need to give myself grace and release.

IT'S NOT PERSONAL, BUT IT IS PERSONAL

I no longer need to hold on to the old belief systems.

Mail

6:50 am

Wednesday

8.25.2021

My dearest love of my life

I ran today. Before sunrise.

I am in an extreme tug-a-war with my heart, soul, spirit, and mind.

It pains me to say this.... But I need to step away again. As much as I love hearing your voice and talking to you, I notice at the end of it you're not here and I keep slipping into a dark hole.

I get anxiety waiting for the day you can call...

I am happy when we speak

I am heartbroken when the call ends

I keep putting myself in this constant cycle

I am now removing myself from this broken record

This last week I struggled.

I slept all weekend

During my breaks and my lunch, I climbed into bed to sleep

I am extremely depressed again

I cannot let this take over

The only way I know how to help eliminate it is by separating our worlds. :-(

I can't keep dying every day, a slow death

I love you with everything in me, I wish it was different.

You asked what I needed from you and I said, " I need you home."

Come home NOW... FUCKKKKKKKKKK!

Yet this life we are currently in... is not so simple.

I still have a kid at home to raise.

And I am slacking, BIGGGG TIME. I know this because I choose to hide out in my own room if I am not working. I need to snap the fuck out of it and glue what's left of my heart together so I can be somewhat of a parent to Jr. Since I am the only one here, but somehow have not been...

I take full responsibility for this.

Phone calls

Let's back up

To once a month

...and if we absolutely have something to say... let's write.

Shana C

Journal entry

Aug 29, 2021

11:01 am

Rob called me back

We spoke 2x

At the end of the second call I said call me in a few weeks ...or write to me if you want to talk.

The call ended

He called back a third time

He said I am going to make this easy for you because I can't keep going back and forth on this teeter-totter. We are done. I will let you know when court happens and what the outcome is and if you decide you want to work on this marriage with me at that time you can let me know, so you have time.

I immediately went into defense mode by saying, "You can't do that anymore?! Teeter-Totter back and forth, that is exactly how I feel all the time!"

He said well he can't do it. (my heart shattered again)

Journal entry

Aug 30, 2021

About yesterday

Rob made it official.

He said, "Let me make it easier for you. I'm done."

...then he proceeded to say he would keep me in the loop of when a court date would actually be set again and what the outcome would be

...and if at that time I want to let our marriage work ...we can see what this looks like at this point.

I don't know how to feel about what he said. My heart hurts again. More pieces keep falling from my heart and I cannot seem to find the slivers that fell to glue them back together ...or the strength.

Part of me is appreciative he put a stop to it and the other part is upset that it came so easily.

I feel sad, exhausted, grief, unsure, guilt, fuck... I am struggling with the damn guilt and I know that feeling is not welcome here because I did nothing wrong yet it is at my damn door again!

My body, heart, and mind feel achy ...like each part has the flu.

I hope and pray I am making the right decision for myself and my higher good.

I really am doing my best to let go.

...I am still hopeful, even through this pain. I guess I need to go back to one day at a time.

Journal entry

Sept 6, 2021

New moon

New moon in Virgo

What does not match... fit... we need to let go.

...I need to rest more

There is a new wave, a new chapter emerging

Expect a powerful change

I need to invite ALL the new in and try to look at the bigger picture ...with new intentions

...I need to focus on ALL the NEW while remaining flexible

...I need to look at my physical health, and my daily habits. I need to fit in more rest and put a plan in place... put that plan in play, take one step at a time. Give myself 6-8 weeks to reemerge and reassess.

Under this new moon in Virgo, I am inviting in, a stronger foundation, an abundant amount of joy, love, laughter, peace, harmony, health, wealth and to travel & explore in gratitude.

It is time to over feel, overfill, and keep filling ... feeling, my own cup. Fill it up with love to myself, love, love, and more love.

Shana LOVE yourself MORE!

Journal entry

Sept 13, 2021

4 am

Nightmare

I remember I felt death or someone leaving me ...like they died. I woke up crying, with my heart shattered...

IT'S NOT PERSONAL, BUT IT IS PERSONAL

I was walking in downtown Portland at night. There were people wondering ... heading to parties. Then I met up with Rob. He was across a dark street ....it was hardly lit up, almost like an alley. Felt like after midnight. We were having a conversation but for some reason, we were not next to each other. We were walking and talking, but he was across the street as we did this. We ended up on a bridge overlooking the water. I remember he said I can't stay out here ...it was getting really bad ... a bad feeling was coming and it was getting colder.

He kept looking up at a building and the water, gazing at both as if he were planning to escape and swim for it.

We walked back to the building, this time slightly side by side. (yet there was still distance)

We saw a guard head into work through the back door up the stairs, the same door Rob came out of. After the guard went in ...Rob began to walk the stairs to head back in, too. 2 flights of stairs. When this happened I walked away slowly ...then a random guy said something to me, to get my attention, because I didn't respond the guy said something mean to me, this triggered Rob and Rob said something as he began to walk back down the stairs the guy headed towards him. They got into an altercation. They were fighting.

...but the guy had a weapon. A sharp object stabbed Rob under his left arm near his heart ...then the guy ran. Rob was gasping for air. I ran across the street to him, to only have him die in my arms.

In my dreams, I felt compelled to put my wedding ring back on and then immediately thought how am I a widow now?!

I kissed him one last time as I was screaming, and yelling for help. Telling him not to die.

I woke up crying. Hysterically.

About a week or 2 after this dream, I had a session with my counselor and she gave me a new assignment.

After reading, and telling her the dream, she said, "Now go back, and switch all persons to myself or I, and reread this dream to me."

So I did. ...it looked and went like this, once I crossed words out.

I remember I felt death or ~~someone~~ I was leaving me ...like ~~they~~ I died. I woke up crying, with my heart shattered...

I was walking in downtown Portland at night. There were people wondering ... heading to parties. Then I met up with ~~Rob~~ ME. ~~He~~ I was across a dark street ...it was hardly lit up, almost like an alley. Felt like after midnight. ~~We were~~ I was having a conversation but for some reason, ~~we were~~ I was not next to ME ~~each other~~. ~~We were~~ I was walking and talking, but ~~he~~ I was across the street as ~~we~~ I did this. ~~We~~ I ended up on a bridge overlooking the water. I remember ~~he~~ I said I can't stay out here ...it was getting really bad ... a bad feeling was coming and it was getting colder.

~~He~~ I kept looking up at a building and the water, gazing at both as if ~~he~~ I was planning to escape and swim for it.

~~We~~ I walked back to the building, this time slightly side by side. (yet there was still distance)

~~We~~ I saw ~~guard~~ MYSELF head into work through the back door up the stairs, the same door ~~Rob~~ I had come out of. After I saw MYSELF ~~the guard~~ go in ...~~Rob~~ I began to walk the stairs to head back in, too. 2 flights of stairs. When this happened I walked away slowly ...then I ~~random guy~~ said something to me, to get my attention, because I didn't respond to MYSELF ~~the guy~~ I said something mean to me, this triggered ME ~~Rob~~ and ~~Rob~~ I said something as ~~he~~ I began to walk back down the stairs I ~~the guy~~ headed towards ~~him~~ MYSELF. ~~They~~ I got into an altercation. ~~They were~~ I WAS fighting MYSELF.

...but ~~the guy~~ I had a weapon. A sharp object and stabbed MYSELF ~~Rob~~ under ~~his~~ MY left arm near ~~his~~ MY heart ...then ~~the guy~~ I ran. ~~Rob~~ I was gasping for air. I ran across the street to MYSELF ~~him~~, to only have ~~him~~ ME die in my arms

In my dreams, I felt compelled to put my wedding ring back on and then immediately thought how am I a widow now?!

I kissed ~~him~~ MYSELF one last time as I was screaming, and yelling for help. Telling ME ~~him~~ not to die.

I woke up crying. Hysterically.

My counselor then said, this was a really good dream, that I was learning to let go and I was healing.

It sure didn't feel this way when I woke up.

Then she suggested I draw the image.

I did.

It looks just as bad as I felt.

A Nightmare.

Journal entry

Sept 21, 2021

Reflecting on my well-being and time

time heals and healing is never-ending

mental health is just as important as physical health

...when you do the work, the reward is healing. Peaceful. Love will show up.

YOU. I. Will be a better person, mother, friend, partner, daughter, sister, human ...because of my never-ending healing work.

I need to keep the following questions in my forefront.

How do expectations cause suffering in my life?

Where do they show up?

How do expectations limit the experience life can give me?

Chapter Thirteen
Fall Apart Of 2021

J *ournal entry*

Rob called me today. I missed the video call.

I am sad.

Yet ...I was happy he thought of me to call.

Then several hours passed by

He called again

...this time I felt hesitant to answer ...and when I did pick up the phone... I was at a loss for words. Not because I didn't want to talk, but because of what he shared. He said he heard some new information about court. They are asking him to take a plea bargain. 10 years.

...he would serve 8 years (the way the system works with good behavior and whatnot, probably less)

Then he says, "So I can be home in 5 years and 7 months."

...I do the math in my head, this is one year shy of me being 50! (doing 8 years)

I am not sure how I feel about this.

...then he says ...he doesn't expect me to wait, but wants to let me know. He also wanted me to help him decide if he should take the deal.

I cannot make this decision for him and I told him this.

Journal entry

Oct 2, 2021

Michael would be 40 today!

I am on very little sleep again! Yet I have to share before I go on my first backpacking trip with Justina! I fell asleep late last night, maybe shortly after eleven. Only to be woken up by the fire alarms in the house, shortly after midnight! At first, I lay in my bed thinking it was the girls cooking. Because this was normal when they were home. They would cook in the middle of the night and set the fire alarms off. Yet I realized they were not here at the house. It was only my son and I. So, then I waited for my son to figure out how to stop the constant buzzing screeching alarms, because sure enough he must be the one cooking! A few minutes passed which felt like 10. Still, the alarms were blazing obnoxiously. I decided I would climb out of bed and help my son air out the house. As I opened my bedroom door I could see across the hallway my son was half asleep slowly opening his door too, at the exact same time! My thoughts came rushing into panic mode! Wait! If you are just now barely waking up too, why are the alarms going off?!

"You are not downstairs cooking?!" I said out loud. I then ran downstairs opening doors and windows, still half asleep I grabbed a towel to wave near one of many fire alarms that were still beeping! They did not stop! I did not understand. There was no smoke, no smell of gas or fire. My son is easily a foot taller than me, so we grabbed a chair and I had him undo the alarms one by one to disconnect the batteries, throughout the entire house. Once we were done it was close to 1 am. I thanked my son and let him know I needed to try to sleep, I had to be up in a few hours to go camping.

Once I was in bed I realized what had happened.

It was my brother, Michael! Today is his birthday! He woke us up to make sure I knew he was 40 today! NOT 39! I mistakenly mentioned this a few times this week. He turned ON all the alarms to say, "Wake up! It's My Mutha Luva 40th Birthday Sis! Let's Party!"

Of course, it was him, it had to be.

To make sure I knew he was joining me in the woods.

Oh, Michael you always knew how to show up with a BANG!

Journal entry

Oct 5, 2021

First backpacking trip! For one night!

On my brother's 40th birthday!

Justina and I arrived in the new parking lot built for the now popular 'Mirror Lake & Tom Dick Harry' Trailhead. Witnessing the aftermath of a handful of cars that were sadly broken into. Glass shattered everywhere. A heavy feeling came over both of us. This sucks!

Yet, we both decided there was no way the person or people who did this would do it twice. Besides the cops were on their way and most likely had a mess of paperwork ahead of them. Which meant the cops probably would still come back and monitor the area.

We felt our angels near! I mean shoot my brother has been screaming, "It's my mutha luving birthday" all night and day now!

We hiked up to Mirror Lake a little under 3 miles and I had not one backpack but 2 backpacks! Very heavy, may I add. Clearly, I have not done this before! We laughed so much at my lovely hiking look! One on the front of me and one on the back of me.

We found the perfect spot to set up and the birds came to feast! They ate seeds and pizza right out of our hands! There was even a wedding occurring across the lake. The day truly was a celebration all around us.

The weather has been in our favor, for the last several days. Low 80s with the artist of fall nearby. Reds, golds, some green, and orange danced all around us in the trees and bushes of the camp.

We had our crown and other drinks! Made a few toasts! Walked around the lake near the dancing leaves, then grabbed more drinks, snacks, and lemon bars in honor of my brother. We trailed up another incline of 2 more miles to Tom Dick & Harry. We wanted to catch the sunset.

Did we ever!

It was one of the most enchanting sunsets. There was a handful of women who also hiked up to the top to set up camp. Then later joined us for a drink and howling at the sky once the sun kissed the earth goodnight. Each of us was there in honor of someone who passed. We were remembering and celebrating our loved ones.

The feeling of strangers connecting by death was magnified by healing love from our angels. This moment at the tippy top of a mountain with 7-9 women, was SOUL powerful and grounding.

Once it was dark Justina and I hiked back down to camp. It was breathtaking. The moon was just a sliver in the sky and we could see all the stars reflecting off the water! It felt like we were in a blanket of stars. I am so grateful I got to celebrate my brother out in nature with one of my best friends, and her angel momma. Oh, and all the birds! We were like Snow White out there. When dawn showed, they were ready to eat from our hands again.

Our first backpacking trip will never be forgotten, thank you, Michael and Justina's momma! We love you both!

Journal entry

Oct 7, 2021

New moon in Libra

This is an opportunity to set boundaries for the next 6 months

Any energy coming in will need to match what my heart is aligned with ...now.

-some goals I need to implement

Pausing before I proceed

Find and feel balanced

Rebuild my foundation, so I can feel safe and have safety

Protect my safety, follow my intuition

Under this new moon in Libra, I will invite in better, healthy relationships, starting with myself.

Journal entry

Oct 20, 2021

Full moon

Full Moon Workshop in Aries

The overall energy will feel like a New Start

Any commitments will be tested. Surrender to the divine.

Clarity + communication = new doors opening

Any old patterns or relationships that no longer provide good energy ...need to be released

Remember to commit to a healthy vision

Under this full moon in Aries, I am letting go of any heartbreak, anxieties, toxic relationships, and grief.

I am grateful for the lessons and now I am permitting myself to release those that are not aligned with my energies and new path.

As above so below

Journal entry

Oct 24, 2021

A Dream

I was on a beach. It was beautiful, warm, sunny, with clear blue skies. A beach that I had never been to before. The water was crystal clear and every time the waves crashed and the tide came in I could see this glow. It was a majestic aqua-teal color. It felt and looked decadent.

I felt at peace. It was so tranquil.

I was the only one at the beach, for the longest time. There were 2 baby turtles that had dark blue shells.

Every time I would attempt to take a photo... is when people would start to arrive. Then the beach slowly turned into some type of resort, because now when I looked around there were lawn chairs everywhere.

I woke when my peace was interrupted by 3 guys play fighting and one almost stepped on a turtle. I screamed at them to leave and to do that elsewhere.

I shared this dream with my counselor on 11/04

I guess it was another really good dream

The crystal clear water = emotions, because it is clear, it could be felt as lighter or healing. The blue turtles were most likely Scarabs which also equals healing, adapting, and good luck.

Slow and steady wins the race.

Journal entry

November 4, 2021

new moon

After speaking with my counselor, some more truths ...again, were brought to light.

I am slowly accepting the idea of a possible divorce.

The hard truths shared.

Rob is in jail/prison. Once a person is locked up, the experience of life and growth is at a standstill.

10 years later or 7 years ... when he is back home. I would have to go backwards with my life. To meet him at where he is in his life.

All of this is sad.

This is all heartbreaking and I am exhausted from grieving the last several years of my life.

She also said. I am not only in love with Rob but I am deeply loyal, so very loyal.

So very loyal to our past. Why is this?

My answer... to her. Because I love him.

My answer to me...

Because I love him deeply. He is my twin flame, we have been through life now and in our past. I just don't know how or if we will stay together in this life ...the struggle is too much and there is no 50/50, or 40/60, FUCK not even a 20/80 right now.

-

Later

New Moon in Scorpio

It's time for deep transformation and clearing

Figure out what my fears are and clear them! Now is not the time to waste more energy, time, or money!

I need to truly commit to myself. My mental health and my well-being.

Set my boundaries and tell others what I need.

Under this new moon in Scorpio, I invite peace and healing. serenity, love, and more traveling. It is time to start saying yes to more, Shana.

Mail

11.12.2021

My Dearest Love of my life,

My Love - Justin Timberlake

Kiss Of Life - Sade

Make Me Feel - Skip Marley ft Rick Ross

Get You - Daniel Caesar ft Kali Uchis

At Last - Etta James

Still Ray - Raphael Saadiq

Comfortable - H.E.R.

Really Love - D'Angelo & The Vanguard

I wish this wasn't on paper. I miss you

I love you always & forever.

Love always in all ways

Shana Christine

xoxoxoxoxoxo

Ps

thought & hoped this could

make both our hearts sing.

Wishing both of us love and peace on this priceless anniversary!

I fucking miss you and us!

Journal entry

Nov 13, 2021

Yesterday was 8 years of being married.

I got no phone call

I got no mail

...and I expected it. (sad face)

Why?!

I let myself down. I should not have had these expectations!

I was happy all day too, because I was so grateful I was able to experience such a deep profound love. I was expressing gratitude all day ...even on the way to the beach solo. I remember feeling extremely happy and blessed to feel loved.

Then nighttime came

One of my girlfriends and her best friend happened to be out at Lincoln City, for the weekend too! They invited me over for wine. We laughed, talked, and shed a few tears from laughter and sorrow. Then I realized it was after 10 pm...and I had yet to hear from him.

I excused myself early and went back to my room, solo.

I got in my feelings and felt hurt, angry, and sad. Again.

But why?! Why should I feel this way if I broke up with him?

...is it because I had expectations ...and I shouldn't have had those?!

Now I have the feelings of death and I have to clean up all the shattered heart pieces... again.

...this feels like a forever-healing battle! (broken heart)

Journal entry

Nov 14, 2021

Today I will leave the ocean. Lincoln City Beach was just what the Dr ordered. At this moment I am feeling gratitude.

Yesterday I listened to my body ...and I rested. I somehow napped most of the day. I read The Body Keeps The Score. I walked the beach for a little and instead of going out to eat; I ordered room service. I was in bed by 6:30 pm. Fast asleep.

I was out of bed around 5:30 am.

Yesterday the skies were blue. Even though I am glad I rested, I am recognizing the gray sky today is showing me how I felt yesterday and the ocean is currently whispering loud stories, with the wind at bay.

...saying, what a beautiful emotional messy journey, we call life.

Journal entry

Nov 19, 2021

New Orleans

My sis last minute invited me down to Louisiana!

Plus there is a full moon lunar eclipse in Taurus tonight!

I am releasing my broken heart.

Old habits

And what no longer gives or serves a purpose.

Journal entry

Nov 28, 2021

IT'S NOT PERSONAL, BUT IT IS PERSONAL

A LOT has happened in one month

Memories were made and travel took place!

Kinda feels surreal, yet I know it all happened exactly as it was supposed to.

The solo beach trip for the weekend of 11/12.

Then the following weekend, I flew out to New Orleans to connect with my bestie! That was not a planned trip and it was on a full moon! We explored the French Quarters and hung out on Bourbon Street on Friday and Saturday night. During the day she had to work, so I explored solo. It truly was rich in culture and I absolutely loved every minute of it. I felt at home. Even the raw pain I saw, I recognized it in me. Yet, the music, the art, the dancing, the love, the energy, I could feel the healing go deep in my bones.

Yesterday I drove out to Eugene with my little brother Alejandro. We spent the whole day together! We met up with Nonni and pre-gamed before watching the Civil War game! Finally, I got to watch a college game! Nonni made sure of it! It was just the 3 of us!!! It was a day full of laughter and smiles! I loved every minute of it! Even the detours in the beginning and end!

Today.

Then I heard from Rob. We just got off the phone. The last time we spoke was a few weeks ago.

and... sigh... Today, we made our separation more final. Without saying the words. Which is weird. But he knew ...and I know it is unhealthy to stay in this constant toxic cycle. It hinders both my growth and his. Because I love him so much, it hurts like fucking hell!

Yet we can no longer be together because it is unfair for both of us.

This last week I filled out a form with a company called Make A

Wish, donating wheels for families.

My 2008 Mitsubishi Ralliart Galant Black Special Edition. Is gone. It is now being donated to good use.

The car has been sitting ever since Rob got locked up. That is two and a half years now.

The reason it was sitting. He wrecked the car right before he left and I had to figure out the maintenance, cost, etc. Insurance wanted to total it, instead of fixing it. Anyhow, I had someone fix it. I was driving it until my mom gifted me with a new car.

As I mentioned earlier, I have come to some realizations. This is one of them. It served its purpose and it is time to let it go. Man, I loved that car! Ironically ...maybe, but I had the car the same amount of years I was with Rob. 14 years.

Life and its full circle.

Journal entry

Nov 30, 2021

I woke up thinking ...I have a little over 30 days and then 2021 is over.

How is this?

I set a few goals and one was bigger than me. It was HUGE! Choosing to heal. Now I am waiting for the part...where I feel better.

I dove crazy deep into this and now my life will look different moving forward.

I can feel the dark heavy cloud try to follow and attach to me, so I don't slip and let it take me back to depression I decided to make a commitment to myself. I will move, walk, or exercise every day. For the rest of this year and do some reflection writing or gratitude journaling.

IT'S NOT PERSONAL, BUT IT IS PERSONAL

Journal entry

Dec 1, 2021

December 1st. I did it! I went out into the dark cold before 5:30 am and power walked almost 2 miles, on a school track near the house. I am grateful for Londrelle and his healing meditation music. It helped me open my 3rd eye. I am grateful to work out of the comfort of my own home ...even if I only rent for now. I am grateful for my son hugging me on his own today. It feels good to be loved and thought of. I am grateful for my brother. He is extremely busy and made time to come over to cut Jr's hair. (even though I did not want to see it go, his hair was sooo long) ...it's all gone, for now.

I am grateful for the view of the moon and the strength I pulled from it.

Journal entry

Dec 2, 2021

I am grateful for my kids and seeing Destiny's beautiful face. I am grateful I had the energy this morning to walk and jog!

Journal entry

Dec 3, 2021

I am just happy I got through the long day. I have been working from 5 or 6 am till 7 pm. When Friday is here I wish I could live a carefree life without working. I am grateful for my job... It is just exhausting.

Journal entry

Dec 4, 2021

I am grateful for Londrelle's affirmations, and music. Listening to this during my walks/morning jogs is truly helping me level up and stay grounded all at once. I am excited for the New Nu chapters because I know and feel the shift of abundance coming my way. I am grateful for all the lessons. It is time for new seasons.

New Nu moon eclipse, in Sagittarius by Yazmin Boland3:30pm

What am I striving for and how true is my aim?

I am striving for peace in my heart and mind. I feel like I have been very true to myself and regardless of how dark it has been or gotten I keep lighting my own candle.

-Om Durgayei Namaha

A blessing of protection and love, which will bring courage and strength from the divine mother

Keep writing and breathe through any tension

Later... New moon workshop in Sagittarius & eclipse season, by Chris Corsini

It is time to listen, inwardly. There is a higher learning that is happening.

Shana, DO NOT go backwards!

It is time to slow down, go with the flow, and be in your own alchemy. Trust yourself. Keep using the tools to help during the challenging times. Expand my knowledge, communication, and even the culture of the world around me.

Resources

Self-help

IT'S NOT PERSONAL, BUT IT IS PERSONAL

Tools

Counselor

Neptune is direct. I need to stay aware of how I feel. Wait and be patient. Mercury is acting like a mirror which gives us the chance to communicate.

I need to fix and fill all the cracks first. I need to be honest with myself. Follow my intuition. Deep connections will come as long as I focus!

It will be very hard to drop all bad habits.

I have learned that any karma is already done.

Under this New moon in the Sagittarius eclipse, I invite in a life of freedom, peace, joy, abundance, travel, and new happy solid relationships.

Journal entry

Dec 5, 2021

Today I am thankful for the sauna at the gym. Such a great decompressing tool! This is an absolute must in my new home! I am grateful for the visit with my mom today. Time spent with her was good and not triggering.

Journal entry

Dec 7, 2021
7:37 am

I needed rest.

Day 6, I did not work out or write. I listened to my body and rested. I am grateful I have finally recognized this. That it is okay to actually rest.

Later...same day

I am grateful today is Tuesday. My normal day off, which means I have the choice to work or not work the OT that is being requested of the team. Having time off allowed me to go to the gym and not be limited to my day. I cannot wait for financial freedom! I need to figure this out.

Journal entry

Dec 8, 2021

I worked a long day. 6 am -7 pm.

My son stayed home from school today.

I am grateful for his smile and pure joy when his new snowboard arrived early! I am grateful for my brother and mom getting us a charlie brown Christmas tree! And for all the small moments, like cooking tacos and chocolate chip cookies this evening.

Journal entry

Dec 9, 2021

Thursday

I am thankful for my son's smile and joyous energy as we ...well he... decorated our smallest tree yet! It looks beautiful. I am grateful for Brene Brown's podcast and the new book that comes out! I can't wait for it! I am also grateful for my counselor, she provided some great tips on how to communicate my needs and to help me not go back into habits of codependency.

Journal entry

Dec 10, 2021

IT'S NOT PERSONAL, BUT IT IS PERSONAL

I woke up early ...before 4:44 am and I walked in the crisp cold dark morning. Which honestly felt like nighttime still. I walked a little over 2 miles while listening to Brene' Brown for the 2nd time on Atlas of the Heart featured on Super Soul, so grateful for the language and hearing this!

Journal entry

Dec 11, 2021

Today I went with the flow.

I went to the gym and worked out. Exercising or moving my body is huge! It always reminds me how I can balance my emotions. This action helped tremendously, especially on a day like today.

...a very close friend of mine, his brother crossed over at a very young age, his name was Michael. Today was Mike's service, this was done through Zoom, from California. I cried for almost 4 hours. The service itself was 3 hours long. It didn't even feel like it. The stories shared were such an honor to hear. I am so grateful I had a chance to meet him, laugh with him, be in his vibrant energy, and hang out at different family functions. Now my brother and he are the best of friends in heaven. I am sure of this.

(angel heart drawing)

Journal entry

Dec 12, 2021

I am grateful for solid friendships that are open to spreading their wings and healing. Today I hung out with Justina. All the signs aligned. We got new ink today! It is a full circle with a maple leaf and the coordinates of our first backpacking trip to Mirror Lake, Tom

Dick & Harry Trail. Split in half, we each have a coordinate.
(drawing of the ink and coordinates,
121.80023 *W, 45.29233 *N)

Journal entry

Dec 13, 2021

Today I am grateful for working from home, at home ...so I could nap on my 30 min lunch break! I am starting to be mentally exhausted. I can't wait to be financially secure and never have to clock in and out for someone else!

Journal entry

Dec 14, 2021

...late entry

I am grateful my son DOES NOT have covid. Tested again today because of the stress of a simple cold!

Thankful for being home on a Tuesday. Thankful for a last minute lunch date with my Destiny! (hearts)

Journal entry

Dec 15, 2021

I rested.

Journal entry

Dec 16, 2021

I am grateful for my awareness.

I walked/jogged this morning before work. Only to have a dog and I am pretty sure a homeless man... sneak up on me. Yet, I saw this from afar when I noticed a small red light in the distance out on the track nearby (where I know the trash bins are). Which was the far opposite side of where I was when I saw this. I had already walked and ran around 4 times, then to feel a presence approaching the back of me I stopped, turned around to see a pitbull gaining momentum towards me and then the man was in the middle of the track field calling the dog's name. Mind you they must have been hiding in the shadows. Because every time I would run or pass this area I would look, yet I never saw anything, but I could sense it. Especially since I originally saw the light when I showed up. It is still pitch black at 5 am.

I did not get to finish my full few miles. I chose to go home and no longer walk or jog this route while it is dark. The man scared me more than the dog. He clearly knew what he was doing. Hiding out in the shadows to then wander to the middle of the field.

Journal entry

Dec 17, 2021

I am thankful I made it through the week.

Destiny and I got some one-on-one time after work and a little shopping with dinner too! It was a good evening!

Journal entry

Dec 18, 2021

Full moon

Full moon in Gemini

Gemini -a mutable air energy.

I need to go with the flow while connecting.

All my new ideas and my awareness needs to be applied. Keep taking baby steps, this is a better alignment for me.

Venus is going in retrograde (this happens about every 1.5 years) This will last for 40 days and 40 nights.

During this shift, I need to slow down and ASK myself how do I feel? Check in with my energy, Is this where my energy should go?

Do not act on impulses!

Last full moon of 2021, I am releasing 3 things in the form of balloons

...I actually now relate balloons to death. After my brother passed away we all brought balloons to release into the sky. Looking back to that date that truly was not the best thing to do for the earth. Yet it was done. 100's of balloons were released in honor of my brother's life.

...so the energy being released tonight under this full moon as 3 balloons are

– any negative self-talk

– I need to work smarter, not harder

– and my never-ending broken heart (Rob) (sad face)

Journal entry

Dec 19, 2021

I am grateful for a warm home, a roof over my head, buying gifts for the holiday, and having them all wrapped except for one ...that needs to be delivered.

I am grateful for the space I am in mentally. I now recognize my strength and endurance to heal is showing up.

IT'S NOT PERSONAL, BUT IT IS PERSONAL

Journal entry

Dec 20, 2021

10:55 pm

Today was a really good day. Instead of jumping out of bed, I rested. I slept till almost 8 am. I baked most of the afternoon. I made cookies, cupcakes, and a cake! My Nonni came home for the holidays! She got here shortly after 5 tonight! I am grateful to just be still and present without working and outside distractions. Oh and the Raiders WON!

Chapter Fourteen

Silent Winter Of 2021

Journal entry

Dec 21, 2021

What an amazing heartfelt day!

It started with me taking a short brisk walk in the morning to witness a beautiful sunrise with Luna near. I hung out with Destiny, Nonni, my cousin, and her daughter. We all got mani & pedis. Then after we ate lunch at Pastini's! It was a great time catching up. We laughed, talked, caught up, and shed funny tears! I could feel and see it was good and very much needed for each of us.

I am grateful for the time we spent together and the new fond memory. I am very rich with the love of my kids and family.

Journal entry

Dec 22, 2021

I am grateful for Nonni being home and our late night visits.

IT'S NOT PERSONAL, BUT IT IS PERSONAL

Journal entry

Dec 23, 2021

I am grateful for the next 3 days off of work.

Extremely grateful my son is home safe! He went up to Timberline to snowboard with the new board he bought. When he came home he told me he had got lost at the tippy top of the mountain near a different group of people. It was his first time up. So he just followed with them back down. He was really happy about the experience overall and it was nice to hear him share his excitement.

Journal entry

Dec 24, 2021

Today was a great day!

We spent Christmas together today. It was a first, doing it this way. It was to help relieve any stress on my kids, having to split their time between homes.

I am happy they all got to be home with me today,

At night I went to visit Marquita and her family. We watched a movie called Cantar, which means to sing in Spanish. Crazy thing, so much of this movie reminded me of my dream from last night. Maybe I was in Columbia and not Mexico.

Journal entry

Dec 25, 2021

Today I am by myself.

Which has happened often on this day.

Rob called, and we had a good conversation. My heart hurt at the end of our call when we got off the call. I am still crushed by how things are. I am still learning to be grateful for the lessons. Whatever they may teach.

I am grateful I can see more ...with my intuition and by listening. I am grateful my kids are home safe. Nonni and I got to cuddle and watch a movie tonight. I am grateful for a warm home.

Journal entry

Dec 26, 2021

8:20 am

It finally snowed! Last night after 10 pm and right now! It is coming down hard. ...outside there might be 1-2 inches. Not a whole lot, but it sure is pretty! It feels like I am in a snow globe and it feels so peaceful. (heart & snowflake)

..late evening.

Hanging out with Nonni and having a snow day was good! Tonight we spoke for a few hours. We spoke about what it was like growing up and my cousins. The bond we have and why everyone was not raised by my Auntie. Nonni might be the only child who knows more details from my childhood.

I am grateful for our time together.

Journal entry

Dec 27, 2021

I only worked a few hours today. I have a sore throat and I wanted to be there for Nonni. She drove back to Eugene around noon. I am grateful for the person she is becoming.

My brother stopped by late after work. I think it was almost 9. He had to pick up the snow gear he let Junebug borrow. I asked him to come inside for a few minutes, he stayed maybe 5.

I told him I called Michael's phone on Christmas. He responded, with a, "Ya, it got disconnected a few months ago."

I said, "How do you know, you called?"

He said, "J, sent me a text and said we are turning Mike's phone off tomorrow, if you want to call for the last time, I just wanted you to know."

And of course...

I was hurt that he did not share that information with me.

He said, "I was more caught up in the text from her, than what it actually said and I did not think to share."

I realize most people will not do what we think they should do and this is where I need to let go of expectations.

I am grateful for the 5 minutes spent with my brother.

Journal entry

Dec 28, 2021

I am grateful for alone time.

That my son decided to agree to play a board game with me. We played scrabble. I am grateful for the lessons taught in 2021.

Journal entry

Dec 29, 2021

I have permission to take back my power.

I am grateful for all the lessons, even the unbearable ones.

Journal entry

Dec 31, 2021

Last day of the year

I went to the Tualatin River National Wildlife Refuge Trail to watch the sunset.

I reflected over the year. It's been REAL.

How heartbreaking, beautiful, chaotic, raw, and unfiltered you were.

I am grateful for the lessons and no longer hardened by the heartache.

I am open to the new chapters that will arise and will continue to work on no longer being sad about what could have been.

I Am

Exactly

Where

I Am

Supposed to be ...on to the next!

During 2021, I hiked 13 different trails, some more than twice!

The trails were ~

Silver falls 2x

Angel rest 3x

Dog Mt 2x

Trail of two forests

Beacon Rock

Naked Falls 2x

Sahalie Falls

Koosah falls

Mirror lake 2x

IT'S NOT PERSONAL, BUT IT IS PERSONAL

Tom dick & Harry 2x

Falls Creek Falls

Wahclella Falls 3x

Tualatin River National Wildlife Refuge 11x or more

I Traveled solo often and a few places with my kids,

California, Sacramento, Alameda, Lake Tahoe, Bend, Issaquah, Washington, New Orleans, Florida, Tampa, Orlando, Eugene

My 1st Backpacking camping trip was on 10.02, my late brother's birthday! He turned 40 and he made sure to let me know! All the signs were surreal.

I saw my 1st meteor shower

Tattoos - My 4 Elements that I drew, and the coordinates of the Mirror Lake trail

Summer here was insanely HOT in the triple digits, several days, up to 118

My Nonni graduated college! UofO

It snowed in February and we had an ice storm directly after with a huge wind storm that knocked down hundreds of trees throughout Oregon

We got snow again on Christmas

I volunteered during April to help coordinate the COVID-19 vaccines at the coliseum on Tuesdays and weekends.

Destiny made her 1st 12k in 24 hrs

Jr got his 1st tattoo w/ his sister Destiny in Florida

Jessica started working at the same company I work at and my cousin Alicia moved to Oregon

Rob and I separated in March. (sad crying face)

Chapter Fifteen

Still Cold, Just A New Year 2022

*J*ournal entry

Jan 1, 2022

New Year and Nu moon is tomorrow!

I am committing to a 30 day practice of meditation.

I will connect with the earth

I will write affirmations for the year (12)

I will set intentions for my intuition

Journal entry

Jan 2, 2022

Affirmations

I. I am full of abundance

II. I am LOVE

III. I am divine

IV. I am spirit

V. I am divinely guided

VI. I AM RICH

VII. I AM healthy

VIII. I AM successful

IX. I AM overflowing in peace

X. I AM evolving

XI. I AM a reflection of my BEST Self

XII. I AM JOY

My Intentions

I. Remember my boundaries

II. Keep healthy relationships

III. Nurture my inner child and spirit

IV. Practice daily gratitude

V. Walk in my true purpose

VI. LOVE myself unconditionally

VII. Volunteer

IX. Let go of expectations

X. Let go and let it be

XI. What is meant for me will never pass me by

XII. Honor and trust myself

...later same day

Super New Moon and Venus are retrograde in Pisces

The energy put out is attracting more caring healthy people, my soul tribe. (which truly is who is already in my circle, I guess we will see if there is anyone new)

Need to continue the cycle of rest and reset. This is very helpful during full moon cycles or anytime your body calls on this. Listen.

Juno is the zodiac sign of marriage and commitment. Comes from

Roman & Greek mythology. Juno was the wife of Jupiter (aka Zeus), she was hailed for her unbreakable loyalty to her husband. She is also responsible for the pairing of soulmates, her feminine hands are behind most marriages that occur.

Nunki is a star that gives truthfulness, optimism, a religious mind, and a proclamation of the sea.

The asteroid Juno helps us see through the water with direction and precision to facilitate and improve what is necessary for our lives.

Under the new moon in Capricorn, the first of its kind this year I invite in 3 seeds.

Love, health, and ALL are covered in abundance.

Journal entry

Jan 9, 2022

2022 will have a handful of breakthroughs.

When anger shows up, I need to transition. Pay attention to the triggers. Pause before speaking.

When sadness shows up, this is a product of pain.

My story does not end here. I still have energy from last year that will rise within me. Heartbreak, loneliness, pain, and grief.

A reminder to myself that this too shall pass. I recognize that I am processing a lot of sadness. Sometimes it feels like it is more than I can handle.

One constant motion in life is change. Separation is change.

Through this process, I am and will continue to gain lots of wisdom. I need to tap into my skills to benefit and recognize my spiritual gifts. I am going back to my core, the depth of me and my past souls. The soul would have no rainbow if the eyes had no tears. Happiness

IT'S NOT PERSONAL, BUT IT IS PERSONAL

+ Sadness = Rain + Sun

All the pain and struggle will switch to a rainbow this year.

Lightworker. Follow my intuition, if I cannot find the light ...remember I am the light. I am the solution. I will guide my own way during any storms because those too shall pass.

Lots of lucky breaks will come! I am powering UP THIS YEAR!

Journal entry

Jan 15, 2022

8 am

Empath class

Aucashit records with Tonesha Sylla

This shows us how to merge past and present

...while accepting spiritual guidance.

What am I seeking?

　　　　　　...Healthy joyous balance.

What is my intention for today?

　　　　　　...to be present and open to the gifts.

Inner child - my 5 year old self

Outer child - my 15 year old self

The Adult - age 43, needs to do a vision board

Manifesting and creating

-Use tools that were already created, so we are modeling

-Creation in the human sense is used metaphorically

-We need to align with our highest energy

　　1. Listen

　　2. Surrender

3. Patience

Clear any agreements
What worked for me well last month?
Moving daily for a minimum of 20 minutes and my daily gratitude writing
What have I learned about myself in the last 30 days?
I am still on a healing path which could be forever yet I now have healthy boundaries that include letting go of what no longer serves me.
What beliefs do I carry that are holding me back?
The old me believes I should never divorce ...and never marry.
What are the dreams I want to manifest now?
Good healthy habits, use my tools and strengths, travel, buy my own home
What steps can I take toward my dream if money and opportunity presented no obstacles?
Prepare myself to succeed
Listen to the messages
Write them down
Make the vision board, complete the actions

Journal entry

Jan 17, 2022
Full moon
Full moon in Cancer
Jupiter is in Pisces which means luck and lots of options for expansion in growth, love, and connections.

IT'S NOT PERSONAL, BUT IT IS PERSONAL

The full moon creates safety and foundation, it will be good to get outside barefoot. Walk in the dirt or grass near a tree. The new start for the year with potential soul messages coming through from our guides or ancestors.

DREAM BIG

Under this full moon in Cancer, I choose to release any stagnant one-sided relationships, unhealthy habits, codependency, and the NEED to go back.

Journal entry

Feb 1, 2022
New Nu Moon

New Moon in Aquarius

Currently, the energy is stuck in 2021...getting closer to the actual new year. 2 more months.

Mars is in Capricorn and asking us to slow down.

Mercury is still in retrograde. Which is having us think about what we want long term.

Evaluate the old perspectives, and how I value my time, money, and resources.

Once all the planets are in direct alignment, we can make more changes and we will see the results.

This new moon is conjunct with Saturn, and Saturn has the energy of slow and steady.

Pluto's energy is deep. There is a light shined on the traumas we have held onto which helps us identify with what to face, any triggers, and how to take action. We are asked how to trust and learn ourselves on a deeper level. When the wounds and pain arise we need to meet them where they are at and establish a new identity once we release them.

Mar's energy is strong, it wants war, to fight and protect. We cannot control what is around us.

We can be intentional about how we think and put steps in place.

I need to connect with water, take some time for myself, and be in nature. Do some breath work, create, write.

Do not carry the baggage with me. Let it go. DO NOT GO Backwards!

Trust myself

Under this new moon in Aquarius, I invite in balance, travel, love

Journal entry

2.2.2022

6:06 am

Dream

I am still sitting in the dark trying to wake up and write at the same time

My counselor suggested anytime I do have dreams to immediately write them down once I wake to not interrupt the flow.

I dreamt of the ocean. I was near the ocean ...getting ready to hike a mountain.

...we ended up at my grandma's home (that was the feeling I had) which made me know that we were there but it was very different, by the looks of it.

I was going with a group I never met and it seemed I was the youngest person in the group. My cousin was there too.

When it was time to hop in the van to drive there, they drove off

...without me. I was still inside searching for a bottle to fill with water.

I wasn't worried because I knew my cousin would tell them they forgot me and turn back, which they did ...and then I woke up.

...later the same day.

Today is Wednesday

I am working at home... have been for the last year and a half.

Today my son does not want to go to school. This triggered me. I did not want to call him out of school, again! The reason he gave me is because all they would be doing, 'is be on their phones,' and he can do that from home. IDK!

Yet, I do know it triggered my anxiety and this was 2 hours ago. It is now 10:28 am and I am on my break writing.

Trying to calm down. I did essential oils, breath work, and meditation music to help bring this to bay ...

My mind is also all over the place with so many different thoughts and I keep thinking of Rob the last few days. He called the other day saying he wants to do a video tonight but my phone does not work because it broke a while ago and the video function does not work. He asked me last night to download the app on my IPAD, this caused me anxiety. I do not use apps on my IPAD and I don't want to!

Then there is the thought of Reno. I am anxious about whether I should go for my birthday or not. I thought I wanted to go but the cost is overwhelming and then this means I would be leaving my son.

I recognize this would be the first time leaving for my birthday solo. Reno means old friends. Old lovers. Maybe I just need to close ALL the old doors. Why do I keep going to my past?

Journal entry

Feb 3, 2022

4:40 am

Dream

It was dark, I was driving all night, and I remember being in the hills and seeing some city lights.

Then I woke up, apparently, I was sleeping at my grandma's house. I was in her kitchen sitting at the table with all my kids when they were small… except they looked exactly like my little brothers. When they were small. My cousin and Rob were there. My grandma made this huge breakfast, she looked happy and healthy. She was skipping around and she kept serving us food. Omelets, waffles, and fruit.

Everyone sat at the table to eat except me. Jr was there except it was really my brother Alejandro at age 4. We sat in chairs facing opposite of the table.

My mom was somewhere in the house, but I never actually saw her, I could just feel that she was there.

Journal entry

Feb 4, 2022

4:55 am

Dream

I dreamt of being inside my grandmother's house. Again.

This time my grandparents were not there.

IT'S NOT PERSONAL, BUT IT IS PERSONAL

Journal entry

Feb 11, 2022

I met with my counselor

My dreams are about being stuck.

Feeling stuck

Feeling pain and being locked up

The suggestion is to have a complete separation. I need to speak to Rob again. Have an honest conversation. I wish this could be in person, we really need to see each other. I feel we do.

An assignment from my counselor - I need to write about freedom. How I will feel when I am free and not stuck.

Journal entry

Feb 13, 2022

How will I feel when I am free?!

Free of heartache

Free of pain

Free of financial worries

I feel lighter. I have the freedom to travel, laugh, and feel happy as I enjoy life as it is. I am grateful for all the stories I have been part of. ..and alive to still share them.

Freedom is only checking in with myself to see where I am at on this journey ...called life.

...later, 2:22 pm

I decided I want to write out a short Birthday Itinerary since I will be off work from Feb 19 - the 23rd.

2.18 - face masks, red wine, or tea

2.19 - Hike

2.20 -Kennedy Soaking Tub

2.21 - Do a reading, buy a lottery ticket, eat cake

2.22 - Mani and pedis

2.23 - Plant 2 seeds, one for my brother Michael and one for Mac

Journal entry

Feb 16, 2022

Full Moon in Leo

Lots of old ideas showed up in the last few weeks.

The awareness is the external has not caught up with the internal

I need to connect with my inner child and my heart space.

The energy is to pay attention to the cracks so I can integrate the work I have done

How am I using my energy?

How am I investing my time? Money? Thoughts?

Be aware.

I need to think of long-term pleasures, not short-term

More energy needs to go towards my passion

More action needs to be applied to do what I love

Under this full moon in Leo

I release any fear of change

I release the broken Shana

I release my marriage

...I am gluing myself back together <3

IT'S NOT PERSONAL, BUT IT IS PERSONAL

Journal entry

Feb 22, 2022

One day in being 44

I know there is a huge shift/ change is coming. I can feel it. It will be a happy change!

Journal entry

March 2, 2022

New moon

...it is after midnight and officially March 3rd! My sonshines birthday!

Under this new nu moon in Pisces, I invite in the following~

Healthy habits

Joy

Love

More Sunshine

Adventures

Travel

Peace

Riches

Home

Abundance of harmony

Journal entry

March 4, 2022

6:36 pm

I just finished speaking with my counselor

Today's conversation was about my mom and how I always feel guilty after our interactions due to her constant guilt trips.

I hesitated to share what I got for my son's 18th birthday with my mom because I knew what was coming after. Yet, I did share. I gifted my son a trip to Hawaii at the end of this month!

My mom's reaction was extremely challenging to navigate.

I have always known that I played a parent role with my mom and that our roles were reversed. It just sucked hearing it out loud with my counselor. I somehow have always been her parent.

It hurts to truly sit in the facts. It makes me feel sad because I never got the mom who loved me unconditionally, it was always ...what can I do for her? Love with conditions.

So basically I have always just parented myself.

No wonder I am at where I am at ...I have had to raise myself. What child can truly survive that long thin trail at the edge of a tall rocky mountain cliff with no parental guidance?

Journal entry

March 13, 2022
Sunday
Daylight savings day

Rob called me today.

I was hoping to speak with him yesterday. Yet it did not work out that way on his end.

It was good to hear his voice, but then the call ended abruptly. I was then reminded of how much this all feels horrible. It feels like death! This truly feels like one thousand knives pushed through my chest, again.

IT'S NOT PERSONAL, BUT IT IS PERSONAL

All this heartache is due to the sorrow of reality.

He is in prison

There is still no sentence

There is no end date

With no connection

... I can feel my heart shattering ...down to the aorta. (literally) The last time I spoke to him was briefly for about 4-5 minutes on Junebugs 18th Birthday. 10 days ago. (sad face)

Journal entry

March 18, 2022

Full moon

Full moon in Virgo

It is finally the last moon of 2021 ENERGY! Thank gawd!

I need to be in my highest vibration

It is time to

Clean, change routine, restructure, tap into resources!

Now is a great time to start New habits!

I need to reflect on all that has happened this last year and make some changes that I want to see.

Follow my intuitive self and apply my energy. I will speak on it. Act on it.

What does safety look and feel like?!

Under this full moon in Virgo, I am letting go of

Fear

Fear of being, of not having enough, ANY and ALL fear!

My broken heart

SHANA CHRISTINE DILLON

My broken relationship
The thoughts that I need to constantly work ALL the damn time
I am letting go of all these toxic cycles
Releasing all of last year's bad juju and from the years before

Chapter Sixteen

Signs In Spring Of 2022

*J**ournal entry*

March 20, 2022

5:30 am

Flying out to Hawaii today with my Sonshine!

Dream

I had some very vivid dreams again.

... the 2nd dream I remember everyone was in a panic. There were fires everywhere. I was in a van heading to a shelter when an announcement was made to evacuate because we would be bombed. We were riding near a huge river that looked like the ocean due to the constant crashing waves, from other bombings. It felt like I was in Mexico or Guatemala, it was not the U.S.

A person kept asking how many were in my group to evacuate and I said 5, but it was actually 6 of us, counting me. Marquita, my mom, my girls, and Jr.

I got our names on the list to leave next. I decided to go grab some stuff from the partially still-burning apartment. People were randomly walking through it when I heard my mom yelling over and over again. My name.

SHANA! SHANA!

When I got to her I said please stop yelling my name.

She said, "We are leaving! Where were you?! Did you grab my wine?!"

The request was for me to grab wine and any food. At the time my mom said she only needed wine. 2 bottles because we were all going to die!

I remember in the mix of the chaos and panic I asked if they would please let Rob out.

I prayed for my kids' safety. I prayed if we were hit, to let it be quick and not painful, or actually please DO NOT let it hit where we were.

...then I woke.

Journal entry

March 23, 2022

Kona

My son and I have been on the big island for a few days now. The time on Hilo's side was beyond magical.

Then we came to Kona.

Why did I book the same place I was married!?

I have been drinking since we checked in.

I can only think of one person!

Rob

Rob, I need to say goodbye. Until you are here again with me. I love you, with every part of me ...and it hurts like HELL to even say this. Yet, I should not be expected to be ALL ALONE, YET married while you are locked up! I am not going to remarry or find a new life partner. I can't! It is supposed to be you! For life! Yet, the current struggle is too much for me! It feels like death. I am in our room solo, as Jr swims out in the lagoon. Out the balcony is a view of a wedding ceremony that I can hear.

I am so fucking torn!
I haven't stopped crying since I got in this room!
Is this closure?!
Is this a sign to STAY and say let's stay together?!
I AM so FUCKING confused
The wedding reception is now unfolding
It is quite beautiful
...heartbreaking and ALL!

Journal entry

March 26, 2022
Saturday
8 something am

Right now I am outside on an itty bitty balcony. Maybe 3 by 4 feet. 23 floors up! One block away from Waikiki Beach.

It is noisy from all the city life, nothing like the peaceful Hilo farm we stayed at. I can see the beautiful aqua-teal water with boats and people wading it out for waves to arrive, yet I cannot hear the ocean. That is how loud the city is. I am trying to imagine I can hear it ...but I can't. I need to physically be on the beach, as I was yesterday.

Lol

The only reason we are on this island... was for my son's 2nd birthday gift! A tattoo! Which he loves! It turned out amazing! He got his new ink yesterday, it took 6 hours. His whole right forearm now has a beautiful dragon! On our way to the shop, it rained, a beautiful omen and a blessing for sure!

Oahu is nice and all but I prefer the slow down vibe and with fewer folks. The beaches on this side of the island are sandy and not too rocky, which is nice.

The last time I wrote in here I was struggling. I had an emotional breakdown. It really was beyond difficult to walk down paths that Rob and I said 'I DO' My heart was ripped into pieces all over again and thinking about it causes me deep grief and pain.

I don't want to question my moves anymore. I simply just want to live without shame, sadness, or guilt. I want to feel joy and love and walk through life with peace in my heart.

I cannot promise anyone I will be there for them if they are not there for me.

It is an awful painful truth because I do love Rob so deeply. Yet, the life I am living will slowly kill me if I do not separate myself from him.

I cannot believe I am still talking about this heartbreak!

I am in Paradise. So I should be smiling, not crying.

Changing and shifting my mindset, right now!

I am grateful for the blue ocean view.

I am grateful to see my son so happy.

I am grateful we have 2 full days left here, away from reality.

I am grateful to have experienced such a deep profound love.

I am grateful.

IT'S NOT PERSONAL, BUT IT IS PERSONAL

Journal entry

March 28, 2022
Monday

Today we travel back to the mainland.

I didn't know how much this trip was needed until I was knee-deep in it. Life has a funny way of unfolding as the path ahead aligns for you.

I am grateful for the small yet big settled signs brought to me on this trip. A few doors of opportunities opened. How my life can further expand and be lived if I stay in tune with the signs and gifts I already have.

I am grateful for the time I got to spend with my son even though it was not every day. Ironically or maybe just aligned ...one of his best friends was on this last island. They got to hang out, walk, shop, and just be. While I sat and reflected during my time on Waikiki Beach. When I was 16 years old. I lived here briefly. When I left I never wanted to come back, due to the struggle I endured during that time in my life. As an adult, I now see it differently. I see how and why things happen. Not everything ...but most things. Including this newest chapter... separation.

I will no longer feel shame for saying this or having this be part of my story. Because life unfolds as it should.

Let go ...and let god take it from here.

Journal entry

April 1, 2022

New moon

New Nu Moon in Aries

New healing will occur

Time for a fresh start, get creative, find more passion, and focus on new projects.

Get excited about a new nu vision with new energy and keep choosing SELF.

Under this new moon in Aries, I invite in the following

Grand uplifting ENERGIES

Abundance

Joy

PEACE

Love

Strength

Fitness

Wealthy health

Genuine connections

ALL YEAR!!

Journal entry

April 16, 2022

I am in Reno, NV. I am staying at my little sister's new home.

Full moon in Libra

Neptune in Jupiter is conjunction in Pisces! The last time this happened was 150 years ago!

IT'S NOT PERSONAL, BUT IT IS PERSONAL

Time to change our plan! This portal and energy door will close forever.

We all need patience. Tis the season to show up and change!

Bring in positive affirmations! Keep dreaming BIG! We. I. Will change my life.

Note to self ~ keep taking action with love, kindness, and respect. Do not forget to be kind to myself.

Balance is NOT always 50-50.

Pluto is still in Capricorn, this is where we can help parent ourselves. Establish healthy cycles and habits. New rules, structures, and routines are to be implemented.

Under this full moon in Libra

I release

Attachments

Broken relationships

Self-doubt

Hardships

I am grateful for the lessons, and now it is time to release them.

Journal entry

April 19, 2022

My brother's twins are 11 today!

They are celebrating in Mexico, on a Cruise ship! At one of the ports, I think the plan is to visit with our dad. I am glad they get to do this. I know he will be so happy to see the familia.

Yesterday on the 18th

Rob called.

He told me he took the deal. 10 years. So ...he has about 6 years left. I will be 50 by then. A whole decade will come and go before he is released. He told me they said if he didn't take the deal he would be facing a mandatory 22 -27 years!

Then he said, he doesn't expect me to wait. And he knows he messed my life up. He hopes I will take his calls once in a while and hopes I will keep his last name. He said please do me a favor, don't change your last name. (sad face)

I don't know how to feel right now. But we finally got closure on a date. Well kinda. With good time served ... maybe he will be out in another 4-5 years.

Journal entry

April 30, 2022

I landed in Vegas yesterday

Right now it is 8 am, and I am sitting at the pool at the Hilton Resort World.

Today is Rob's 46th birthday!

...a little later. I just got off a video call with Rob. I was happy to see him on his birthday. Sing to him. Wish him a happy birthday. Let him know I will have a sip of Macallan, just for him, and make a toast to wish him a healthy peaceful birthday. Then after the call I began journaling again and this song started to play Lovesong, by The Cure. Quite fitting. I will always love you.

My original plan was to sit at the pool and do my New Nu Moon workshop and then he called. I am glad I didn't miss the call.

This is such a heartbreaking tough thin line ...our love story.

But it has to come to completion.

IT'S NOT PERSONAL, BUT IT IS PERSONAL

For now.

Life.

What does it mean?

Life is graciously accepting all the lessons. The highs and lows. Life is living in the moment each day, being present, being kind, moving with love in the heart, and not hatred or resentment. Life is about failing yet succeeding in purpose with purpose. No expectations.

Meditated for 10 minutes with the beautiful sun kissing me out here in Las Vegas.

Giving gratitude

I am grateful to have experienced love

I am grateful for the hard lessons, this helped me become softer and kinder to myself

I am grateful for the new nu healthy year that will unfold

I am grateful for my health and becoming the healthiest yet

I am grateful for all my new wholesome tools for navigating my hardships and mental breakdowns

9:09 am ...I will complete the moon workshop later

Mail

(Birthday Card) was copied on paper

because the facility will no longer allow mail "as is!"

Front of Card - Flat stones /rocks stacked near water

Seek BALANCE... Find HAPPINESS... live WELL.

Inside card -

WISHING LIFE'S BEST TO YOU on your BIRTHDAY.

4.30.2022

My Dearest Robert,

Birthdays = the meaning.

The anniversary of the day on which a person was born, is typically treated as an occasion for celebration and the giving of gifts.

I know this one might be one of the hardest yet... with all the puzzle pieces going into place, yet the picture is missing what you need most. The whole heart. (sad face) The completed puzzle is a sad one.

Regardless of the completion. I. AM. SO. Grateful YOU were born.

I always loved celebrating birthdays, especially the ones who meant the most to me. It gave me the chance to be thankful for the day a person is born. When I would celebrate YOU, I wanted you to know how much you meant to me. How grateful I was and how special you ARE! I wanted you to know you were loved and I wanted you to feel LOVED. What better way than to do it on your day? Your Born Day!

During ALL the birthdays we celebrated I truly hope you felt loved, wanted, valued, appreciated, cared for, and like a King. Because you truly are one of a kind.

I know it's beyond challenging to feel joy in the space you are currently in. My wish -birthday gift - for you is to seek within yourself and find peace. Make peace with your heart and soul. So your body can heal and your mind can get rid of any clutter or damage that continues to linger. You deserve this. You deserve love. LOVE yourself again. This small token is the Biggest gift you could give yourself. Before you moved to Oregon you once shared. If you don't take care of yourself, then you are no good for anyone else. Rob, take your own advice. You need to start filling your own cup with love, first. I use your advice... monthly if not daily, now.

IT'S NOT PERSONAL, BUT IT IS PERSONAL

Thank you! I am grateful for the gifts you shared. I am grateful you were born. You are a human who is worth celebrating and I know without a doubt, YOU WILL TRIUMPH! As life continues. I know you will, I can feel it! Feliz Cumpleanos! Happy Birthday, King!

with all my love

Shana C

Xoxo

Journal entry

May 1, 2022

9:09 am

New moon workshop in Taurus season

Venus rules Taurus

Ask, trust, believe, receive, grand opportunities will arrive ...observe and think before choosing.

During eclipse season, is when our feelings connect with ALL the changes and notice I am moving in the right direction

When Neptune and Jupiter came together in Pisces for the 1st time since 1856, this alignment made a shift in the energy. Clearly this is extremely rare since we have yet to experience it in this lifetime.

Pluto is retrograde in Capricorn, this creates an opportunity to move through the energies of death and rebirth.

We are asked to look at our values and structures. What do I value now?

There is a deep mental energetic shift... after we will feel it in the body, and as we flow and move forward with intentional steps, we will gain clarity.

We need to pause and reflect. Digest what is happening.

Eclipse energy is heavy on the body, so it is ok to rest.

Be creative and try not to indulge too much. Find some balance, maybe it looks like 70-30. Remember it is not truly always 50-50.

At this time it is ok to journal how life has changed in the last 6 months if I am called to.

Journal

May 16, 2022

5:33 am

Total Full Moon Eclipse in Scorpio

Scorpio is the deep subconscious mind, connected to power, sex, drugs, and old fears

Now is the time to clear it out

Eclipse is a portal, a door

Hidden truths will come out

Time to establish rules

Keep my circle small (lol, this is already the case, but I will continue to do this)

Get rid of all toxic people and habits (I clearly want to sting, because this feels like I have to remind myself daily)

Clear the negative energies before leveling up

This next chapter in my life (the next 6 months) will LOOK VERY different!

Trust and just watch!

Eclipse season can cause confusion, exhaustion and it is tough to navigate for some due to so much energy moving around

The current placement of Saturn makes it extra challenging to release

IT'S NOT PERSONAL, BUT IT IS PERSONAL

Yet we can take baby steps while we clear. If I feel blocked this is ok.
I have been doing the work. All will come exactly as it should. I can
take it one day at a time.

Journal entry

May 28, 2022

5:26 am

DREAM

The sweetest cutest baby looked so angelic, maybe 3 months old
with beautiful sea glass light green eyes, and when he smiled, I could
see my brother Michael. I could feel his energy. I walked with this little
baby. Holding him, talking to him through the hallways of a school or
fun center. In the back, a few people were playing basketball and there
was a water slide. Then the baby said, "Oooh water."

Which surprised me because of how little he was. I was so happy
to hold him as I walked towards the front of the building my brother
Alejandro said, "Ok, Shana we have to give the baby back, he belongs
to Jenny and her new husband."

As I was heading outside of the building, the sun was shining and
it was really warm out. People were coming and going ...in and out of
the building.

Then I guess I went to bed.

...and then I woke up, but I was not fully awake as I was walking to
open my bedroom door. I caught a glimpse of something on the wall.
My eyes adjusted and I could see the words. I love you. I <3 you. I love
you, Shana. I LOVE YOU. I love you. On EVERY surrounding wall
in my room.

I was astonished. I was happy. My brother came to give me a message! I couldn't believe it. I could barely speak and was still trying to wipe sleep out of my eyes. In my room, the writing was all in RED, like spray paint or marker! From the floor to the ceiling! When I finally got my door open. I see it does not stop! (smile face) The hallway I am walking down to try and get my brother's attention, to come see what I am seeing! The entire hallway is covered in tagged words. My brother's name. Alex. Alejandro. Michael. Perez. Freak. In blues, greens, and purples from the floor to the ceiling again! It looked like art. Beautiful art. It was even on the ceiling! Literally all over the ceiling! And I finally got my little brother Alejandro to wake up! And then my son came to look too!

I kept saying, "See! Michael was here! He came to visit us! Go look at my room!"

And then I got closer to look at words graffitied in the hallway, he wrote ...I love you, Alex. And I screamed for Alex to come look!

"LOOK!"

It was all the way down the hallway into the dining room, then there was this cool picture my brother put up! I had an idea to go grab my phone to start taking pictures of everything. So I did, and when I got to the photo. I snapped a picture of it. I realized it when I looked at it through my phone. Everyone in the photo was moving around and then a few people began to disappear. Then I would look at the photo without my phone. There were a ton of people, like an action shot of my entire family and friends and extended family. Yet on the phone ...only certain people would fade away.

This photo on the wall was huge, maybe 40x30! I couldn't believe what I was seeing.

IT'S NOT PERSONAL, BUT IT IS PERSONAL

So I yelled for my brother again saying, "Look what is happening when I take this photo!"

He just kept being silly saying sissy, not looking at what I was trying to show him but trying to pose for the photo.

Then I went back through the hallway and to my room. I was so happy and in awe that my brother came to visit me. It felt so real. It feels real.

I love you, little brother! I love you, Michael Angel Perez! I <3 you!

...stopped writing at 5:55 am

The colors translated in the dream are connected with the chakras.

Red is for the root (which is the foundation), Purple is the third eye (which is spiritual, the divine wisdom), Green is the heart space (which is the ability to love and come in and out of balance), Blue is the throat (which is the ability to express and communicate clearly, also brings awareness of balance)

Journal entry

May 30, 2022

New moon

New Nu Moon in Gemini

Mars is in Aries, and Jupiter will bring luck when I take action ...this will invite in more opportunities.

Keep following my intuition

Do not act on impulse

Choose how I want to respond

...make sure my thoughts and words match with the action

Allow the universe to show me where I need to go

In this next major cycle, the new moon in Gemini I invite in
Good health, new skills, travel, self-love, yoga, joy, strength,
courage, an open schedule, and healing.

Journal Entry

June 14, 2022
Full moon

Full moon in Sagittarius
...there is a lot changing
Change is coming
Sagittarius is connected to our belief systems & the south node is
in Scorpio
We are releasing things with Scorpio energies, such as fears, manip-
ulation, sex, and giving power to others.
Time to release it all. Again.
The new me is emerging!
During fall I will notice all the hard work and fill the shoes of
change!
How do I spend my time, energy, and thinking?
Time to invite in new energy

The north node is in Taurus, Venus is in conjunction which can
allow us to invite better foundations
Slow and steady
Under this full moon in Sagittarius -
I released 5 things.
This time. I burned them.

IT'S NOT PERSONAL, BUT IT IS PERSONAL

...side note. I don't think I ever mentioned this. I decided to sign up for school. I have been going since June 7th. I am currently taking virtual classes every day through August and then in October or November, I will finish in person. The schooling is to become a certified yoga instructor. A lot of discipline is required and a ton of information to memorize. Yet I feel this has been one of my callings since I first stepped into a yoga room, 20 years ago! I can't believe I signed up to be indoors on Zoom, staring at a computer screen during Summer! It is first thing in the morning. For a few hours. Every day.

I got this.

Right?!

Mail

June 19, 2022

My Dearest Robert

Today is Father's Day and Juneteenth. I hope this letter finds you well and in some kind of good spirits.

It has been 2 weeks since we have spoken. A lot has happened in 2 weeks. Jr graduated high school, he quit his job, and bought his first plane ticket to travel by himself to a different state. Yes. You heard all of this correctly. Life. I guess it doesn't stand still. Everyone keeps moving, living, and all at their own pace. Which is to be expected. I mean shit, I bought my 1st plane ticket when I was 16 and it was not a round-trip ticket. So...with that said. I am not too stressed out. Yet I am very aware of life and growth, for me to let go of my own tendencies of wanting to control everything and that each (human) needs to be free to make their own decisions in life.

Codependency is no joke. I have some very ***REAL*** tough habits to break. And... I guess he is really not going by himself out of state, he will be traveling with one of his close friends. They are flying to Colorado to meet up with another friend. He invited them out for a week. And for quitting the job part, I guess that place was not for him. (shrug) Live and learn.

How bout this! (ugg face) The water heater broke. For the last 2 days, we have been taking cold showers. Fucking freezing showers actually! (ugg face) Because summer has NOT shown up here yet! LOL, It's cold here! 50 degrees! Tonight I could not take a river shower so I went to my mom's for a hot one. I just got home. Cold is ok for the morning. Then I might not need coffee, because I will be awake from the ICE water! LOL but seriously. It sucks! Hopefully these folks fix this fast!

Nonni ...she officially moved. Well, partially. She is in Idaho with her boyfriend and his mom. They just got there today. No more Eugene drives. Or Oregon (sad face) for right now at least.

Yesterday... on Saturday I went to Cyn & Jarred's. They had a birthday party for Aries. He is 2 years old on the 22nd of this month. It was nice. They had a little mini petting zoo, Kinda. (smile face) They rented 4 little goats and the kids seemed to love it. There was a small fence put up by a farm in the front yard and the goats and kids ran around inside that little fence, for the hour that I was there. The last few minutes it began to rain, then downpour. Apparently, goats don't like rain, so they pulled out umbrellas and the goats ran for cover. LOL

This moment reminded me of Jr's graduation. It dumped buckets of water that day too! Yet it was absolutely beautiful... even with the event all outside. We were all soaking wet by the end. I will send you pics once I get them and once you are at your next location. Since I am not sure how this looks right now. What you are taking with you and what you are sending back to me.

Speaking of ...what happened on June 6th? I thought I would hear from you or the lawyer. (sad face)

Well... I guess I will go now. There is a lot more that has happened, but I can save that for later.

Again I hope this finds you in better spirits.

I miss you and will always love you

Love

Shana

Chapter Seventeen
Healing Summer Of 2022

*J**ournal entry*

New Nu Moon in Cancer

How do we protect our energy and meditate the high good feeling vibration into our soul circle?

Solstice is big on balancing the light and the dark. My goal here is harmony.

The world is asking us to level up and we need to take better care of ourselves.

We are currently in a stage where there is a lot of anger, it is time to burn the old bad toxic energy so our buildings can be on a healthy foundation.

The healing collective knows what we want ...it is ok to ask for support while standing in our power.

Under this new moon in Cancer, I invite in the feelings of safety, security, healthy compassionate love, and unlimited support.

Journal entry

July 5, 2022

Today is Tuesday

A LOT can happen in 48 hrs!

On July 3rd my son had horrible pain! He couldn't stand or sit! I took him to the closest Emergency Room, the hospital in Newberg. Due to the holiday weekend, they were not fully staffed and because of the nature of what was occurring my son was then transferred by ambulance to another hospital 19 miles away. Which depending on traffic can take 20 - 40 minutes, to drive. I drove by myself, in my car ...with the heavy weight of the unknown to Portland, Oregon for an emergency surgery. While my son was in the ambulance all drugged up to help manage the pain, heading to the same destination.

How did I arrive before the ambulance?! Only by a few minutes, but still.

This was HARD!

This felt surreal. Felt like another part of my heart was breaking to the floor. It was tough to keep my mind from thinking the worst. I found that my core and foundation were shaking. During the minutes and hours of waiting for my son to recover I prayed. I walked the hallways and read the sister's mission of Providence and found that the faith of my son was in good hands. I entrusted that he ...WILL recover. I began to repeat these words. He will recover. He is safe. He will be okay. He will recover. ...repeating for a few hours.

We are now home. He is safe and healing. I realize during all of this I held back tears and now as I release them, I feel the weight being lighter, the burdens are now floating away in my never-ending river of tears.

Journal entry

July 13, 2022
Full moon

Super Full Moon in Capricorn

Pluto will return in about 1-2 years

There will be some heaviness during this shift and the U.S. will feel it

How can I keep my boundaries and adjust as I need to?

The toxic cycles from my past, my ancestors, the foundations, ME, and any bad habits NEED to change!

Capricorn is meant to be a father role, and Cancer is the mother role, with these 2 conjunct ...it will bring in past parent experiences.

Now is the time to dig in even deeper to figure out the root of any toxic behaviors and remove them.

Drop the OLD structures

Capricorn is with Saturn. I need to follow through with what I say I WILL DO!

The current placement of Pluto ... let's just say, the last time it was in this position was when the Declaration of Independence was signed! HUGE shift.

On this full moon in Capricorn, I am releasing OLD habits, negative energy, and broken structures.

IT'S NOT PERSONAL, BUT IT IS PERSONAL

Mail

7.28.2022

Thursday morning, 7:48 am

My Dearest Rob, the love of MY LIFE

Good morning

I hope this letter finds you at peace and maybe a little lighter as you move through your day.

After our conversation this last weekend, you ended with a question. Do you love me? Do you really ...love me?

(very sad face)

I.NEVER. STOPPED. (crying sad face)

I am so sorry I placed this thought and feeling in you. I am definitely not 100% over here. I struggle daily with a hole in my heart and depression. The last three and half years spiraled out of control... and now I am slowly trying my HARDEST to piece it all together.

I don't know if the steps I took were the right steps, yet I know I needed to take a different approach if I had any chance of actually living. I truly felt like I was dying. As I explained before, the pain was and is unbearable.

I have now found many tools that I can use or turn to when I have this feeling and pain. (Is it easy? NO) It's fucking hard. It takes A LOT of digging deep within me and it's WORK! But it will help me move forward in my life with all relationships starting with myself first.

So I am learning to love myself again 1st. Unconditionally. (To myself, it is hard) Loving my kids unconditionally is easy. Loving you unconditionally is easy. Easy like Sunday morning. Again, loving me unconditionally is a hard act for me to do. I constantly shame or blame myself and I am learning to shift away from this. Like I said it's fucking

HARD WORK! Yet I am trying.

I say this because I lost love for myself and I was hurting and in an extreme amount of pain. So I disconnected from you to reconnect with the facts and myself. I thought at times (because I was in an emotion of agony) if I did not say the words I love you. It would all go away. I know now instead I was punishing you and this way was not the healthy way. Despite how much pain I felt or anger I was experiencing. It was brutal. And. I am sorry for this.

I do love you. Very VERY DEEPLY. I NEVER stopped loving you. You truly are a huge part of my heart, spirit, and soul.

I am only asking for baby steps, to mend any damage I was part of to start by recognizing who I was and how I reacted to the trauma I was experiencing.

...again. I am by far 100% I would like for us to start with our friendship, and get to know each other again, in a loving, kind, healthy way. If this is okay with you...

And Rob, I LOVE you. I always have, I always will. This part (this part, right here) has NEVER Changed. It never will.

I just wanted to share and say this piece since we didn't talk on Tuesday, as planned.

Sending my love

With a grateful heart

Shana C

Xoxo

Ps

I listened to the podcast

w/Bruce & Obama (smile face)

Pss

IT'S NOT PERSONAL, BUT IT IS PERSONAL

I miss you
I love you

Journal entry

July 28, 2022
New moon

New Nu moon in Leo

Pluto is retrograde in Capricorn, asking us to release any old structures. Time to learn how to tame the beast.

Huge new beautiful changes will occur now that I am learning to keep a solid strong foundation. I just need to keep paying attention to the truth, any red flags, and follow my intuition.

Keep releasing the old patterns and addictions
Under this new moon in Leo
I am planting healthy seeds of who I want to become
...slowing down and enjoying the small moments.

Journal entry

Aug 1, 2022

Yoga is my anchor. Why?

I circled back to this a few times. The reason why yoga is my anchor is it saved me more than once. This practice truly has saved my life. An anchor reminded me of the steady solid foundation I am rooting myself to.

I can't believe I only have 2 weeks of schooling left online. I also could not believe I signed up for this commitment during the summer! But I did it! I will do the remainder of school in Bali, Indonesia. During November.

Journal entry

Aug 11, 2022

Full moon

Full moon in Aquarius

...a glimpse into next year. The foundations we have been building now will show up next year with creative energies. These energies are showing up now for us to start planting our seeds of stability and healthy structures.

The huge theme right now is to detach

Detach from anger

...detach from the ego, being mad, revenge seeking, any negative energies, release the limitations

I need to remind myself to no longer look backwards

The current emotions feel like huge tidal waves

Lots of downloads happening, people are noticing how others are freaking out, and I need to stay rooted in my truth, my new reality, my newfound identity

Use the healthy energy to plant seeds of love, creativity, and light energy

Under this full moon in Aquarius

I give myself permission to release shame, judgment, fear

I am releasing it all

...and giving myself gratitude

IT'S NOT PERSONAL, BUT IT IS PERSONAL

Journal entry

Aug 27, 2022

New moon

New Nu moon in Virgo

There are several planets currently in retrograde.

Keep purging and releasing ...keep clearing.

Under this new moon in Virgo

I am inviting in

Love

Stability

My truth

My voice

...and courage.

Mail

8/31/22

5:33 pm

My Dearest Robert

Where do I start? I guess what prompted me to write to you in the middle of work. Finally got that call you said I would get. We were on the phone for 36 minutes. Longer than our calls. (sad crying face) the call came in at 4:33 pm

LOTS of questions were asked...

Probably all that were asked of you and then she asked at the end if I wanted to add anything or say anything. I still have a lump in my throat and chest. And my heart hurts. I cried. I am still crying and emotional.

I did manage to ask for your court visit to be by video. She said your lawyer needs to request this and put in a motion. I just sent them an email with this request. Ultimately it is up to the judge, but it makes the most sense to appear by video with your health.

I hope you don't mind that I requested this on your behalf.

The other thing I wanted to say or ask...what happened Sunday? I thought you were going to call... (crying face)

There was a question asked by the P.O. I said, "How would I know the answer to this? We don't get to live and communicate like a real relationship or what the normal status is /does."

I guess this call really triggered me and I am all up in my feelings and the only way I can get it out is by more horrible writing because of my arm. (sad face)

I don't know if I should put this in the mail. (sad/disgusted face)

All I want to do right now is crawl in a ball and cry, climb in bed, and never get out. That's how I feel. How much pain I feel.

But I can't. I have to keep doing life. Work. and complete this long checklist before I leave on this road trip tomorrow.

I wish our communication wasn't like this. (sad cry face) I wish it was - heart-to-heart in person, free.

I love you. I miss you.

Love Always

Shana C

(Postcard of Reno, NV) copied on paper

Sept, 2022

Where it all started. Now coming full circle, sending teenage love your way. Aka slick rick

Love you

Love Shana C

IT'S NOT PERSONAL, BUT IT IS PERSONAL

Journal entry

Sept 2, 2022

...late entry. I was in Reno, Nevada. It was my Nonni's birthday! She now lives in RENO!

Life.

Full circle.

A big part of my life was spent in Reno, my old stomping grounds. Many life and death experiences.

Love found. Love lost.

All in good ole Reno.

Journal entry

Sept 10, 2022
Full moon

Full moon in Pisces

...I need new pens

You can barely read my writing.

Mars is in mercury... Scorpio is in one of the nodes ...for a whole year.

ASK: What is bringing me success? What is bringing me joy?

I need to be intentional about how I want things to unfold moving forward for short and long term.

Say what I want and need.

I no longer need to lie to MYSELF.

It is ok to say we are NOT on the same page.

Look at this date, this timeframe, last year.

I need to speak up

I need my voice

Do not go backwards, I need to invest in ONLY myself, in order to succeed

...I looked up this time last year. I was in a deep dark sea of depression. Drowning and I wasn't sure if I still knew how to swim. I found a small life raft when I hiked Dog Mountain right before the summer of 2021! I kept climbing till I no longer felt the quicksand swallowing me in that dark sea. I saved myself and had help from the wisest souls that day and the days to follow. The strong rooted trees in nature during each hike and trail I embarked on. This space was my healing raft.

Last year vs this year. We are not in alignment and that is ok.

I will keep trusting in myself and this new chapter. I know true legitimate joy is near.

Under this full moon in Pisces

I am letting go and releasing

Pain, depression, loss, heartache, and any loneliness

All those broken pieces ... from age 2, 3, 6, 10, 11, 12, 13, 14, 15, 16, 17, 19, 21, ALL of my 20's, 35, 36, 37, 38, 39, 41, 42, 43, and 44 ...releasing them all to be mended with gold.

...Outside right now, the sky is a hazy orange-gray color. The fires are back. Undoubtedly bad, as of yesterday!

IT'S NOT PERSONAL, BUT IT IS PERSONAL

Journal entry

Sept 13, 2022

3:43 pm

This morning, I ran.

On Sunday, I also ran.

I decided to pick up running again.

...back to today. I saw J when I ran past my brother's tree.

I shared this experience with Destiny. She thinks I should have stopped and spoke to her.

Then I shared it with Marquita. She is surprised I didn't cuss her ass out!

Right now I feel sad. Many emotions have resurfaced. I am questioning my actions a little. At first, I was proud because the old me would have stopped to please that other person. Yet this time I chose me. I guess I am a little hurt that my daughter does not see it this way.

I feel ok with my decision to not stop. To speak that is. I waved hello, goodbye...I just kept running.

I also just found out. Rob's official court date has been moved.

Again.

It will now be next year. Jan 23, 2023. Yes, he did take the plea deal, yet he has not gone to court for this yet, which means he has never been sentenced since they took him into custody in May of 2019!

Just another broken record.

Chapter Eighteen

Aligned Autumn Of 2022

*J*ournal entry

Sep 24/25 of 2022

New moon

I backpacked with Justina during the New Nu Moon in Libra

We were on the Indian Heaven's trail

We hiked a little over 15 miles this weekend with 45+Lb kids on our backs. In my opinion "to say it was hard the 1st day is an understatement!" The kids were our backpacks! Packed to the seams!

Yet

We did it!

a n d ...

The moments were healing

The sights incredible

The stillness priceless

...and all the pain, well worth it!

Words by Adrienne Rich

painted the last 2 days beautifully

"No one has imagined us.

We want to live like trees,

sycamores blazing through the sulfuric air,

dappled with scars,

still exuberantly budding,

our animal passion rooted in the ~~city~~."

(lets change city to *forest* or *wilderness*)

We had our lunch at Blue Lake and continued our hike over to Bear Lake, where we set up camp.

Bittersweet to leave. We always seem to need more time beneath the stars.

...it truly was heaven though.

Journal entry

Sept 27, 2022

New Nu

2 days late, only because we had no service out in the woods

Which is exactly how it is supposed to be

Disconnect

To

Reconnect

New Nun moon in Libra w/s and meditation

This new moon energy has to do with relationships and money

All my learning has paid off, I have a new story now

It is time to focus on balance

Mercury is in retrograde in Virgo,

now until mid-October

...the puzzle pieces will slowly come together

I can gather all the information and then decide later how this all fits ...this will continue to help me with my boundaries and create a healthy balance.

During this retrograde, I might be triggered by old traumas

Keep exploring myself, unfolding the layers

I will evolve into my higher self ...that I have been working towards

Under this New moon in Libra

I invite in an abundance of love, freedom, and money!

Journal entry

Oct 9, 2022

4:40 am

Full moon

Full moon in Aries

I am making space for the new me. I am recognizing all the work I have done so I can continue to grow with a different experience.

In 2 weeks there will be a new moon eclipse in Scorpio

What shadows in myself do I see, that will need tending and healing too?

I need to no longer abandon myself.

I need to no longer create crutches or keep taking care of others before myself.

Do not fixate on the past

Pay attention to the present and some of my future

I have done a lot of work ...to get this far.

IT'S NOT PERSONAL, BUT IT IS PERSONAL

Keep going

You got this Shana

Under this full moon in Aries

I am letting go of people ...that no longer match my kind of energy

Under this full moon in Aries

I am inviting in New Healthy energies and more abundance from all directions!

Journal entry

Oct 20, 2022

Thursday night

I just finished a session with my counselor

She asked me...

"Why are you still holding on to the relationship with Rob, and do not say because you love him?"

"What are the good things the qualities that are brought by him and what are the bad things?"

"...and WHY is it ok for those bad things?"

...me- because it is normal. I grew up around it. It was okay...

"Shana. You deserve to be loved all the way. Not halfway. All the way. Not once in a while. All the time."

I need to say. I love you and this is not acceptable ...

My 5-year-old heart and my 44-year-old heart /self ... are broken again.

Journal entry

Oct 25, 2022
New moon

No work today

They asked me to, I said no thank you.

...proud of placing my boundary.

New nu moon in Scorpio and an Eclipse

There is a lot of dark, heavy energy and I am trying my damnedest to NOT get sucked in!

I will change and work on only me

No more OLD toxic patterns

I want new rules

New action

New positive karma

I will not entangle myself with low vibrations

What do I truly want?

I want long-term healthy abundance, freedom, joy, and health, with unconditional love.

Pay attention. Any actions need to match the words.

Level UP!

I have something HUGE to celebrate

Keep doing the inner work

On this New nu moon in Scorpio

I accept the following into my life

~peace

~equanimity

~love

~balance

IT'S NOT PERSONAL, BUT IT IS PERSONAL

~travel

~joy

~freedom

~more money

~abundance of grand energies

Journal entry

Nov 8, 2022

Full moon

Full moon eclipse in Taurus, also known as the Blood Moon

Right now all my new identities are not aligned with my past.

Just keep releasing and purging Shana, clear and cut the cords

Mars is in retrograde in Gemini

Pay attention to who is telling me things, yet not following through

Keep speaking my truth

6 months ago my needs looked different than how they look now

I gave and gave... for many years

Under this full moon in Taurus

I will release the pain from my broken heart

Under this full moon in Taurus

I am stepping into the new version of me

Radiant and full of love

Journal entry

Nov 18, 2022

In-person 200 YTT

Bali, Ubud

The first class is with Persia, Throat Chakra

Exercise is to practice speaking with active listening for 3 minutes each

As a kid - no problems only solutions, and now we have learned active listening

Use heart and throat chakra to express myself

Feel the vibration of the throat working through the open heart (the bridge) and throat, implement shoulder pose

Class with Vijeth

Vijeth is the only instructor I have had the entire course with since June! He was extremely helpful virtually. I can feel his aura in person and had this awareness during the online course. He is highly grounded and healing. What an honor to be taught by such a profound soul.

Today – Self-study, study oneself

Integrate what I hear and experience daily

This is the practice to integrate what my heart is singing

Release any judgment and let go of the bad ego

Awareness is the key.

This is the divine calling ...intensifying the awareness, always

The last 8 yama's is pure consciousness ...surrendering

Read the Zen stories

If you love immensely you will no longer have the ego

LOVE is the highest self

Trust in life completely

IT'S NOT PERSONAL, BUT IT IS PERSONAL

Never question
Allow self-reflection

Class with Punnu, Meditation
Exercise the heart muscle
What makes life, to be a full experience
...the greatest ...being fully aware with happiness?
When the root is not well and not healed, then the relationships do
not go well or have joy
If the relationship with parents is not right, set them right
If the relationship with Dad is bad - this equals no money
If the relationship with mom is bad - this equals needless obstacles
in life
Divine intervention is always within you
After the lecture, Punnu led a meditation that involved each of us
speaking out loud to our parents about any heartache, pain, neglect,
or any feelings we have held onto that we have not healed yet.

This was a very deep dive. WE are all with our eyes closed and I
could hear the crying, the yelling, the banging on the floor, the sobbing
of the tears. I knew when I first walked into the room the energy was
heavy, and now I know why. So many of the students are just now
beginning their healing journey. I am grateful I started years ago and
I have the knowledge that this road is neverending. My heart cries for
their pain and burdens.

I am grateful we are in a safe healing space.

Journal entry

Nov 19, 2022

Saturday

Bali, Ubud

It is day 2 in Bali, Ubud 6:45 am, and currently, there are 7 of us gathered in the Shala preparing for class. The music playing in the background is the beautiful sounds of Mother Nature. Just this sound alone makes me want to move here. Regardless of how many spiders I cross, that are bigger than my brother's hand.

Journal entry

Nov 20, 2022

Bali, Ubud

Reflection from Sunday, we were off from classes all day.

This is our one day to explore.

I joined 6 of my classmates to hike NungNung Waterfall. The drive was a winding path for about 45 minutes. All 7 of us were snug in a little car. Talking, laughing, and listening to music. The trail itself had over 400 steps...stairs that led down to the center of the mountains where 2 bodies of water flowed from the tops of the jungle. The waterfall was enchanting. I even saw the most beautiful teal butterfly flutter around me. All of it was quite magical. After hanging out in the water for an hour or so, we attempted the climb back up the 400 + stairs. Much harder than getting to the destination. We decided to check out another viewpoint at the top that had breathtaking views. On this short yet dangerous trail, we saw a black cobra in a small coffee tree. The locals were walking us back there and made sure we stopped and got off the path stating it was a very dangerous snake and to please go around.

Connecting with my Bali family and Mother Nature was food for the soul.

Journal entry

Nov 23, 2022
New moon
...in Bali

New Nu moon in Sagittarius

Mercury and Venus are in Sagittarius. Jupiter is now direct, this combo creates lots of travel!

Under this new moon in Sagittarius while in Bali

I invite in

An abundance of joy

Safe travels, stability, and new riches with my Bali familia

Journal entry

Nov 24, 2022
Thursday
Thanksgiving
...in Bali

It is 6:33 am

I am currently in the Shala preparing for class. The only sound I hear is the humming of the insects and the rooster occasionally reminding us it is a new day.

I am grateful for the safe travels. The beautiful people I have met. The constant LOVE and fulfillment of abundance. I am grateful my kids are well, safe, and supportive. I am beyond blissful for this next huge chapter to unfold. Thank you, God. Thank you universe. Thank you to the higher spirit.

Meditation today ~ <3 ~

We have 114 chakras. Yet most folks only know about the 7 chakras.

Today we meditated with 7 chakras, the imagery of having gold being poured into each while chanting 7 times for each one. I saw fire gold, a white lotus with gold trim on every petal, gold fire pouring down the sides of a black stone mountain, trees, forest, and the 3rd eye with a stream of beautiful rainbow colors.

Journal entry

Nov 26, 2022
Saturday
...in Bali

My alarm was set for 4:44 am

To get ready for finals.

I arrived at the Shala at 5:55 am. Dhruv and Simona were already there setting up the class. I helped braid all the ladies' hair before we taught. The day came and went. It was full, gratifying, and went way better than I imagined. I taught with 4 other classmates. Afterwards, we were given feedback. I was humbled by the responses. I was told I should make a YouTube channel. That I was ready to teach Yin or Meditation. I am glad I found my throat chakra. The biggest gift here truly was crossing paths with so many beautiful humans. I will forever cherish this experience.

Journal entry

Dec 1, 2022

Kuta, Bali

I am now solo.

Staying in an Airbnb in Kuta, Bali. No room-mates.

It is nice, and a little too freeing.

Yesterday I got new ink! When I was in Ubud with Gatlyn, at the Karma House. I got Kali! The Goddess of change, power, and destruction! It was very fitting for this chapter of my life. The day before I took a boat with 6 other classmates to Nusa Pinda. We stayed at a hostel called Nyuh Gading in Nusa Lembongan.

This journey has been beautiful, enchanting, exhilarating and healing. I am so grateful I did not talk myself out of it. This was exactly what I needed to help me stay on a genuine healthy path.

Journal entry

Dec 7, 2022

Full moon

I have been home since late Saturday night. Sunday I learned I caught Covid and my son fractured his right shoulder snowboarding.

Under this full moon in Gemini
I release this illness
any pain my son may be enduring
...and ALL negative energies

Journal entry

Dec 10, 2022

Today is Saturday, and I have been back in the States for almost a week. I went to a mindfulness retreat from 9 am - 2 pm today.

It was exactly what I needed.

We meditated for 5 hours. Silence. Clearing all the rubbish from the mind, that gathered in one week and that icky C was a mess. I had a high fever for 4 days! Stayed in bed. No appetite. Just glad to be back on the mend.

The retreat was medicine for the soul for sure.

We did some sitting, standing, walking, eating, and chair yoga. All in silence.

Aside from the instructors leading the next mindfulness step.

I just got home now and it's almost 6 pm. I went food shopping and made spaghetti when I got home. My son joined me for dinner, this was a treat. Then I decided to open all the mail that the kitchen table was collecting.

Lol

I got a legal document saying instead of $3000.00 I will get another $2000.00 for my permanently disabled arm. Which I have been dealing with since the end of October 2019. 3 years now. Our government and the system are beyond backwards.

IT'S NOT PERSONAL, BUT IT IS PERSONAL

Mail

Dec 11, 2022
Sunday night, 8:18 pm

My Dearest Rob

I truly hope this letter finds you well and seeking peace.

I am a little surprised I have yet to hear from you... by letter or phone. Then again... maybe I shouldn't be.

I would love to share everything with you... yet I do not know where to begin.

... maybe I can start with not assuming and ask a few questions.

Why have you chosen to not communicate by pen?

Do you still have anger towards me and/or a grudge?

Can we both be honest with each other about where we are at? To the best that we can...

Our last conversation ended abruptly due to time not on our side... and I wrote to you on 11/15 to apologize for how my tone of voice was, the choice of words I used, and how it was delivered and probably received.

Yet... I was rushing to get to the airport and forgot to mail it out. When I remembered, I was on my 2nd plane heading to Taipei, Taiwan. A 12 hour flight. When I was in Bali I attempted to mail it out, but it's way more complicated when you're in a different country. And time was not on my side. I had school from 6 am -6 pm daily except for one day out of the week.

So... I just decided I would talk to you when I got home... but that has yet to happen too... So here I am writing.

When we were on the phone and you said you would call me (what

I should have said was) I am sorry Rob I already told everyone that I normally speak to (kids, my mom, etc....) that I will not be taking phone calls during this trip. I didn't realize that you did not know that part and I snapped. My message could have been delivered in a more gentler way. I apologize.

Truth is. Even if I said yes, I would have never got your call. There are 2 ways to get calls there, purchase their SIM cards or download WhatsApp. I already had WhatsApp because that is how I talk to my dad, so before I left I asked all the kids to download it and that was how I was able to communicate with them. And with the time difference, there were slim windows to chat. Which was fine. I was looking forward to sharing my journey in person.

There were soooooo many good things. Good omens, signs, messages, gifts... It truly was a beautiful experience. The only obstacles I faced were in the Singapore airport and the Canada airport. And what I will NOT miss in Bali, or should I say Ubud, are ALL the lovely creatures. Not one or two but in packs or 100's. Ants, mosquitos, bees, spiders, LOL any insect trying to join me on my mat for yoga! Then there are the snakes, a scorpion, and the really big lizards, maybe a komodo dragon. I don't know. I did get a few pics and videos. And that was just walking to and from the Shala or to get my meals. The property I stayed at was in the jungle with several rice fields in between and a few bridges to walk over the creeks, running down from the river. This part of it ...was breathtaking. I truly wanted to bask in mother nature for hours if I could, regardless if I got bit 20 times in less than one minute. It was so lush and green, the fruit trees were full of color. There were bananas, mangoes, papaya, and even dragon fruit trees! The sounds, aweee the sounds were like music it was enchanting and hypnotizing. I can see why people choose to come and never leave.

I almost forgot about all the birds and butterflies! There were so many beautiful colors flying around. Butterflies as big as my hand, spiders as BIG as Jr's hand, I even saw a teal butterfly ...again... simply breathtaking.

I am glad I did not cancel. I am glad I did not listen to my voice of doubt because it popped up many times. Another big reason I chose not to take any phone calls while I was out there was that I needed no distractions or I would 2nd guess myself on what I was doing. By placing a few boundaries and prioritizing myself, it worked.

I graduated from my 200-hour teacher training for Yoga! They say schooling is required every 2-3 years (any type of training/ education geared toward this) really.

So now I am just taking it one day at a time and maybe putting a plan together for next year on what I have learned so far.

Before I go to bed I guess I can circle back to the questions I asked.

...actually. I can wait till you respond.

...again I truly do hope things are lighter for you and you're doing ok.

Sending my love.

Love

Shana C

Xoxo

Chapter Nineteen
Winter Of 2022

Journal entry

Dec 23, 2022

New moon

~ under this new nu moon in Capricorn

I am inviting the following

New healthy habits

Returning back to running, yoga, meditation

...and an abundance of love, freedom, travel, and joy with a solid, safe, and healthy foundation.

2022 Travels/ Hikes/ Events

Hikes -

01.01 - Silver Falls

01.08 - snowshoeing Trillium (w/Justina)

02.20 - Spencer Butte (w/Nonni)

2.26- Beacon Rock & Wahclella falls (w/Kenzie)

3.21 - Wai'au River 2x (solo & w/Jr)

3.21 - Kulaniapia Falls -solo

3.22 - Kulaniapia Falls REPELLED with my son!

3.22 - hiked down Bamboo Trail to see Mua Loa Falls, Waena Falls, & Mahana Falls

5.22 - Spencer Butte (Nonnie & Louie)

5.29 - Labyrinth (w/Justina)

7.09 - Tamanawas Falls (w/Justina & Amy)

7.10 - Wahclella falls (solo)

7.19 - Wahclella falls (w/LuLu)

7.26 - Wahclella falls (solo)

08.14 - Sunset hike at Angels Rest w/ Justina

09.04 - Lake Tahoe w/my kids

09.24 - Indian head trail /Thomas Lake trailhead -to Bear Lake (Backpacking) w/ Justina

09.25 -Bear Lake/Indian head trail to -Thomas Lake trailhead

11.20 - Nung Nung in Ubud Bali w/ my Bali familia

Books- I read

Jan. Signs by Laura Lynne Jackson

June - Atlas of the Heart by Brené Brown

Aug- Four Agreements by Don Miguel Ruiz (a few times now)

Sep- Meditation for Beginners by Jack Kornfield

Dec - Alchemist (8th time, completed) by P. Coelho

Traveled to and events!

2.20 - Eugene, Or

3.20 - Hilo, Hi

3.23 - Kona, Hi

3.24 - Waikiki Hi

4.15 - Road trip Reno, Nv w/Jessie

Parámetro

4.29 - Las Vegas, Nv w/ Justina, Jenah, Amy

5.14 - Sunset beach - clean up/ seaside w/ Suzzi

06.10 - Jr graduated high school

7.02- Del Rey beach w/ Cyn & her family

8.06 -Del Rey beach w/ Cyn & her family, E/ Jr, and friends to celebrate Aria's 4th Bday

8.06 - Cannon Beach w/Jr & E sleepover

09/01-09/05 Road trip w/ Jr, E, & Z, to Reno, NV

09.04 Lake Tahoe

09.24/25 Carson, WA Indian Heaven's backpacking trip with Justina

10.14- 10.16- Reno, NV- solo to see my Nonni

11.15- 12.03 - Ubud, Bali- solo. For my 200hr Yoga Teacher Training

11.28 - 11.29- Nusa Penida, Jungutbatu, - Nusa Lembongan

11.29 -12.01 - Ubud

12.01-12.03 - Kuta

12.03- transfer in Canada to head back home (this was fun, NOT)

Concerts- Events!!

04.30 -Sway Lee Dj pool party @ The Virgin Hotel / The Elia Beach Club

04.30 -Michale Bublé in Vegas w/ Justina & Jenah

08.05 - Jazz Musiq Soulchild in Portland w/Marquita

11.25 - Punnu in Bali

12.31 New Year's Eve - Digable Planets w/Justina at the Crystal Ballroom

New INK

5.15 - Me & my bestie Marquita, got our key is honesty & flower
Anam Cara - in Oregon at Pussycat Tattoo

11.30 - Kali -at Karma house in Ubud, Bali

Chapter Twenty
Stormy & Brutal Winter Of 2023

Journal entry

Jan 6/7, 2023

Full moon

Full moon in cancer

Ready and accepting the new change for this new year

Journal entry

Jan 8, 2023

8:18 pm

I am ready

I will have a safe beautiful home near water that I can call my own

I will give myself more love

I am open to teaching meditation and yoga

IT'S NOT PERSONAL, BUT IT IS PERSONAL

Journal entry

Jan 16, 2023

...in one week Rob will finally have court.

Almost 4 years later...

Mail

Jan 16, 2023

Monday, 3:33 pm

My Dearest Love of my Life

How are you?

I missed you! I miss you.

I was hoping I would have heard from you last week... or this weekend again. (sad face)

You must have used the free call or it didn't work.

I am sick and depressed knowing next week is finally here and not being rescheduled or canceled. I wish I could be there and a part of me doesn't because I know either way I will be depleted. We both will.

Please call me.

As soon as you get this letter. I am not sure you will get it before or after Jan 23... it doesn't matter. Whatever day please call.

I hope you are doing ok or at least a little better than the last time we spoke.

I truly cannot wait till this is ALL over and I (WE) can have a normal conversation in person. I miss this so much!

Only the nice, caring, loving version of you. Not the grumpy version. But if the choice was a grumpy version of you or nothing I WILL take grumpy. (smile face)

My handwriting is all over the place... I hope you can make out this mess I am writing. I have been meaning to mention this artist I came across... I think 2 years ago now. The artist/musician's name is Londrelle. I truly like his albums from 2018 and 2020, the music is different... more of affirmations, meditations, and healing.

Last year when I was walking every day for a month, that is all I played on repeat.

Guess what?

I have no more cactus plants. (sad face)

The last one out of 6 died this weekend. Either I am not a good plant person or cactuses are not my thing. Ugg!! (sad/angry face)

I was thinking about printing some photos from Bali, to send to you. But I will wait till we know where you get transferred to. Hopefully, you can have normal photos there. And I hope visiting is allowed now since we are kinda out of the pandemic!

This is the worst letter ever!

Sorry

I just miss you! And wanted to talk to you. I always do... even when I say I don't want to... but .... Well that's why I decided to write. Tired of holding things in.

Let's think of something good to say... before I end this letter.

Hmmm... Tupac Shakur! I listened to both of his albums yesterday. All Eyes on Me and Me Against The World!

He was soooooo WISE at such a young age! His path is similar to you and me ... we grew up too fast. We were both adults ...when we were kids.

When I used to introduce myself and my background. It was... my name is Shana and I have been an adult since the age of 2.

Hmmmm... ya. Crazy.

Now this year I will be 45.

Do you have a favorite song from his albums? I used to think I did... but he has so many good ones. It's hard to pick just one. I can tell you what my first 2 songs are that will be played first! It's from the album Me Against The World. 'Temptations' and 'Can you get away.' Then there's 'How Do You Want It' from the other album. I listened to the whole song, 'What's ya phone #' The end when the girl is talking and she is talking dirty and his response is "Do a bear shit in the woods and wipe his ass with a fluffy white rabbit?"

What?! Hahah!!! I had to double-take triple-take!! I don't know why I don't remember that part! He is wild for that! ...then he mentioned fucking on a balcony and that took me right to our 1st spot on Hill Street! Mmm!!! That felt sooo good!

K.... gonna go. I will meet you on that balcony! & until we talk soon. I LOVE YOU SOOOO FUCKING Much! I Always will!

Love Always

Shana C

xoxo

Journal entry

Jan 17, 2023

The last 3 days ALL I have wanted to do is cry!

I finally allowed some tears to come down yesterday after my walk.

What is the season I am in today teaching me about gratitude?!

This can go 2 ways ...

Currently, it is winter, in the middle of January after 2 months of holidays and I am in an empty house. It is cold out, yet warm inside. I am thankful for a roof over my head, a warm bed, a warm meal, a hot shower. ALL the small simple things people (most Americans) take for granted.

The season my heart is in ...is a lonely ice storm.

I am grateful I am still alive, that I can recognize the suffering ...and that I do have a heart.

Journal entry

Jan 18, 2023

7:30 pm

I just finished a session with my counselor

I asked her about the homework assignment that was given to me in October... (the last time I saw her) It was on YouTube called Crappy Childhood Fairy which speaks about CPTSD (Complex post-traumatic stress disorder)

I then asked her, "What is your professional opinion on the meaning?"

She replied, "Didn't I give you the Ace's Test?"

"...uhhhh NOPE," was my reply.

So ...we did the test tonight.

I scored 9.

The highest score is 10.

...then I reread the questions and realized I answered one wrong. Actually, my score is a 10 out of 10!

After hearing and seeing the score, she said, "Wow, you have been through a lot as a kid. A LOT. Try not to let this detour you. You have come a long way. No wonder you can not let go of Rob. I am surprised you are not in jail, Shana! Or doing drugs."

(very sad sobbing face)

I am not sure how to feel about all this surfacing truth.

It feels heavy on my chest.

Journal entry

Jan 20, 2023

Late...9:35 pm

Dream

My brother showed up in my dream last night.

He was riding a bike. I was on the sidewalk hiding under some type of canopy. I saw him riding by and called his name out, he found me. (happy face)

It is the end of Friday ...and only 2 and a half more days till the 23rd!

Journal entry

Jan 21, 2023

New moon

8:11 am

New Nu Moon in Aquarius

I need to make sure my foundation is solid.

What are the benefits of any connections I currently have?

If it feels beneficial to me then this is a good energy exchange.

Finally = in the next 4 months, ALL planets are moving direct!!!! This is the time to take action!

Pluto → and the north node in Taurus, is suggesting to release all old unhealthy structures. This used to protect me. It is time for something new.

I am not responsible for cleaning up anyone else's life.

I am responsible for myself. My heart. My foundation.

Under this New Nu moon in Aquarius

I invite in the following

   Healthy mind, soul, heart, and body

    ...peace and love.

Journal entry

           Jan 24, 2023

            8:49 am

         ...in my car writing

Last night Rob finally called.

...around 8:23 pm.

Court finally happened, a little after 3 pm.

I was not the first person he called.

This made me feel some type of way.

I was hurt, angry, and frustrated.

I finally cried last night.

I had so much anxiety all day waiting for the answer we already knew was coming yet it took hold of me throughout the day.

I remember when I was cooking pancakes for my son, I felt relaxed and at ease because this was my only focus.

I do have to remember to not let my thoughts consume me.

They will only do harm.

So 10 years.

Rob says every year there should be 53 or 54 days subtracted. Which could make his time be reduced to 8 and a half years. (8.333) per my calculator

So maybe instead of May 2029, he will be released in the summer of 2027!?

...either way, this is heartbreaking and feels like an eternity!

Journal entry

Feb 5, 2023

Full moon

Got out into nature today.

I was with one of my dearest friends, Justina. We hiked the Balfour-Klickitat loop, and saw so many Bald eagles! It was beautiful and healing.

Then we headed over to do a second hike. Little Maui Falls & Old Ranch Road trail, off the Coyote Wall.

Since today is a full moon I made sure to bring some paper and pens.

We both wrote what we wanted to release under the full moon in Leo and then we burned the lists.

It was healing... and very much needed, for both of us.

Later during the evening, I completed the mediation portion of the Full Moon in Leo workshop, my son hung out in the room during this time. This made my heart happy. I felt the benefits traveling through both of us.

Journal entry

Feb 9, 2023

7:11 pm

I just finished a session with my counselor.

We spoke more about the Ace's Test and she sent me homework.

She mentioned that I still need to be angry or mad at all that I went through when I was young. That I was not put in safe places and that I am lucky to be alive.

Then she said, "I remember when you told me that you donated your eggs ...sold them to buy a gift for that man who abused you. I thought how sad. I was so sad and heartbroken for you Shana. That you thought you had to sell yourself, to please another person."

When she said this. When I heard this out loud. ...my heart broke as well. I never saw or even thought twice to see it from this view.

Journal entry

Feb 17, 2023

6:46 pm

I just finished my therapy session

...I forgot to do my homework

I need to make a list of the old identity and the new identity

...at the end of our session, the realization and question asked was

HOW does Rob fit with my new identity?

AND how I still have so much SHAME of all my own past life experiences that happened ...for me to survive.

She also mentioned that I would be a great mentor for any woman in jail. That I have a great back story. That I did survive.

IT'S NOT PERSONAL, BUT IT IS PERSONAL

You can't see it ...or feel it. ...or see me. ...but I have been crying for the last hour or so straight.

< —---- Old identity

—---- > *New Nu identity*

...to the left, sharp hard path

...to the right healthy path

Person who holds guilt & shame

Makes healthy choices

Has NO boundaries

Asks what are the healthy choices?

Codependent

Thinks before saying YES to EVERYTHING

BAD unhealthy habits are normal

Has boundaries

People pleaser

Understands I am not responsible for everyone

Assume I am the caretaker

Has more love for myself

Of all that I am and love I understand I deserve to heal and receive healthy love.
Checks in w/my heart and self 1st
I let go. I no longer need to try & control ALL things
Follows my intuition

Journal entry

Feb 19/20 2023

...late

New Moon

New Nu Moon in Pisces

I need to look at all the progress I have made. Reflect on the last year, and see what is working for me and what is not working for me.

I need to invest in good karma.

I truly am aware of all the toxic and disconnect ...reasons I can no longer participate.

I need to have trust.

To appreciate and pay attention to my intuition and harmony

No more blocking my blessings! I need only BIG Queen Energy!

Under this New Nu moon in Pisces, I welcome in

...my new identity, healthy safe foundation, love, and riches from ALL elements.

Journal entry

Feb 21, 2023

10:18 am

I am 45 today.

I am so grateful my little brother Michael joined me to watch the sunrise! He brought the party! 100's of birds showed up singing Happy Birthday in the sky above me! This was right after I requested a sign from my brother. I asked for roller skates! Because that is what we used to do on my birthday! My brother showed up with our song, 'Lovely Day' and SKATING an hour after the request!

IT'S NOT PERSONAL, BUT IT IS PERSONAL

During episode 9 in season 3 of Dead To Me, while watching with Nonni!

I couldn't believe it!

I mean I could, I can! I just was in awe of how quickly he showed up for me.

…later evening

We decided to all go skating tonight! And it just so happened to be adults only! My little brother Alejandro showed up too, and all my kids were with me! It was so much fun! I even felt Michael out there with me on the rink!

Mail

March 4, 2023
wrote on the app email

Rob Good Morning

It is nice to see you, yet it is triggering. The time is always cut short and the constant reminder of the truth is piercing. I need to be honest with myself and you. We both agreed we would continue this open truth of conversation. I need a week or 2 alone.

Journal entry

March 5, 2023
Soul day

Sunday

Currently, I am in SE Portland at a meditation retreat. I just finished lunch outside with the trees. The location is off of SE 43rd on Catholic grounds. This place is beautiful. I fell in love with it when I was here last year in December after my travels from Ubud, Bali.

It is always good to pour into yourself.

I did invite my bestie this time. We get to reflect together later since this is a no-talking retreat. It is crazy weird not being able to speak with her right now during our lunch, mindfulness eating practice. Yet refreshing to know we both can practice this self-healing skill, intentionally. Spread the love to ourselves so we can share it with others.

Journal entry

March 7, 2023

Full moon

Full moon in Virgo

...end of the astrology year!

Today Jr passed his driving test, and now officially has a driver's license.

Today Saturn is in Pisces till 2026!

Also, there is an angel's birthday today, JaySean.

Marquita, Johnny, Jr, and I went roller skating tonight.

Truly it was a beautiful day full of riches and love.

Under this full moon in Virgo

I am ready to release and willing to release ANY and ALL old negative habits, and one-way relationships.

ALL released...

IT'S NOT PERSONAL, BUT IT IS PERSONAL

Journal entry

March 14, 2023

5:44 am

Tuesday morning

...before work

On Sunday it was daylight savings. I decided to go to my old yoga studio I used to love going to. Where I found myself 20+ years ago. Crazy 2 decades. I went again yesterday and I will go again tonight. I bought 2 weeks worth. I am not sure I will go back after my 2 weeks are up though. The energy is off. It is very different from what I fell in love with.

I guess the true goal currently here... is to get my body moving and the energy to flow so I am no longer stuck in depression.

I know this is the right path.

Journal entry

March 18, 2023

7:43 am

Saturday

I caught the sunrise and locked it away in my heart. Just in case I need a few rays of strength later, I know where to go.

From 2- 5 pm, I went to yoga class again.

Today we did 108 Sun Salutations

It was hard, beyond challenging, yet I made it, I dug deep!

This was followed by Yin Yoga

...then mediation

One of the instructors opened and closed with such a beautiful reading and knowing of the ledge #108, revealing how we are all connected to each other and the universe. The significance of the heart chakra and we opened the energies from this space and connected with each other's heart through the class.

It was one of the biggest classes I have attended.

Today's class I enjoyed.

Happy Spring Equinox ...coming Monday.

...later. It is now 11:28 pm

When I got home around 6:15 pm I called my mom to invite her to watch the sunset.

We went to Snyder Park and sat on a bench to view the sunset. She seemed happy. I listened. There were too many clouds to see the sun, and there was a smokey haze. The visit was still a beautiful painting of warmth.

Chapter Twenty-One

Spring Of 2023

*J*ournal entry

New Nu Moon in Aries

Now is the time to jump in, use my skills to lead, and level up! Anyone in my circle needs to level up too, or it is time to let you go.

Saturn (is harsh) and is in Pisces, during this time I can make things come true and keep planting seeds.

Under this new nu moon in Aries

I invite in ALL the abundance and welcome the universe to provide what is needed.

Journal entry

April 4, 2023
Tuesday
12:30 pm

Today and yesterday I did not work. Friday night I flew out to Arizona to connect with a new friend. Her name is Elena, she is a Pisces and shares the same birthday as my son. We speak all the time through work on the phone, yet never really hung out yet. When I met her in person at the company picnic during the summer I knew instantly we were meant to be friends. That she would be part of my soul familia. We did hang out a few times, for lunch and dinner. Currently, she is out in Arizona for 2 weeks working at the Bike Fest in Cave Creek.

I was fortunate enough to spend time out there. The whole time I was there so many signs appeared that reminded me or came from my loved ones that crossed over. My grandparents and my brother. It was a beautiful feeling to feel them near.

Sunday we hiked the Echo Canyon Trail to the top of Camelback Mountain at sunrise! We started way before the actual sunrise, we got there about 5 am, and the sun rose at 6:14 am. We missed the actual view from the top by 25 minutes, yet got to see a few glimpses through the canyons and cactuses as we climbed, hiked, climbed, crawled, and rock-climbed some more! This trail was so healing and worth the aches and pains. It was heartwarming to see the different people and ages traveling this trail. It showed how we can all conquer difficulties in life and push through when determined and through nature's healing powers.

There was a 360-degree view at the top!

...remember I mentioned the signs. My brother seems to show up as a hummingbird on most if not all the trails I hike. As we ventured back down, I was telling Elena that I was surprised I had yet to see a hummingbird, at that exact moment one flew up to us. Fluttering near our heads!

This experience truly was grand.

Made me think of how I want to move with intention...

What are my intentions?

I want to create a ripple of kindness. So others can adopt this to apply to themselves and to naturally be kind to others.

Coming home Sunday night in the Phoenix airport I was sitting. Waiting. There was one open chair next to me, yet it appeared to look like 2 open chairs because someone stepped away but left their items in the chair. A lady came and asked if she and her guy could sit. Instead of saying that another chair was spoken for, I decided to just give up my chair, so they could sit together.

One small gesture of kindness will ripple and go a long way.

I witnessed it after I did this kind act.

An older gentleman saw what I did and wanted to give up his seat, so I could have a seat. And he could have easily been my great-granddad, offering up his chair.

...there is still good out there.

Journal entry

April 5, 2023
Full moon

Full moon in Libra

Aries season, the new year is officially here.

Take time to look at the last 9 months and view how we can match each other's needs. How do I want to show up in this world?

How can I relate to people with my new identity?

Eclipse season will open doors soon and make a forceful change.

Be prepared and/or ready during the eclipse season, things will surface and come into view to help invest and create healthier relationships.

Invest and start with myself first.

What does balance look like for me?

...it will feel like peace and harmony.

Under this full moon in Libra

I am letting go of the following ...broken relationships, codependency, and any old structures.

Journal entry

April 6, 2023

12:32 pm

Thursday

I just finished leading my 2nd mindfulness meditation virtually at work.

I am grateful, yet I do wish I did not have so many nerves leading up to the event.

...my adrenaline seems to shoot through the roof right before speaking and at least the first 15 minutes of my talking. It used to not be like this. When I was a teenager I never had this problem.

IT'S NOT PERSONAL, BUT IT IS PERSONAL

Journal entry

April 19, 2023

New moon

New moon nu in Aries with 2 eclipses

It is time to trust myself and make small steps towards the new energy. I need to drop short-term comfort and start something new.

I will trust the process by making small changes daily.

Under this New Nu moon in Aries, what will I integrate into my life?

Health

Wealth

Abundance

Love

Joy!!!

Journal entry

May 1, 2023

...middle of the day

Rob's birthday was yesterday.

...and I did not hear from him.

It is extremely hard to live life daily when there is a person you love dearly locked up.

It feels like death.

I am truly tired of this dying circle.

Logic over love.

(sad face)

...I need to be practical.

...but, HOW?!

Journal entry

May 4, 2023
...afternoon

I am expecting mail and packages. Two of them. However, not this package.

Rob's mother decided to send me an apology letter with a hand-made turtle.

...and I don't know how to feel about it.

Actually. I do.

This apology letter should go to her son. For putting him in the position he is in and making him think he needed to disobey the law and his heart, again!

This makes me angry! Sad! Annoyed!

ALL these feelings. I want to be done with feeling these! Done!

Journal entry

May 5, 2023
Friday
Full moon

Last eclipse in Scorpio Full Moon

ALL the hard work I have done for the last 18 months, will now pay off.

When I speak my truth!

IT'S NOT PERSONAL, BUT IT IS PERSONAL

The energy will shift, starting internally and then working its way externally.

Pluto is also in retrograde in Aquarius.

Journal entry

May 7, 2023

Soul day

It is sunny out

...yet I am still a constant dark gray cloud ...fighting depression.

I did run today.

A little over 3 miles

The first 2 miles I was stuck in my head.

...the last mile I had to try something new. I did affirmations in my mind.

I am enough

I am strong

I am healthy

I am ...

This small shift did help some.

...and Rob called yesterday and today. We got to do a video call today. It felt good to see him and hear from him. ..yet each time I can feel a piece of my heart fall to the ground like glass, and shatter.

Journal entry

May 19, 2023
New moon

New Nu Moon in Taurus

...

...I switched it up. I listened to the workshop during the morning and then did the mediation at night. I also did some grounding today.

It felt healing.

I envisioned a huge park as my backyard, sitting still embracing the healing energies of the wisest souls. The trees.

So thankful for a New Nu safe cozy home.

I feel it.

I see it coming to fruition!

Journal entry

May 24, 2023

Yesterday I got mail from Rob.

...but it wasn't for me. (sad face)

It was only phone #'s ...that he will need back.

This last week they finally moved him.

4 years later.

He was in Prison with NO sentence, for 4 FUCKING YEARS!

FOUR YEARS!

I never got to see him in person. They do not do in-person visits! The place he was at did allow you to come to visit, but once you were there it would be a FUCKING VIDEO VISIT! You heard me right! Smh.

I laughed and cried when I found that out the first year.

Now he is heading to FCI in Florence, Colorado.

No one we know lives in Colorado.

This week has been exhausting. To say the least.

...last week I got pre-approved to buy a home. Again.

Journal entry

May 31, 2023

Wednesday

Today I spoke to Rob for the first time since he was moved to Florence, Colorado. He called at 5:13 am.

It was tough.

It was like the beginning all over again.

He questioned if I was even going to be there for him and basically asked why I wouldn't allow a conversation with his mom. ...because in his words ...she made you a turtle, she is trying to mend the relationship.

I was caught off guard and I know I do not want to be in ANY false relationships. There is no reason for me to pretend I am okay with how things played out before Rob left with his mom. That is not the energy I want to be around. I am only going to give my time and energy to people who are genuine and truly live by what they say. Those who are trying to do better and not be stuck in their old ways.

Journal entry

June 3, 2023

Full moon

Under this full moon in Sagittarius, I release my ego and any relationships that no longer serve me.

Rob did call again.

We spoke.

The last 4 days in a row.

Today he said, "Maybe we need to figure out what we are doing, but the conversation needs to be in person."

I genuinely do want to see him. This part, this part right here ...is long overdue.

...I went roller skating tonight. 3rd time this year.

Journal entry

June 6, 2023

7 am

Today is my dad's birthday! He is 66! And today is 6/6!

I called him this morning, and we spoke for about 20 minutes. He seemed so happy. We did a video call through WhatsApp since he lives in Mexico, that is the service that normally works best. He was so excited to walk around his house and backyard to show me all his fruit trees! He has grapes, lemons, and peaches growing in the backyard. It looks beautiful. He also said I was the best daughter. This made me emotional. I still have tears. I really REALLY want to figure out how I can go visit him! I know he wants my little brother to join. As do I. His schedule is just a bit more complicated than mine. Yet I want to make this happen.

It was good to see him smile and be so happy!

Mail

June 7, 2023
Email App

Rob

I should have expected you would have not been able to follow through with your call. (sad face) Considering the dynamics, we never truly know if you can call when you say you will. This is my own fault, which has caused me frustration and heartache again. I know better than to expect the calls now.

This part sucks.

My original reason for hopping on here was to let you know to check your books. I placed $$$ on them and that I will not answer my phone from June 11 -20.

Today is your little sis bday, so probably want to save the call for her.

Journal entry

June 13, 2023
Tuesday

I am currently in Kona, Hawaii.

I flew out here with one of my besties, Lulu, and three of her kids. We are staying with her parents in a cozy 2 bedroom condo.

The day we arrived we went to their pool for a few hours and yesterday we went to Lulu's favorite beach! Well... one of her favorites! It was beautiful.

I am learning that the Hawaiin's are all about community and everyone is family. Even if you are not blood. Right away they will call you Auntie or Uncle, after being introduced.

I wonder how life would have unfolded if I stayed in 1994 when I moved to Oahu. If Destiny would have been born here ...instead of Reno. How that would have all played out. Today happens to be her birthday too!

We Facetimed earlier and I watched her open the gifts I left for her to unwrap. She looked beautiful and happy. Happy born day to my first baby!

... instead of wondering how it would have looked if I chose to stay and raise her here. I will choose to just be in the now. For now, I am grateful simply to just know how to be present. To be more aware of my gifts and the gifts that life shares. The life lessons that are mine or the ones that are shared from others, they are all gifts.

Journal entry

June 15, 2023

Thursday

...morning, 8:08 am

This morning I did some yoga outside and then walked a bit. I found a bench to sit on beneath the wise souls on the Waikoloa Golf Course near hole 15 or 18.

The birds are busy and deep in conversations, and the small warm breeze feels good against my skin. This moment of time feels like peace and harmony.

Journal entry

June 17, 2023
New moon

New Nu moon in Gemini

I am currently sitting in the backyard on Hilo side at Auntie Maggie and Uncle Clayton's house next to a Lychee tree!

This home is sooooo beautiful, with so much love tended to all the trees and plants outside. You can feel the love in every step from inside the home to outside on the grass. And it is a must to be barefoot. How else will I feel connected and rooted with the healing powers of Hawaii?!

This place.

Has called to me so many times in my life.

I wonder if I lived here in my past life.

I just finished listening to the workshop and mediation for the new moon. Jupiter is in Taurus. Which shifts us to dream big! DREAM BIG!

I need to make more available space for the new big energy that is arriving.

Any limited beliefs, release them!

Under this new moon in Gemini

I am open to the possibilities of more money, more movement, more meditations, writing my book, and getting it published! (9 hearts)

Chapter
Twenty-Two
Soul Summer Of
2023

Journal entry

June 20, 2023

Maui airport

I am transferring flights now, there is a 2 hour layover.

While I was waiting I decided to crack an oyster open at the jewelry counter. The one I chose had 2 pink pearls inside, twins. The lady said she had yet to see that and that I was lucky. I will get them set in pendants and give them to my daughters.

So many beautiful different synchronicities occurred while I was out here. So much magic. Even a few firsts for Lulu and she grew up out here.

The last evening it was just Lulu and I. We got new ink a wave with the coordinates of one very special beach we hung out at, and I got my honu. (In the Hawaiian culture the turtle represents wisdom, a connection to the natural world, and astonishing resilience.) We then grabbed food and caught the sunset on the beach where our ink is now reflecting the coordinates. That evening we saw an eel slither half out of the ocean near the shoreline to grab one of the many crabs that were roaming the sands! I just happened to be videotaping the ocean, the moon and then this wild scene took place!

I looked up the meaning later and found that an eel represents our emotional nature. That we are to check in with ourselves and confirm we are interpreting encounters clearly. The eel has a similar body to a snake and this is associated with Kundalini power. Having and seeing an eel show up is HUGE for the spiritual growth and the soul. This is no small matter.

I am beyond grateful for this late birthday trip.

Journal entry

July 4, 2023
Full moon

Yesterday I went to Naked Falls, out in Washington.

...Justina, Sarah and I released dry leaves into the water speaking the words out of what was to be released, under this full moon.

The words I spoke... hardship, any financial burdens, and ... divorce. (sad face)

Under the full moon in Capricorn, it is time to release any relationships that truly are no longer there...

My intentions for the next 6 months will be to invite more grace and love towards myself.

I will start taking small steps daily towards this.

Mail

July 6, 2023
an email by app

Rob

I don't know what to say.

I am so angry and frustrated right now. Your current situation is beyond worse than the last 4 years! :(

THIS is making me drown and have a feeling of anxiety and anger. I am beyond pissed. I know it is out of my control yet I cannot take it. And now it sounds like if and when I go to Colorado there is a chance I will not be able to see you. (Another slap in the face) Time and energy are constantly being wasted. I don't know if I have any more to give.

I feel like you just got locked up again. I know you have been gone. AGAIN. It feels like the very beginning. It's a broken record. To the tune of repeat. What you absolutely don't care for and ...I honestly don't either now. Now that I see and feel it happening. Again. (sad face)

I am sorry.

I do not have the strength, Rob. I wish I did, but I don't. I don't want to be bitter towards you, but me hanging on ...is doing this. I know you can't change the fact of the matter. The truth fucking sucks right now.

(sad crying face)

It kills me to say it

I have to let you go.

I recognize this situation is not healthy. And I cannot go back into depression.

IT'S NOT PERSONAL, BUT IT IS PERSONAL

If it is meant to be. We will find our way back... once we (you) are free.

I will not be using this email/app for communication unless it is urgent.

Letters are more than welcome. If you are truly trying to communicate.

In the meantime do your best to stay well

I will forever love you

with love

Shana

Journal entry

July 6, 2023

I wrote an email to Rob. (sad crying face) I said I had to let him go.

I am shattered and depleted. Again. Because it is now real. I really wanted to go see him. Visit him. When he called and apologized for not calling when he said he would, he could not due to being in lockdown. I was triggered. I am so angry. I feel agony on so many levels and the only way I think it will stop is to stop holding on.

I can not stop loving him. Yet I do need to let him go.

Journal entry

July 17, 2023

New moon

New Nu Moon in Cancer

Scorpio is leaving the south node. The last 18 months have come to this point right now.

There is a lot of confusion and this new moon feels quite emotional.

It is time to clear and clean up all the pain, all the old trauma, starting from when I was small ...and could barely walk.

The new me can only focus on doing good healthy habits. I give myself permission to choose the new me.

Mercury is in Leo, this is where I shine without regret! Saturn's position says wait, do not jump forward, go slow and steady. Then there is Mars who wants to go and make changes!

I just need to get really intentional on how I want to spend my time, love, energy, and money. I need to be mindful and intentional as I continue to move forward in a healthy way.

Slow down, protect myself, and invest in myself.

I need to only pour from my overflowing glass, not a half empty glass.

I need to focus on ME.

Small steps towards me again.

So I can be stable and keep my foundation solid.

~ ~ ~ I am open to receiving financial freedom, and an abundance of healthy love and habits.

Journal entry

July 18, 2023
Tuesday

My heart hurts again. Why do I have to feel so deeply?!
I want to cry, but I won't.

IT'S NOT PERSONAL, BUT IT IS PERSONAL

The reason this time... I had a conversation with the loan officer to buy a house. I have been looking since May. It is just not in the cards again this year unless I have a winning lottery ticket hiding! The cost of moving and buying is insane right now anyways. The interest rate is a mess! It is not like it was back in 2020 or even when I bought my first house back in 2001.

Back to the drawing board next year.

Also, I can't remember if I mentioned ... back in May when I started looking for a house, I was told by my mom, that she would no longer be able to help with the down payment. Per what she said she would do 3 years ago. She said, "I already gave you a car, you can sell that for a down payment." Mind you this car was a gift I had no idea she purchased and actually did not want to take the gift because I knew it would be held over my head or with strings attached.

Funny how our gut knows exactly what to do, but we do the opposite for that instant gratification and/or hope that we were not wrong.

Journal entry

July 23, 2023

7:48 am

Soul day

I went out last night, on a whim.

Earlier yesterday I went to an event my best friend was volunteering at in Portland. On my drive to Portland, I told myself if anyone asked for my phone number I would say yes instead of no this time.

Well at that event, the DJ hit me up and invited me to another event that evening. I was supposed to go with my girl, but she stayed back at the last minute, so I went solo. I was there for maybe 2 hours. When I decided to leave, is when I got hit on. At different times. It was quite flattering and felt good to know I still got it.

I am not sure where it will lead, but I am letting go and allowing the universe, the higher power or god intertwine my path.

Journal entry

Aug 2, 2023

6 am

Writing for Aug 1st Full Super Moon in Aquarius

Many planets are in retrograde and Mars is in Virgo. Small changes every day are needed.

This Leo season is about me getting excited about my power and new chapters.

Everything I have learned I have been reprogramming to the best I can with the tools and skills I have come across. This will help me keep aligning with my energy, my soul, and what truly feels good in my body.

Uranus is squaring Venus during retrograde. Any squares will feel off, it feels like a struggle. I need to pay attention to any friction or tough tense feelings. Readjust and make notes. There is no need to make any big commitments, just take notes and circle back later. If this is an option. I need to practice not applying my old bad habits that feel like a quick fix.

Under this full moon in Aquarius

I give myself permission to release the old me, codependency, and loneliness.

IT'S NOT PERSONAL, BUT IT IS PERSONAL

Journal entry

Aug 6, 2023

6:37 am

...morning, Soul day

Yesterday I led my first official yoga class with strangers.

Actually, only some were strangers. I knew the folks I worked with and I say this because I have already led and taught a few classes with my daughter.

I helped lead at the Mindfulness meditation retreat. I taught twice. Once early for the morning flow and then in the afternoon we did chair yoga.

I am happy to say I still reaped the benefits of an all-day meditation.

I am grateful I saw many signs during the drive out to Portland yesterday morning, my brother is always with me. It is always such a huge gift to see the signs and finally be in a space to recognize them. He truly has been a guardian angel. This confirmation always brings my heart peace and strength to live greatly in this life.

Journal entry

Aug 11, 2023

Friday

Afternoon

God forbid if I died tomorrow!

What, who, how would I like my loved ones to remember me... or what would I be known for or remembered for?!

I do know I am kind and I love deeply with no conditions. I always gave my best in areas of life that meant the most to me. I genuinely tried hard! Especially over the last 9 years to walk with kind compassionate intention. To mend any wrongs I have done and forgive myself and others for any guilt or shame placed. My heart has always belonged to those I love and I would DO just about anything for my beautiful children, familia, and soul tribe.

I am grateful for all the life lessons. Even the hard ones! They do not define me, however they are the reason I choose to walk lighter in this hard world.

I hope they will remember me as a light. A person who genuinely cared and loved deeply while intentionally carving space from my heart to place with theirs. Even a stranger I would give my heart to if that was what was truly required to help them feel peace.

Journal entry

Aug 15, 2023
...Tuesday evening

Tomorrow is the new moon ...

I am open to joy, wealth, love, and happily ever after.

Last month... out of the few guys who requested my phone number, I have texted and talked on the phone a few times, with one specific person. It feels like maybe we have a connection. I wonder how this will unfold.

IT'S NOT PERSONAL, BUT IT IS PERSONAL

Journal entry

Aug 16, 2023

I went to a sound bath retreat tonight.

I did a lot of grounding when I got home in the front yard. I completed the New Moon workshop and gave myself gratitude for the person I am becoming!

Journal entry

Aug 18, 2023
6:13 am
Friday

...few things I am grateful for
I am grateful for my healthy children
My family
My extended familia
...and to feel joy.

Journal entry

Aug 20, 2023
...morning, Soul day

...what I am grateful for
I am grateful for my momma's homegrown tomatoes
I am grateful to choose how my day will flow
...and I am grateful for L's conversation yesterday and the wisdom shared.

Journal entry

Aug 24, 2023

...gratitude

I am grateful for my bed and a roof over my head

...last night's sunset, it was so magical with all the birds. Luna was out and the sun was glistening the color red in the pond nearby. I didn't want to leave the trail. It was so peaceful.

Journal entry

Aug 25, 2023

I am grateful to witness Mother Nature at 5 am, to see the storm and lightning perform as confirmation that it is okay to feel angry or gloomy. Then the sun's rays shine through with a statement of, "This too shall pass."

I am grateful for the reminder of having feelings

...and a warm embrace.

Journal entry

Aug 30, 2023

Full moon

Super Blue Full Moon in Pisces

I saw the moon rise!

The full moon is saying... right now, it is time to pay any karmic debts.

I need to step into my new identity, the new me, the one that I have been working on for the last several years!

Under this Super Full Moon in Pisces

I am releasing any old versions of myself.

Journal entry

Aug 31, 2023

What weighs my energy down or drains me?

...the constant unknown, any negative energy, people who are not kind or only take for selfish reasons, anyone I love or care for that is not conscious of how they may impact others by their actions.

What gives me energy and makes me feel lighter?

...kind gestures, self-love, love, giving love, yoga, healing practices, meditation, good energy, less chaos when things flow, genuine people with good intentions, nature, the sun, the moon, the trees, unconditional love.

What energy will help me release fear and allow me to trust more?

...my true authentic self and aligning all my chakras

What energy will help me align with my highest intuition?

...me, myself, my own energy.

I am open to an expanded view of my life.

Journal entry

Sept 9, 2023

8:55 am

Saturday

I was supposed to see my counselor last night. It was canceled. The next one won't happen until October 19. My choice. I need to dig deep to help myself to survive when things feel off balance.

I am truly wanting and missing love... and a partner who chooses me. I miss Rob, but I can't tell him. I will confuse everything. Besides... he must not miss me, he has yet to even write.

With all the growth ...I am still learning, yet I now know to be selective. That person I spoke to is nice, yet I am realizing we are probably in different spaces. I have decided I no longer want to talk to him, I just need to say this. I am recognizing I am trying to fill a void. I need to resort to healthy tools. Love myself deeper and go to my healing spaces. I need to get out into nature more!

Today I will get out. Go hike. Be with my wisest friends. Again. The trees.

Journal entry

Sept 10, 2023

I am on a call with my counselor RIGHT now because

...of seeing a person die, last night   ...taking notes

Tomorrow is Monday

Call the Dr.

Call this Trauma therapist, she will help

All brains are different. Exposed to traumatic events ...usually the

third day is the worst. I might have many extreme flooding feelings
...the first phase is shock!!!
EMDR
The new therapist specializes in trauma healing
...this will help with acute stress disorder

Journal entry

Sept 12, 2023

I just finished a video visit with a PA to get sleeping meds.

I broke down crying when she asked how I was doing. I couldn't talk, I was too emotional.

I guess I am not me. I feel sad, broken, and not me, at all. Why am I in this space? I don't know, yet I am grateful I do have the support and resources to navigate this tragic event.

Crazy to think I thought my counselor could help me. I mean she said she would still help, but it would be best to see a therapist who specializes in trauma. Hasn't the majority of my life been of trauma?!

I guess seeing death is different. Watching a person die ...possibly killed, or in a freak accident, will do something to a person. I just wish I could stop seeing that horrible event in my mind, so vividly.

When I shared what I witnessed with my brother and how I had to stay outside for hours until I could go home. (mind you home was maybe 1.5 miles away from this horrific scene)

He said, "Shana, that is absolutely horrible. Never ever repeat that story again! To anyone."

I listened. ...and took it with a grain of salt... yet, the image feels like a grain of assault.

Journal entry

Sep 15, 2023

I am home now

The drive I just completed was anxiety-producing!

I have not driven since ... since I saw that woman die. Plans changed, so I ended up being the driver at the last minute to Washington. I know things happen for a reason, I just did not anticipate anxiety while driving for many hours. To and from.

I am going on one hour of sleep in 24 hours. Lulu bought us tickets for my birthday, and ... the concert was last night! We were in Seattle to see Beyonce! An exceptional experience! The concert was amazing!

Music therapy was right on point! After the concert, I got to hang out with Soul. We talked for a few hours, actually until the sun came up. It was divine ...and timely. It felt seamless ...as if we had known each other before.

The sleeping meds prescribed to me did not work. I only took them that first night, and instead of resting, I was awake half the night. That shit did not work. It doesn't matter, I would rather take nothing anyways! Eventually, I will find rest at night. I hope.

The new moon in Virgo was last night, it was an invitation to expand with abundance with love and to continue to choose wisely with energy that is aligned with New Nu Bigger and Better Versions!

Chapter Twenty-Three

Abrupt Autum Of 2023

Journal entry

Moving at the speed of trust. If we move with ease while being grateful... will we always receive?

Yes, I believe so. There is so much that unfolds in service of life, even if we feel lacking ...we should always have something to be grateful for. Many people would ask for one more day to experience the simple pleasures of living. Or ask for one more day to wake up.

It is time to just rest in the heart. Just like the body, let's allow it to expand with strength, compassion, and resilience.

I will heal.

Life is a gift.

Journal entry

Sep 28, 2023
...day /night b4 Full moon
11:05 pm

It feels like forever and yesterday ...all in one.

Not sure where to start. ... I worked 10 hours, I cooked enchiladas and I exchanged conversations. I think I am ...well ...I am trying to feel normal and navigate mindfully again. Whatever normal truly is.

... it is now 12:06 am, I just got off the phone with Soul. He makes me laugh and has very interesting topics and views that we discuss. His spirit and energy are vibrant. I value his insight and knowledge. Anytime we talk I seem to have a huge smile on my face and my heart. This could be healing.

I leave tomorrow, on a cruise with my mom to Hawaii. Fly out on 9/30!

Marquita and I discussed this yesterday.

I will be on a life test.

Journal entry

Sep 29, 2023
Full moon

Last Super Full Moon of 2023!

I release all the pain and trauma

...I release any old attachment styles.

I invite in my inner strength, power, and love to myself. So I can heal for the remainder of my time on Earth side.

Journal entry

Oct 1-8, 2023

on the ship

Reflecting...

9.30- We arrived in Oahu

First evening on here... during and after sunset I longed to share this moment with another soul, a partner, a lover. My heart. Yet, Rob and I are worlds apart, separated, (for real this time) and I now need to act as so.

...next day.

The morning with my mother.

My patience was tested. Again. I will not go over the details of our travels during each airport and getting to the actual cruise ship to board, but it was a lot, to say the least.

Our Room is 9172 on the 9th floor

Day 2

10.01/10.02 -Maui

My mother and I walked the cruise ship together and later I went to a beach solo.

Day 3 -in Maui 10/02 - my late brothers 42 birthday

We took a tour trip to Hana, with many stops. We traveled up to 13,000 feet of elevation. Witnessed the majestic beauty of 8 waterfalls or more, a few eucalyptus rainbow trees (my absolute favorite part), walked the black sand beach, saw 2 turtles at the beginning of the journey, and ended with 20 something honu at the end. Soul many spiritual signs.

...later back on the cruise ship

I joined my mom for dinner so she would not have to eat alone. She decided she wanted to get a hamburger, my choice at this restaurant would be french fries and I felt there were so many more restaurant choices on the ship that I would find one with a substantial vegetarian option. So I sat with her while she ate. After the cruise ship took off I ate by myself and I am very teary-eyed. I guess I am just processing the day, my brother's birthday. How much time has come and gone since we lost him. I did finish a glass of wine and now I am on my 2nd waiting to eat, 2 hours after my mom did.

We had a good day ... but once we got off the tour it was challenging. Big time.

I met Norman & Kathy from Tampa, Florida while waiting for my dinner. They were surprised I was sitting alone.

I said, "I am not alone, my brother is here in spirit and my mom is resting in the room."

They both smiled at this and we all talked a bit until my food arrived.

10.03/ 10.04 - Hilo, Kona, Hawai'i (saw familia, Lulu's parents)

Day 4 - we are docked at Hilo, Hi

During breakfast outside on the dock my Mom said, "We have movies in our room we can watch today."

I said, "I am not sitting in a room on a cruise ship to watch movies. We can do this at home."

She said, "I bet when you're 75 you will."

... Hmmm note to self at 75. Will I?!

By the way, my mom is still a decade away from this age.

Day 5

I have been awake since 5:20 am. We are now anchored in the middle of the ocean at Kona, Hi. There is no actual port here, the reason for docking in the middle of the ocean. If anyone wants off there are little taxi boats that hold about 200 people at a time, to take you to the island.

...later

Out of all the stops, my mom decided yes she wanted to shop on this island and get off the ship. Let's just say today's test was times 100. I am still trying to calm my vagus nerve. It is after 8 pm now.

10.05/10.07 - Kauai -

Day 6

My mom got us tickets for a Luau.

Yet we forgot the tickets in our room and did not realize this until we were waiting outside in line to get on the tour bus. I had to run back for the tickets not once but twice. Since I am not partial to the elevator I ran 9 flights of stairs and down the long hallways of the ship, twice, or maybe that is 4 times. You do the math. I made it back just in time to board the bus. We had fun. The stories told at this Luau were historically enchanting. Seeing my mom smile during this event was heartwarming. I am grateful she put this trip together even through the tests. I do wish my little brother Alejandro was here with us, too.

Day 7

10.06 Kauai - Kīpū Farm 3000 acres zip lining highest for me was 1800ft & jumped into a Bamboo swim hole (only for Mike)

I went zip-lining for the first time. I was solo, but not really because I was with a small tour group. It was healing to be with all the wise souls of Kauai. The feeling I had zipping above nature was profound.

I am grateful for this captivating experience, my mother gifted me.

...later during the evening, I had a fancy dinner with my momma and we took photos afterward.

Day 8

We are traveling back to Oregon and the test continues.

Reflections from the trip are summed up by the words of *Maya Angelou*

"You may encounter many defeats,
but you must not be defeated.
In fact, it may be necessary
to encounter the defeats,
so you can know who you are,
what you can rise from,
how you can still come out of it."

This year's birthday celebration for my brother who crossed over and is now an angel to many was celebrated with my beautiful momma on the healing islands of Hawai'i, Oahu, Maui, and Kauai

...the trip itself was grounding with many gifts of gratitude, and YES I *was* tested, yet I would not change any of it.

We LOVE you, Michael Angel Perez! Thanks for being with us, always in all ways.

IT'S NOT PERSONAL, BUT IT IS PERSONAL

Journal entry

Oct 14, 2023
7:07 am
Saturday

New moon in Libra and an eclipse

Chiron is in Aries and lots of emotions with old feelings will stir up.

I need to follow my intuition.

...and if these hard feelings keep coming up. Say it is ok to let go... and let them go.

(sad crying face)

I need to look at the bigger picture and prioritize 'MYSELF', no more self-sacrificing!

Focus on the BIGGER picture!

Just keep witnessing all my work and all the changes I have made... they will come 6 months from now!

I WILL BE

Rich

Healthy

Fit

and at Peace

walking and dancing in JOY!

I will keep hugging and giving myself healing gratitude.

Journal entry

Oct 17, 2023

Yesterday was my Auntie Paula's birthday.

She came to me as a hawk, in the pouring rain. While I was working inside I could see her outside perched on a tree for almost 20 minutes.

I let Jessi and my mom know. They both were happy to hear this and acknowledged the beautiful sign.

Tonight I will see Wu-Tang and Nas perform with my little brother! I am more excited about just hanging out with my little brother! It was his birthday gift I got him! These concerts sure are timely.

Today at 1 pm I will get new ink from my old artist Rory! It has been a while since I have seen him. I can't wait for this therapeutic session! It will be a lion's face over my left shoulder near my clavicle! The inspiration came from Lulu's beautiful lion on her hand she got when we were in Hawaii, back home in Kona!

The placement I chose is because it is closest to my heart. I have a few Leos in my life that are near and dear to my heart, and a bonus my luna sign is Leo.

Journal entry

Oct 22, 2023

2:02 pm

...Soul Day Afternoon

...in Kintsugi Breaking and mending circle (group)

When I look at my bowl I see ...many breaks mended with time, love, and care.

Every golden fault line reminds me ... of strength, resilience, compassion ...surfacing out of pain.

What my bowl tells me about grief is ...there is no identical path when healing grief and each heartache is rooted in the soul.

What my bowl tells me about gratitude is ...no matter the breaks I can be grateful for each life lesson and experience.

What my bowl tells me about healing... is to start with kindness and love towards any crack within myself and eventually, the healing will ripple outwards.

...later the same day, almost 10 pm

Reflecting -

...last night my son called me at 10:10 pm ...

My heart skipped out of my chest.

He wrecked his car...

...off the street

...in a ditch, on the back roads

He shared his location so I could find him.

It was pitch black out, wet, cold, foggy ...and on a road, I only drove maybe three times since living out here for 28 years. This road had sharp turns, hardly any lights, and it felt like I was driving in the woods. When I got to my son, my heart sank deeper into my stomach.

His car was stopped by huge sturdy trees about 6-7 feet down!

Michael, my Auntie, grandparents, friends, and so many angels were watching over him. I am so grateful he is safe, home, and with few injuries.

Trauma is hell!

I wish to be free of this type of feeling...

I keep mending my heart back ...and I am afraid I may run out of glue.

Journal entry

Oct 28, 2023

Full moon

7:19 am

...Saturday

Full Moon Eclipse in Taurus

This full moon energy is closing out the energy that started back in November 2021.

Note to self, look back at November of 2021... to see how far I have come.

Full moon in Taurus with Jupiter in Taurus.

I am recognizing I need to release attachments and abandonment feelings. I need to love myself more unconditionally, so this feeling of abandonment or heartache does not rise or when it does I can meet it with love and tender kindness.

I am love

I am rich

I am covered in abundance

I am safe

I am successful

I am HEALthy

I am a QUEEN and a light for many

I invite healing love and safety for all in the world

IT'S NOT PERSONAL, BUT IT IS PERSONAL

Mail

November date unknown, 2023

I know it was sent before 11/12

email by app

... (this email got lost or deleted, so I am writing it by memory)

My Dearest Rob,

I went on here a few times to go through our paper trail and was heartbroken to see it was deleted. I am thinking of you and I hope you are well. Sending you healing love. Also, I placed some $$$ on your books.

love always

Shana

Journal entry

Nov 8, 2023

Dream

We needed to get to an event. My mom, daughter Nonni, and my newborn were with me. We hopped on a boat. It was a small sailing boat that had room underneath with beds. Kids were sleeping and I could feel the boat tipping and somehow see (the sea) from the outside looking in. It was night time and a huge wave came and flipped the boat upside down. We swam to a concrete wall or rock that was somehow not that far. I panicked. Looking out into the dark ocean ...there were only a few small ripples and I could see bubbles rising. I immediately dove in and rescued my newborn. She choked and coughed up water, but I was able to save her.

I had this feeling of why did I agree to take this trip, this route to Florida. Later we made it to the event. It was held at a Palace. My baby was part of the parade with the Queen. She was wrapped in all white. Sleeping, precious, and looking unbothered. I felt frazzled from what I knew we went through to get here. After the parade and ceremony, a lady said "Your baby is so angelic and beautiful did you take any photos?"

... she offered to share her videos.

Then I woke.

...date not noted

Met with my counselor, and she said to change ALL the people to me, and all the signs are telling me to keep going.

What it feels like to feel safe instead of a safe place or creating an imaginary safe place

...many synchronicities are occurring keep paying attention

Journal entry

Nov 13, 2023

New Moon

New Nu moon in Scorpio

Saturn is in Pisces ...saying let go. This is the first new moon of this season. This will help us grow and expand when we let go.

Where my attention goes my energy flows.

No more pain, trauma, and old hardships. When we focus on the bigger the better, we will get BIGGER results.

It is ok to talk and say what I truly want and need to establish healthy habits. I need to trust myself and my vision.

Venus in Libra, if it is not equal in any relationship, let it go.

I am grateful for this New Nu moon in Scorpio

I am initiating the following

I am strong and lighter

Happier and healthier

Rich and full of love

Ask myself where do I want to be and who do I want to be in the next 6 months...

Journal entry

Nov 14, 2023

Reflecting on November 12

This date would be my 10-year anniversary of still being married. My time was spent in Seattle, Washington... alone for the day. I walked in Golden Garden Park. Put my feet in the ocean. Spoke and read about the people that crossed over, across many benches that faced the water. Slept. Meditated. Practiced Yoga. Stretched. ...and never cried about today. This day. Even though Rob told me he would never not reach out, no matter what. I never heard from him. I am glad I finally let go of the expectation, even tho... I did wonder. Why he didn't call or write?

Journal entry

Nov 21, 2023

I have been seeing my trauma therapist weekly.

I am still processing and I have noticed I forget a lot more lately

...but she says it is normal with everything I have endured.

Today she gave me homework

An acronym journal prompt: **G.L.A.D.** for what I am **Grateful** for, what I **Learned** for the day, what I **Achieved** that day, and what brought me **Delight.**

I am **G**rateful for the majestic sunrise and conversations with Soul.

I **L**earned a lot about the benefits of food and Soul should be added to my diet.

Achieved - a lot of writing. I ran and I went to the gym.

Delight - nature, the moon, the sun, the joy I feel when I am speaking with Soul, feels like music.

Journal entry

Nov 25, 2023

7:21 pm

...Saturday night

I finally decided to empty the storage. The storage unit I have had for 10 years. I had to get it the first time Rob was locked up, and I have had it ever since due to lack of space.

...the emptying part will happen tomorrow. I still do not have the space, but I'm going to make it happen, cramming it all into the garage! I can't wait to no longer have this bill!

G. L. A. D.

I am **G**rateful I had the strength to empty the garage by myself. I think my right arm/shoulder is at 90%.

I **L**earned after this move. I only want to do it once more. In my own home that I buy and own!

IT'S NOT PERSONAL, BUT IT IS PERSONAL

I **A**chieved more resilience

Delight was felt when Marquita and Johnny showed up to see what tomorrow looks like and we each witnessed the moon kiss the sun good night at sunset at the Tualatin National Wildlife Refuge.

Journal entry

Nov 26, 2023

9:26 pm

Soul day

The storage is almost empty. I have 2 Big items to move.

The Piano and the BBQ grill. I really hope I can rearrange the house so I do not see boxes. I am so tired of seeing and living out of boxes.

G. L. A. D.

Grateful my family and soul tribe showed up to move the heavy stuff!

I **L**earned I need to let go of 'stuff'

Achieved - the emptying of the storage

Delight was with my brother and Johnny- when they were laughing and making jokes. This was heartfelt.

Journal entry

Nov 27, 2023

Full moon

Under this full moon in Gemini

I let go of old habits

I am creating flexibility and inviting in more abundance, love, and flow.

Journal entry

Nov 30, 2023

10 pm

Monday night I went to Seattle and stayed out there for 2 nights. Half of my time was by myself and the other with Soul. It feels like I may have found my match from a past life. It is hard to explain this on paper, yet I can say there is a magnetic pull.

I am grateful our paths have crossed and we stayed attuned and connected without truly even knowing that we were connecting. Now we do.

My heart feels like it might be slowly mending with gold.

Mail

Dec 2, 2023

Saturday

4 pm

My Dearest Rob

I just got your 3-page letter.

Reading this ...I hear a lot of pain, anger, resentment. I am sorry to hear you are going through this.

It was a difficult letter to read and process.

I would like to clear something up. The email I wrote to you in November did not say "I" deleted the messages. "It", the system deleted the messages. All this communication was through an app, it does not show up in my email. I never deleted it. A few months ago

I went looking for the electronic paper trail, to read what you wrote ...since this was ALL I had in writing from you. In a long time. And I was heartbroken to see it was all gone. This is what I was trying to communicate and imply. Which also means I NEVER stopped thinking about you. It was not only around November 12th.

I have written to you many times. I just never put them all in the mail.

This letter from you today is #3 This year. 3 letters out of 350 days. Last year in 2022, I might have received 2 letters from you. Maybe. I say maybe because I could only find one, and I was hoping it was more than that. There were a handful of other envelopes, but empty in my opinion if there was no letter from you. Just you mailing out stuff ...to me, but to you.

I just truly hoped and wished you actually would have fought harder. By writing. You said, "You loved me enough to give me space." you were and ARE NOT physically here, I have enough FUCKING Space! (crying face)

The one request I asked several times. Even the last time, I said if you need me or want to communicate please write. Maybe it was not exactly those words but I know it was very close to this and it is what I meant.

...Roller coaster ride of emotions.

LOVE. That is love for your ass. sigh. (sad face)

You said, "I can not and will not do this roller coaster ride of emotions with you no longer. I am done so please let me go, like you said you had."

Your right

...I did say I'm letting you go. It fucking killed me...and I guess I never truly did... let you go. ...but I will now. The only way I know how to. I will keep you deep in my heart and I will let you go. No matter what... I will always keep you in my heart. I will stop asking you to fill any holes. I will start filling them myself. I might be broken, but I think I can figure out how to mend another broken heart.

I am not going to say one person tried harder than the other... that would be like comparing the love we shared for each other. I know each of us loved one another deeply. I also know I still love you deeply. And I think you do too! Even if you did not write or say it this time. True love does not just go away. My choice of stepping away was not because I stopped loving or caring for you. This was already explained in several different ways. I chose the facts this time. I chose life over death. That choice... took me years to decide and act on it. It was extremely painful.

I guess the next step of done... is a divorce. As much as I despise saying this. Can you please file for a divorce? After reading this letter it is clear that this is the next step.

I truly hope both of our hearts can heal, and find peace in our soul and spirit.

I will forever love you

Shana Christine

IT'S NOT PERSONAL, BUT IT IS PERSONAL

Journal entry

Dec 11, 2023

10:44 pm

...getting closer to the end of the year and I was reflecting.

Looking at old photos... trying to remember how I felt at each moment. Just this one year ...feels like 10 years. ...feels like I am in a time warp or twilight zone.

Tomorrow is the 12/12 portal and a new moon. I need to go out and hike! Get some grounding in!

G. L. A. D.

I am **g**rateful my heart is not solid ice

I **l**earned that I am resilient (more with every year that passes)

Achieved a post of reflection

Delight showed up when I was looking down

memory lane and when my son came to hug me.

Journal entry

Dec 12, 2023

New moon

New Nu moon in Sagittarius and mercury in retrograde

It is time to zoom out and see the bigger picture

Dream more

I need to slow down and pause, how do I want to invest in time, energy, and money

Venus is also in Scorpio, this will want us to know a person more deeply. Deep conversations will be had. Get very clear on what I want in this next major chapter.

I will reap what I sow.

I want long-term pleasure not short-term.

I am inviting in new healthy habits with a better solid foundation that will create new travel, home, life, love, and money. To align with the new me.

Journal entry

Dec 19, 2023
Tuesday

No alarms are set for today.

...yet I was woken up by constant buzzing.

I got 4 missed calls from Rob. It was a little after 6 am. I chose to climb out of bed and start working. I only worked for a few hours. Did some shopping for Christmas Eve dinner. I saw my trauma therapist. At the next appointment, we will start the EMDR

..thinking.

What have I learned over the last few weeks about 'HOME' and my inner sense of belonging?

Home is only within me. All the stuff, things, and furniture does not make a home. My sense of belonging is off-kilt... more so because I have outgrown the space I am in.

There have been unexpected detours, which have taught me I am exactly where I am supposed to be. I have learned to pause, think, and take it all in.

...it is a lot to take in.

Chapter
Twenty-Four

Winter Stillness Of
2023

*J*ournal entry

Dec 25, 2023
10:30 am

Christmas morning

Last night I came across an old song from Nina Simone, Black Bird.

I went to sleep with it playing on repeat... and it has been playing all morning. All while watering all the plants, cooking, and doing some cleaning. The song, and the words, are a raw truth I can recognize. I wonder if the level of pain has anything to do with sharing the same born day.

Jr is home this year, but still asleep. We celebrated the holiday last night. This time Nonni is home, no snowstorm to detour her like last year! It truly has been a gift having her home. Both Destiny and Jr are so happy and wanting to do more activities together as a family. It really has been a great last few days.

Wednesday night after Nonni got home we all went Ice Skating at a new pop-up outside in downtown Portland. Then afterwards we went out to eat. Friday night we all baked different cookies and sugar treats while watching holiday movies. Saturday we prepped and cooked Italian food for the Christmas Eve lunch on Sunday. It truly was full of smiles, love, joy, and not much sleep!

G. L. A. D.

Grateful for so many new memories with all 3 of my kids together

I learned that my 'gift' is to love unconditionally. When it feels right it is ok to share this always with no expectations of anything in return. That I do not need to block my love, it is ok to share.

Achieved more patience.

Delight was all around me pouring out of the seams of the house, each space was filled with smiles, love, joy, and laughter.

Journal entry

Dec 26, 2023

Full moon

Full moon in Cancer

This full moon is an invitation to completely let go and trust the process.

Currently, we are still in mercury retrograde. This full moon in cancer is illuminating the broken structures and scars. I need to not add layers of defense ...no more hard shells. Saturn in Pisces is asking us to rebuild. Pluto will leave Capricorn next month, this will feel like death and a rebirth.

IT'S NOT PERSONAL, BUT IT IS PERSONAL

Under this full moon in Cancer, I am releasing
...past traumas
...expectations
...and the belief of not being safe or enough on my own
Shana, it is ok to let it go.

Journal entry

Dec 31, 2023
I decided I will go to Seattle later today

G. L. A. D.

Gratitude for feeling peace.

I am **l**earning more about my healing path. I typed a few things in my notes. I recognize the strength and resilience I have in me.

I **a**chieved a few small projects today including updating my meditation list and resume.

Delight came in the form of my son's smile after he replaced the lights on his car and the hugs he gave out today.

...later, it is 3:11 am... now 1.1.2024

I am in Seattle, the whole drive here, and back to the city I saw, 444, 999, 777, 222, 111, 666, 333... and I'm pretty sure I saw 5's! Because I saw so many angel numbers all day and night. There seemed to have been a few detours this evening, yet I knew I was protected and on the right path. Soul and I eventually connected and it was all divine timing, traffic and all. I even got to see the fireworks, while driving!

Journal entry

Reflection of 2023

More growing pains, few broken records, several HI times, many firsts,

lots of grounding, applying grace, and

... some doors opened ... because I closed a few.

The year of 2023 ~ the common denominator

was a conscious decision

of choosing ~ me.

Buddha said ... "Nothing remains without change."

I am grateful to be resilient with...

Reciprocity. Joy. Gratitude. Love. Respect.

Hikes ~

1.01 Silver falls

2.05 - Balfour-Klickitat Loop, w/Justina

2.05 - little Maui Falls, old ranch road off Coyote wall w/Justina (& this was a full moon in Leo)

2.20 - Balfour-Klickitat Loop, w/my mom (part of it), and stopped for ice cream at Multnomah Falls

04.02 - Echo Canyon trail -to-camelback Mt 2.5 miles w/Elena in Arizona (w/rock climbing!)

04.08 - Angels Rest -solo

04.22 -On Earth Day, Beacon Rock w/Justina & Sarah

04.23 Rodney Falls, Hardy Falls, pool of the winds /part of Hamilton Mt in WA, w/Justina

4.29 - Wahclella falls w/Elena

5.13- Tom McCall Preserve & Rowena Crest w/Justina & Sarah

IT'S NOT PERSONAL, BUT IT IS PERSONAL

(moms day hike, WE saw a Coyote)

5.16 - Tom McCall Preserve & Rowena Crest w/E'lisia

6.12 - Mau'umae Beach (in Hawaii)

6.13 - Puako '69's' Beach

6.14- Kuki'o Beach, Kailua Kona

6.15- Rainbow Falls in Hilo

6.17- Kauna'oa Beach

6.19 - Kua Bay Beach

7.03 - Naked Falls w/Justina & Sarah

7.23 - Naked Falls w/my son and saw Justina, Amy, Brett, Chris & Sarah -

7/30 -Wahclella Falls solo

8/15 - river at Westlinn w/LuLu

8/27 - paddle board in Estacada w/Justina

9.01- Dahlia farm w/Destiny

9.04 - Dahlia farm w/Elena

9.09 - solo Champoeg trail

9.16 /17- backpacking w/Justina & Sarah - mirror lake & Tom Dick Harry - overnight

10.02 - Maui - road to Hana w/mom

10.06 - Kīpū Farm/zip lining /Bamboo swim hole, solo

10.14 - solar eclipse 9:13 am, solo

10.29- hike Wahclella Falls w/ Marquita

11.11- - Golden Garden - Seattle, WA -w/Soul

11.12 - solo -Golden Garden - Seattle, Wa

12.17 - Angels Rest (sunset attempt - wind got us, w/Justina) Concerts ~

12.31 /01.01 -New Year's Eve - Digable Planets w/Justina @ the

Crystal Ballroom

07.01 - Blues Festival (Ms. Vee, BrassRoots movement, GA-20, Los Lonely Boys) solo

08.06 - Kenyon Dixon w/ Johnny

08.18 - piano -Marcus Johnson at Mimosas w/ Marquita

9.14- Beyoncé w/LuLu, Aveah & Jason

10.04 - Jazz, on Cruise ship

10.17- 50th Bday for hip-hop saw Wu-tang, Nas, De La Sol, Method Man, Talib Kweli, Ghostface Killah, w/my brother!

Traveled to ~

3.31 - Phoenix. Az (solo) stayed w/Elena

4.22-23/ Hood River w/Justina, Sarah, Amy

6.11-6.20 - Kona, Hi - w/LuLu, & the A's!

8.01 - Hood River Drive to see Jace (from yoga school)

9.14-9.15 - Seattle w/LuLu & Aveah (Beyoncé) /Pikes place

9.15 - Seattle, WA Pike Place Market with my LuLu

9.30- 10.7 - NCL (cruise w/mom) Hawaii islands

9.30- Oahu

10.01/ 10.02 - Maui - Road to Hana

10.03/ 10.04 - Hilo, Kona, Hawaii

10.05/10.07 - Kauai -

10.06 - Kīpū Farm/zip lining /Bamboo swim hole

11.11 - Jr new car - BMW in Seattle, WA

11.11-11.13 - Seattle, Wa

12.31-1.02 – Seattle, Wa

Books read ~

- Lighter by Yung Pueblo 6/3

- Yoga The Science of the Soul by Osho 7/9

IT'S NOT PERSONAL, BUT IT IS PERSONAL

- Finding Me by Viola Davis (one of my favorite all-time actresses)
4 agreements 10/2 (this might be the 5th time reading)

Events -
3.05 - mindfulness retreat w/ Marquita
3.19 - Blazer basketball game vs. w/ Justina
5/27 - Helium comedy- Aries Spears
6.19 - my siSTAR Lulu and I got new ink - honu, (4 me only) and
we both have a wave with coordinates of our favorite beach – done @
Packine ink w/Kawai (ink of coordinates in a wave are 156.00111 *W,
19.81882 *N)

7.27 - Helium comedy - Jiaoying Summers
8.05 - mindfulness retreat and I taught yoga! 2x
10.17 - new ink w/Rory - Leo my lion / my heart & moon sign
10.28 - lunar eclipse & work Halloween party w/Justina (dressed
up as sun & moon goddess)
Sound bath a few times!
12.20 Ice skate outside w/my kids
...and now a divorce will come in 2024. The reminder I have to keep
telling myself ...This is not a failure, this is simply a relationship that
has completed its cycle.

Chapter
Twenty-Five
2024 Diverge In Winter

J^{ournal entry}

Jan 1, 2024

9:43 am

I woke up several times after I fell asleep shortly after 4 am. Only me. In a king-size bed. Attempting to sleep yet awake... I am going to head out into healing nature. See what answers I can find.

Same day

...new time 8:33 pm

I hiked Twin Falls. It was amazing! Challenging! And rewarding!

...and then I decided to log back into social media. I have been off IG for a few weeks. I decided to go back on today. Only to see that Rob hit up a handful of people, including a girl he used to talk with back in the day. I saw several calls made on there to her. I think this is rubbing me the wrong way because my intuition and the text trail from him back in the day right before we got married (tell me they did connect). The words I read, "You felt so good." surfaced again after logging back onto IG. PTSD is real.

...ya, I guess the marriage truly is over.

Mail

Jan 5, 2024
Email letter, through an app

Rob,

I decided to respond to you through this app instead of IG since my message is apparently too long of a response for that site.

People die of heartbreak

You connect on social media ... a platform many use daily to connect ... which has been many folks' routine ..while living free. Not something I do daily, yet many do.

You asked me to keep this platform ALIVE for you.

As I did ... a constant reminder of your absence... but I did it. Now you are on here as if you're free. lol, confusing folks. Even Tuffy thought you was free and this part ... This part I don't understand.. and maybe it's not meant for me to. Because I assumed you would be in touch with me ...once you are free. (I know you're not free, but this communication ...this platform can feel this way) Or even some type of outreach at least to say hey Shana ... no worries about logging in to my account every now and then ... as I requested of you.

I get it now.

I respected you enough to never touch any friend requests or comments ...

Yet when I logged in and saw you were active a whole other type of way ...

Again... not for me to understand (at this point)

... I'm not gonna rain on your parade ... of connecting

I know what I said back in 2021!!

I was trying NOT to die of heartbreak.

I also know I asked you to connect another way. And you DID NOT do this. (That part) that part is ON YOU.

I am being honest. I was always honest.

Back to you being happy.

I didn't get it before... but I get it now. I did not read in between the lines. I understand now. You've BEEN talking to that girl.

& No type of remorse ...

You moved on ... lol. And I'm the one free.

That was all I was saying. Not that you cheated. I did not say those words.

I deserve a full commitment

Someone to be fully present

A phone call was NOT convenient... because it was only on your terms. I could never just call...

Where you are currently at ...of course, it was not your choice.

Dammit! I fought too! Over and beyond! I fought for YOU & ME ...

WE had multiple conversations. MULTIPLE. Countless. Conversations. When I came to visit you the 1st go around during 2014 - 2017. EVERY single weekend for OVER 3 years. Then you came home and also assured me YOU WOULD NOT put me in that position ever again. Then ...the choices you made when you came home

...put you in the position you are in. AGAIN.

You said you would never leave me alone like that again...

Like I said before Rob

I love you deeply. I always will. I know this will never stop. My love never stopped. I just chose to survive and be honest with what life presented me.

This is the last time I will say this ...a different way.

I was and I am...

Living by myself. Moving by myself. Packing. Moving. Crying. Moving. Fighting to live. Surrounded by BOXES and PAIN of being alone yet married IS and WAS excruciating! Because I am ALONE. There was no you and me together figuring it ALL out. This last time. It was ME over here hanging on to a thread of life. You over there hanging on to a thread of life. But 2 very different types of LIVING. 2 separate lives. Not a union. Not the way a marriage could survive.

I was constantly in the depths of an ocean... no raft, no life jacket, and no partner to physically help me on all the levels required to survive in 'LIFE'.

Mentally, physically, emotionally, financially, spiritually.

How else was I supposed to swim in an ocean daily without drowning!?

How?

By choosing the facts.

Shana, you are alone!

Figure this shit out by your fucking self Shana!

Now start living by yourself because those are the FACTS. Now start to invest in yourself. Throw yourself a raft or a life vest.

And whatever is meant to be ... will be in your life.

You see where I am going with this?!

God. The universe. Allah. Whoever you believe in for the higher power ...plays a huge part on how the journey of life will go ...depending on what choices we make.

I truly believe in karma... it will never forget a person and the unfortunate part of this... is karma will show up regardless of how good life may be flowing ...if it is still due. Karma will show up.

I also truly believe that if it is meant to be ...YOU and I ... we will come back together.

If not in this lifetime... then maybe the next.

My love for you is too deep ...

It is not surface love

I do love you. I DO LOVE YOU.

Happy.

You said you are happy.

Okay.

I hear you.

I am at peace that you found happiness.

I will let you be. And be happy.

> ...later journal entry 7:18 pm
> Rob called me from his phone
> Finally, at 4:44 pm

We talked, cried, made our voices get louder, listened, talked, and cried some more... for two hours. With no interruptions. Two solid hours of no one interrupting either of us. No recorded voice to remind you that you were speaking to an inmate, that the call was being recorded, and that you only had 2 minutes left of the call. None of the cruel triggering interruptions occurred. It was long overdue. And bittersweet.

He said a few things that hurt deeply. He also said a few things that helped me see what I did. Me 'Trying to survive' and not allowing him to call me, hurt him deeply. Even though consciously I was not trying to cause pain. Consciously I was only doing my best to survive. My chest hurts, yet not the same way. It feels like I found a sliver of my heart ...and glued it back with some gold.

We both did what we thought was in our best interest during the agony years of being apart. Survival mode. We both chose ourselves.

I used to believe if I got a divorce it would create shame and a sense of failure. I have now come to believe the facts. How else do we succeed if we do not fall? This is not failure. This is what society places upon us to believe. A relationship that was in a union and decided to part ways because it is the healthy way, in my opinion, is respect, honesty, love, vulnerability, endurance, intimacy, and completion.

At the end of the May 20 entry of the Codependency book 'The Language of Letting Go.' Melody writes of Sadness and refers to the tribe of being in prison as similar to death.

"The pain will stop. Once felt and released, our feelings will bring us to a better place than where we started. Feeling our feelings, instead of denying or minimizing them, is how we heal from our past and move forward into a better future. Feeling our feelings is how we let go.

It may hurt for a moment, but peace and acceptance are on the other side. So is a new beginning." (Beattie, pg 135)

As much as it has pained me to bring this relationship to a close. I am grateful and content that we have agreed to disagree on a few things. We both have confirmed that this relationship has come to a completion. I know I will survive, rise, and continue to shine. My light does not dim easily. I trust Rob will do the same. Our love story was truly unique, full of endless love, passion, compassion, laughter, tears of joy and pain, and soul many exhilarating moments ...that are now simply fond memories. We genuinely lived and loved deeply, especially when *WE* were *FREE.*

Acknowledgements

I am forever grateful to my family, my soul tribe, and the neverending list of specific individuals who shined their own wisdom and light upon my healing journey, which I now know is 4 eternity. Names provided are not in any particular order. Yet, I would like each of you to know that YOU are valued and I am that much more richer because of our paths intertwining.

Alex Elle

Alejandro Perez

Bali Familia

Bridget Brown

Chris Corsini

Cynthia

David

Deep

Deonna

Dhruv

Elena

E'lisia Destiny

Elizabeth Hartshorn

Grace Liu

Guardian Angels

Jace

Jade Hampton

Jessica Keas

Jr (aka my Junebug)

Johnny Jaramillo

Justina Woods

Kenzie Lamb

Laura L C

Lou

Louise Rodriguez

Marquita Jaramillo

Melody Beattie

Michael Angel Perez

Michelle

Natalie Harper

Persia

Punnu

Rob Dillon

Sheila Glo

Simona Buonomo

Solomon S

Spirits

Tonesha Sylla

Universe

Vejeth

Wildflower

IT'S NOT PERSONAL, BUT IT IS PERSONAL

"All you have to do is to pay attention; lessons always arrive when you are ready, and if you can read the signs, you will learn everything you need to know in order to take the next step."
-Paolo Coelho, *The Zahir*

Alexandra Elle ~ Course group (HYH) Healing Your Heart and Pathway to Peace, Podcasts Hey Girl and This Morning Walk, on IG @alex_elle

Chris Corsini @chriscorsinitarot on YouTube for Full moon and New moon workshops, chriscorsini.com and on IG @chriscorsini

Michelle A on IG @divinespurpose

Poem book, Love Her Wild by Atticus

The Power of Now by Eckhart Tolle

The Language of Letting Go, Daily Meditations on Codependency by Melody Beattie (published June, 1990)

Zen stories Niklas Goke (published in Personal Growth Jan 10, 2019)

About the Author

Shana Christine Dillon was born in Alameda, California grew up in Reno, Nevada, and moved to Portland, Oregon when she was 17 where she still resides.

She was a teen mom and did the best that she could with the tools that she had. A new first-time self-published author who recognized that life is about evolving, growing, and accepting change. She has faced many hardships and obstacles as she navigated raising 3 children. Who are all now adults. Shana is a proud mom, a generous friend to many, a loving sister to few, and a healer to her soul tribe.

The personal healing journey was never to implement a book from it. Yet, events that unraveled at the beginning of 2024 called her to dig in even deeper and transform part of her healing journey that was written; into her first book. Inspiration was the constant pull to walk in empathetic joy again and share her truth with no shame. Shana loves hiking, nature, books, yoga, music, art, and exceptional experiences that permit growth.

TIKTOK: @Spoken4Eternity

Instagram: @Spoken4Eternity

Find Shana Christine Dillon on Facebook

www.ingramcontent.com/pod-product-compliance
Lightning Source LLC
Chambersburg PA
CBHW060402130626
46555CB00005B/1977